SELF-GOVERNMENT IN INDUSTRY

This is one of a group of books
on industrial relations under the General Editorship
of A. I. Marsh, Senior Research Fellow in Industrial Relations
at St. Edmunds Hall, Oxford.

Self-government
in Industry

G. D. H. COLE

with an introduction to the 1972 edition by
J. G. CORINA
Fellow and Tutor in Economics,
St. Peter's College, Oxford

HUTCHINSON EDUCATIONAL

HUTCHINSON EDUCATIONAL LTD
3 Fitzroy Square, London W1P 6JD

London Melbourne Sydney Auckland
Wellington Johannesburg Cape Town
and agencies throughout the world

First published G. Bell and Sons Ltd 1917
This edition 1972

Printed in Great Britain by litho on smooth wove paper
by Anchor Press, and bound by Wm. Brendon,.
both of Tiptree, Essex

ISBN 0 09 114020 X (cased)
0 09 114021 8 (paper)

PUBLISHER'S NOTE

Self-government in Industry was first published in 1917
by G. Bell and Sons Limited, London. In this new
edition, the text is reproduced facsimile except for two
chapters and an appendix which are no longer relevant
today.

Corina.

CONTENTS

PREFACE

I AM profoundly grateful to Margaret Cole for her permission and help in producing a 'new' edition of G. D. H. Cole's classic text on industrial self-government. G. D. H. Cole exerted a lasting influence upon workers in the Labour Movement and appeared as a giant to successive student generations at Oxford. The generational strength of that influence has yet to be assessed by the historian of social ideas. To illustrate with one example only. During the early 1920's, a revolutionary-minded textile labourer fell under the spell of Cole's Guild Socialism, and fought for that vision in the General Strike of 1926: organising a bitter struggle in his neighbourhood with the help of a bright young man—Vic Feather, now General Secretary of the TUC. Later, Cole, as a Fellow in Economics at University College, Oxford, taught that labourer's son (a dyehouse labourer) the history of the Labour Movement, during the early 1930's, guiding him towards service in the Co-operative Movement; and then Cole, as Professor of Social and Political Theory at All Souls, later tutored his son in labour theory during the early 1950's. Since that last experience was my own link in but one family history, I must declare a personal interest before the bar of scholarship.

Yet Cole's vision must be judged neither as a piece of general history nor by its influence on the individual.

It stands as a piece of social theory in its own right. The aim of a new edition is not to celebrate the past. The purpose is to snatch a vision of the future; to present a body of stirring and exciting ideas before a generation which has now rediscovered the debate on industrial democracy.

I owe a debt to my colleague, J. F. Lively, for stimulating ideas on the Introduction and the topic of social democracy, and I am grateful to my colleague, Martin Powell, and to my students for acting as guinea-pigs on the drafts. Last but not least, I am grateful to Janina Corina for her insistence that a 'new' edition of the text should be made available to a new generation.

I dedicate this edition to another person, quite apart from G. D. H. Cole, who holds a leading place in the saga of Guild Socialism—Margaret Cole.

JOHN CORINA
Fellow and Tutor in Economics,
St. Peter's College, Oxford

INTRODUCTION TO THE 1972 EDITION

G. D. H. COLE, scholar, teacher and lifelong political
activist, was one of the most visionary social thinkers of
the twentieth century. One gift, shown in his writing, is
his ability to step across disciplinary borders in the
pursuit of answers to the fundamental ethical and social
problems of our industrial system. He is a humanist
of deep sensitivity. But he also seems to have an
additional dimension of understanding so that, where
others simply analyse, he continuously moves towards
fresh frontiers and resynthesis in building a value
system from the realities of political and economic life.
His vision, partly expressed in *Self-Government in
Industry*, first published in 1917 and slightly revised in
1919, still remains an intellectual *tour de force*. As a
blueprint for immediate Trade Union action, Guild
Socialism was steam-rollered by forces pressing in the
direction of centralisation and the public corporation.
But Guild Socialism, since it succeeded in identifying
underlying problems and in posing awkward questions
about the diffusion of social responsibility, has retained
much of its theoretical vigour and appeal. As a source
of practical inspiration, its pervasive influence still
remains with us (perhaps in surprising forms) to the
present day.

Self-Government in Industry is essentially a manifesto
on the rights of man in industrial society. Just as Tom

Paine's manifesto on the rights of man in quasi-agricultural society appeared on the brink of the French revolution, so Douglas Cole's manifesto appeared on the brink of the Soviet revolution. Both revolutions, spurred by popular aspirations to extend the concept of democratic citizenship into all the group sub-structures of society, ended by denying those rights in an orgy of centralisation and dictatorship. Their mistake was to equate the community with the State. The Guildsmen interpreted the evolution of society as a long series of struggles between social classes, mirrored in the activity of the State, for the possession of economic power—in which the National Guilds were to be the culmination of the process. But they also insisted upon advocating a division of economic and political power to preserve individual freedom against the absolutist claims of legislative assemblies. Guild Socialism ultimately rests upon a pluralistic conception of sovereignty.

In the last fifty years, although its path has been ill defined, pluralism has come in many and devious ways to colour modern conceptions of the State. As economic and social organisation grows more complex and as the 'welfare' State exercises ever-increasing responsibility for economic and social affairs, so it becomes more and more apparent that 'society' is composed of a mass of interest groups and pressures, of group affiliations and powers, of social identifications and interpersonal relationships, which are beyond the easy reach of legislation. Since *de facto* power is diffused in an undirected manner throughout all institutionalised relationships, the constraints upon social control through the State and its agencies become the *actual* limits to *State* sovereignty. The State has consequently changed its posture: from functioning as the centre of a consultative apparatus stretching down into economic and social institutions, into the stance of acting as chief bargainer in the social process. State sovereignty—the right to exercise power—crumbles away at the edges of the social system where the State is unable to exercise traditional power in non-traditional activities.

This historical process has given rise to a present paradox; as the State has assumed wider responsibilities, so it has become less capable of truly fulfilling them. Justifying its extended activity in terms of a general public interest and of individual self-fulfilment, it becomes less and less capable of fostering, or even formulating, these objectives. The paradox is reflected in both a theoretical confusion and a haphazard constitutional pattern. Pluralist theory, posed as the more compelling defence and projection of the democratic system, has been falsely transmuted into the notion that the community interest is no other than the sum of short-run group demands and, in parallel, that the State's function is to effect their reconciliation. No doubt, the political *practice* of the American federal system most closely mirrors this theoretical rejection of the State as representing a multi-dimensional community interest. Where experiments in 'industrial democracy' have been undertaken—in Algeria, Yugoslavia, Israel, and now Guyana—through State sponsorship they have tended to lean in a similar misguided direction.

But British developments point to the identical confusions of theory and practice. As governments have become closely implicated in the process of group bargaining, they have sponsored 'outside' agencies (independent equally of the State and popular control) whose function it is to express or promote the general interest. These organs are neither State agencies nor representative institutions. The resultant constitutional pattern is haphazard, but the trend is consistent. Proliferation has produced agencies with very general responsibilities: such as the National Economic Development Council and the 'little Neddies'; 'change agents' charged with specific tasks such as the Industrial Reorganisation Corporation; and 'umpire' agencies such as the statutory National Board for Prices and Incomes (now transformed into the Commission for Industry and Manpower). The Crowther Commission has found these impossible to classify in terms of representative democracy. The 'Collectivist' process has also led to the extension of union influence into the apparatus of government, while preserving union structure and rights in the industrial base, but without greatly altering the relationship between the Trades Union Congress and the affiliated unions. So the Donovan Commission, while paying lip-service to workers' participation in management, recognised the roots of power at the level of the workshop, but was induced to settle for indirect collective bargaining reform through yet another 'catalytic' body—the Commission for Industrial Relations. Finally, the constitutional tangle has also exposed the deep-seated contradictions between local economic interests, the requirement of co-ordination for national social goals, and the territorial basis of the existing system of local government. The Redcliffe-Maud Commission was forced to recognise the need for decentralisation and the need for regrouping local authorities under the 'Province' concept, while the central State apparatus has been belatedly modified to try to integrate regional planning with local government.

These three areas of democratic ambiguity—
economic planning, industrial relations, and local
government—have appeared because the democratic
threads of accountability, responsibility, representation
and control, have vanished in a cloud of confusion over
the notion of sovereignty. What we have now is neither
the Victorian legalistic notion nor the pure pluralistic
concept. But the test of any social principle is its power
to interpret the present with an eye on the future. If the
National Guildsmen were over-eager to assert that
self-government in industry depended on prerequisite
changes in the concept of State sovereignty, they were
analytically correct in challenging the view that the
rights and powers of all other forms of association are
derived from the State. The analytic strength of *Self-
Government in Industry*, in presenting a case for the
Guild System over fifty years ago, is that it points
concretely at some of our current political and
industrial problems. In arguing the case for the Guilds,
Cole cogently expresses a case for articulated economic
planning which incorporates the bargaining process.
But, he points out, any economic 'partnership to be
worth anything must be a partnership of equals, not
the revocable concession of a benignant and superior
State, and, to make it real, the Guilds must be in a
position to bargain on equal terms with the State'.
Here lies the stand against technocratic conceptions of
economic planning. Cole also strikes a modern tone in
his analysis of the industrial relations system: his plea
for union centralisation and structural change, his
insistence that the bargaining system is centred around
the workshop, pinpoint the problems which confront
us today. In his introduction to the 1919 edition, Cole
becomes almost prophetic in writing that, 'I believe

there is a great future before the region or the Province as an area of local administration, and that it will be both necessary and desirable in a Guild Society to have powerful regional Guilds working in conjunction with regional Councils over large economic areas.'

What Guild theory does, if the modern scene is viewed through its windows, is to articulate the bargaining process, in terms of the internal balance of industrial power; and to turn the pyramid of communication, guidance and instruction the right way up —so that it stands on a social base transparently linked through group consensus to the interlocking flows of decision-making. The Guildsmen do not deny a role to the State. They argue that where the State presumes to become a bargaining partner there should be a rough equality of formal power amongst the industrial parties. The balance of power in industry must be re-adjusted—through the Guild system—in favour of the workers, so that they are given a chance to express positively their full interests as producers, rather than their negative interests as protectors and protestors against the power of capital-controllers in a market economy or a nationalised economy. The State becomes the 'grand co-ordinator' of that class of collective activities which affect all members of that society equally and in the same way. For other classes of economic and social activities other forms of association are vital, and these are no less 'sovereign' in their sphere than the State in its sphere.

The system we now have is a half-way house: a mixed economy where the State assumes the overall tasks of economic management and the broad allocation of resources. But the ownership and control of the means of production still seeks its justification more in absolutist concepts of private property ownership than in concepts of social trusteeship. Within the private sector there remains a heavy concentration of ownership by a very small proportion of the population. The growth of consumer ownership through the Co-operative Movement has been steadily declining. Nevertheless, Collectivism has been reflected in the growing influence of the public sector. Already, one man in four is employed by a public authority, public investment exceeds private investment, and the combined expenditure of all public authorities (including the capital expenditure of the nationalised industries) is over half the national income.

Yet the system has not become one of governing the economy through popular mandate in the sense that it sets out to supersede the activities of privately organised firms by obliging them to conform to the aims of a policy arrived at independently by the State. Neither has it become one in which the activities of firms are left to be dictated exclusively by market forces reflecting the preferences of individual producers without regard to wider economic purposes and longer-term goals.[1] But ultimate authority, in the workplace, is still vested in management. The mixed economy merely provides a bureaucratic framework for a system of pushes and pulls over the social costs and benefits of resource allocation. It remains a system in which capital-owners and managers, in public or private industry, maintain domination over worker interests while continuously appealing for worker co-operation. Public and private management keep one eye on Government and what it will do next. The consumer keeps a wary eye on management and the Government.

[1] See Sir Alexander Cairncross, 'The Managed Economy', *The Advancement of Science*, **26**, 1969-70.

But here the checks and balances end. The trade unionist finds that such issues as job content, job satisfaction and job design—the principle of moulding the technological environment to benefit the personality of the worker—are neglected. The democratic idea of controlling his immediate work environment, by creating a work culture in which things are run by him rather than for him, is squashed into last place as a naïve and Utopian aspiration.

But Guild theory carries an important message for the modern Collectivist dilemma. The modern Guild theorist would argue that since the State has reached a point where it can only work through the co-operation of groups to achieve wider social goals, we must start our analysis again by viewing individuals in their various group contexts—in industry, up through the workplace, enterprise units and industrial unions to the national level. This is the *functionalist* argument for placing management in the hands of producers' organisations, and for sharing control between these and other organisations representing men as 'consumers and users'. This differs from modern modes of the moment such as 'countervailing power' or 'co-determination' since it carries a moral undertone. The moral core is that self-government in industry gives men freedom to express their personality through their work experience. Since human beings desire freedom to make their own choices through experience and education, and the political system recognises that desire through the machinery of democracy, so the economic system should be elevated to the same moral purposes. If management carries the heavy burden of economic decision-making in conditions of uncertainty, then every individual has the right to share in those burdens by becoming fully equipped to share in economic decisions.

The argument for industrial control, pursued by the Guildsmen, is quite distinct from that of the Syndicalists who viewed all economic power as coming, via revolution, to reside in the hands of the unions. The Industrial Republic of Industrial Unions is a conception far removed from the co-sovereignty of the congress of National Guilds. Nevertheless, Guild doctrine sails closer to Syndicalism than to Collectivism. As Cole insists, 'A close analysis of the Syndicalist demand points the way to the only real solution. That absolute ownership of the means of production by the Unions to which some Syndicalists look forward is but a perversion and an exaggeration of a just demand. The workers ought to control the normal conduct of industry; but they ought not to regulate the price of commodities at will, to dictate to the consumer what he shall consume, or, in short, to exploit the community as the individual profiteer exploits it today.' What then is the solution? We come, full circle, to a division of functions between the State, the Guilds, and other associations. That is to say, the Guildsmen have a definite political theory, quite apart from the strategy of 'encroaching control', which differentiates them sharply from the Syndicalists, Anarchists, and crypto-Marxists.

Most Guildsmen were sceptical of apocalyptic change through revolution, which Cole himself describes as 'catastrophe', pinning their hopes on encroaching control, the creation of local Guilds, the direct creation of Guilds by Trade Unions, and the extension of public ownership which would eventually permit the workers a gradually increasing share in management. Whatever the setbacks to the Guild experiments in the 1920's—

when the State accepted no responsibility for the overall management of the economy—history vindicates the Guildsmen's mistrust of revolutionary movements using 'industrial democracy' as a stalking horse in efforts to capture the State. Since the demand for workers' participation is part of 'the human condition' which arises out of an industrial system geared to efficiency, growth and profit, most revolutionary movements will pay lip-service to gain popular support, justifying later repressive actions in terms of a post-dated cheque on the 'Co-operative Commonwealth'. The Guildsmen recognised that 'industrial democracy' would be reduced to a vulnerable slogan unless it was backed by its own political theory. Their perception was uncanny. The Utopian strands in the Soviet approach to industrial democracy, popularly acclaimed by Bukharin and Preobrazhensky, become twisted in the 'conveyor-belt' theory of the Marxist State where industrial organisations and unions existed only to serve the ends of the Communist Party. The Utopian strands in the Anarchist approach proved equally vulnerable in the Latin soil of anarchism, where they became distorted into a perversion termed the 'corporate' State, in Italy—a development which is still mirrored in the economic organisation of Spain and Portugal.

But the Guildsmen were also right in recognising that 'industrial democracy' as they saw it was more revolutionary than the 'revolutionaries' who proved unwilling to change the nature of the wage system. As Simone Weil was to emphasise, the cry for industrial democracy is persistent because it is the cry of a deep-seated human need.[1] Where that need is denied—in the

[1] Simone Weil, *L'Enracinement* (1943).

Communist system or in the West—the undercurrents of frustration boil over into political discontent. The 1960's experienced such a resurgence of excitement and interest in the ideas of industrial democracy; although the watchword of 'participation' still often cloaks a situation where individuals are aware that authority styles in factories, offices and classrooms are faulty without thinking rationally about replacing them with a democratic system. *Self-Government in Industry* illustrates that this debate is not novel. The idea of workers' control of industry is a revival of the first ideas of working-class combinations. It was not new in the 1900's when it was forced to the front by Syndicalism in America and France. It was not new in the debate between the Guildsmen, the Syndicalists and the Collectivists. It is not new in the sudden-found enthusiasm of the Labour Party or the Liberal Party. It represents a return, after a long sojourn in the wilderness of State power and reform, to the idealism of the early revolutionaries. But the pool of ideas, muddied by the clichés of 'participation', calls for as much clear thought as ever before. 'Participation' can still become a cover for the State centralist seeking sugar for his revolution, a pill for the capitalist to seduce the workers, or a cry of futile ambition rather than a focus upon concrete goals.

The hallmark of the true revolutionary lies in his ability to conceive Utopia, not in his ability to sloganise. Those who condemn managerial functions as pure 'autocracy', like those who defend managerial roles as pure 'guardianship', ignore the inherent existence of bureaucracy in social decision-making. Such slogans have a seductive force because they mix up social paradox with economic welfare. But paradox is an *intellectual* device. No social order—unless it runs on double-speak—can be *based* on such tenets as property is theft, democracy is the State, law is crime. Paradox, as Proudhon saw, is useful in *criticising* the established order. Dilemma has to be recognised in building a new one. We can use terms internal to the tradition in order to change it. It is this which Cole does to the theory of self-government in industry.

Like all significant social documents, *Self-Government in Industry* can be viewed against the economic and social context of its time. It is easy with Utopian programmes to dismiss them as a futile dream with relevance only to long-gone circumstances, or to treat them as an aberration in the history of the Labour Movement. But the test of theoretical significance is whether the problems identified are perennial, and, as we have shown, the problems of industrial government are with us today. One cannot dismiss Guild Socialism merely because it did not serve as an incitement to sweeping change in the depressed economy of the inter-war years. Cole's motive was to provide both a programme for action and a theory; and the *theory* must be evaluated in its own right.

Cole's purpose in advocating workers' control was to create an active citizenship out of the labour force, in which he included managers, technicians and white-collar workers as well as manual workers. Unless responsibility were placed upon them squarely, they would remain open to the charge of being too 'immature' to evolve a democratic system of industrial government. *Self-Government in Industry* represents only part of a stream of ideas, chiefly emanating from the National Guilds League. Cole himself underpinned these ideas by initiating, for the first time in Britain, fundamental research into the *roots* of the existing industrial relations system. Unlike the Webbs, he was prepared to expose the minutiae of industrial sociology and labour economics in tracing the character of the collective bargaining system and the nature of workshop organisation.[1] This programme of empirical research, embodied in the Carnegie studies, in *Labour in War-Time*, *Trade Unionism on the Railways*, and *The Payment of Wages*, laid the foundations for most of our contemporary industrial relations studies, exerting an influence which may be clearly seen fifty years later in the deliberations of the Royal Commission on Trade Unions and the reports of the National Board for Prices and Incomes. Yet this labour was only a by-product of Cole's systematic espousal of Guild Socialism, in *The World of Labour*, *Self-Government in Industry*, *Social Theory*, and *Guild Socialism Re-Stated*.

Throughout these theoretical works, Cole continuously revised his position towards an ever-increasing sophistication of the machinery for the functional representation of the citizen. But *Self-Government in Industry* contains most of the essentials of his thought on the problem of creating extra-Guild machinery to determine wider community interest and to co-ordinate producer interests. A young man's book written with a mature man's insight, its purpose was 'to give body and definiteness to the Guild idea even at the risk of being prematurely dogmatic or even absolutely wrong'. It ran through four editions, the message being eagerly absorbed by a militant generation emerging from the holocaust of war and about to face the trauma of the General Strike. Here, the newly edited text is that of

[1] See G. D. H. Cole, *Workshop Organisation*; *Trade Unionism and Munitions*; and *Labour in the Coal-Mining Industry*.

the first edition. Despite the defects of exposition so
frankly admitted by Cole, it retains the full freshness
and appeal of the Guild philosophy which was to
attract a glittering circle of sympathisers including
R. H. Tawney, Leonard Woolf, George Lansbury and
Bertrand Russell. Throughout the succeeding editions,
the theme stands largely unscathed amid an internal
debate amongst the Guildsmen, in which Cole crossed
swords with S. G. Hobson and A. R. Orage over the
concept of State sovereignty.

Whereas Cole stuck to the pluralist position, Hobson theoretically claimed for the State an unlimited
authority. Cole initially made his stand on the idea that
the Central Government and local authorities were
primarily geographical or 'neighbourhood' organisations, and therefore fitted to express the point of view
of the consumer of goods and services. Since the
industrial nature of the unions and Guilds meant that
they had a 'selective' structure, they were to represent
men as producers of goods and services. However, Cole
later came to reconsider the State as a typical 'neighbourhood' organisation in favour of a more decentralised system, because communal needs become
ultimately decomposed into smaller areas than those
encompassed by the State. To find an appropriate form
of political representation, Cole was prepared to
categorise consumption in spatial terms, using concepts
highly reminiscent of modern input–output relationship
matrices. Such an approach may be too hastily
criticised by the latter-day economist, on the ground
that it fails to gather the complete structure of inter-
dependencies within the net of a 'general equilibrium
system'. Indeed, Leon Walras—to whom laissez-faire
economists often bow without realising that his chief

occupation was the promotion of French quasi-Guilds—
spent his lifetime in constructing such an abstract
mathematical system. Be that as it may, Cole was
unerring in his social instinct about the primacy of
locally expressed needs and for machinery to reflect
those needs on the 'national' resource allocation
pattern. As modern centralised States have found, to
their cost, non-representation of the diversity of local
social and economic needs leads society straight into
the swamp of 'environmental' and 'urban' problems
which hallmark the closing decades of the twentieth
century.

Self-Government in Industry is essentially a series of
self-contained essays grouped around the central theme
of industrial democracy. The revised (1919) version
starts with a passionate plea for National Guilds,
followed by the implications for the Trade Union
movement and backed by a social analysis of the power
factors underlying the wage system linking man to his
work. The rest of the book consists of a classic essay on
the nature of the State, a discussion upon State ownership and control, some positive institutional proposals
for the expansion of freedom for producers through
Guilds, and ends with a speculative glimpse of the
relationship between the Guilds and the consumer.

'The Case for National Guilds' is a powerful polemic
in the style of the early radical pamphleteers, in which
Cole was better versed than most. He switches key
in 'The Re-organisation of Trade Unionism', where
Industrial Unionism is presented as the only organi-
sational form which can make an effective claim to
assume control of industry. But the argument also rests
on sociological recognition of the workplace roles in
industrial relations and on a normative view that trade

union government should become an exercise in democracy. The import sounds astonishingly modern to any student acquainted with the theoretical literature upon the Donovan debate over the future of industrial relations: 'The true basis of Trade Unionism is in the workshop, and failure to recognise this is responsible for much of the weakness of Trade Unionism today. The workshop affords a natural unit which is a direct stimulus to self-assertion and control by the rank and file. Organisation that is based on the workshop runs the best chance of being democratic and of conforming to the principles that authority should reside, to the greatest possible extent, in the hands of the governed.' Interestingly enough, Cole also foreshadows the modern revolution in TUC authority, spurred by the impact of voluntary incomes policy, when arguing that since the central body 'cannot bind the Unions in dealing with the employers or the State, and they cannot harmonise with any authority internal differences . . . centralisation is needed not only nationally but locally'.

The 'Abolition of the Wage-system' echoes William Morris in condemning the warping of personality through the existing system of industrial ownership, and differs from Marx in seeing that worker exploitation will not resolve itself inevitably through revolutionary seizure of the State. But its foresight strikingly focuses upon the major elements in the modern controversy over the nature and evolution of the wage system. Cole turns deliberately away from the concept of wage as 'reward', towards pluralistic concepts of work motivation and the development of a socially based co-operative relationship in work organisations. This was far-sighted at a time when 'scientific management', and such practical developments as the Bedaux system of payment, had become theoretically based on a cynical one-motive view of worker 'involvement' in economic activity.

What Cole shows is that the search for *pure* economic criteria of 'co-operation' or 'worker integration', so fervently pursued in private and public enterprises today, is a futile search. The economic reasons for the inconsistency of such criteria lie in the indeterminacy of pay as an economic price. It is intimately related to the nature of the enterprise as a decision-making process. On management's side, the expected or actual 'marginal net productivity' of any individual worker cannot be known or estimated with any objective or scientific accuracy. On the workers' side, an individual tends to accept authority only when it is perceived as inescapable or legitimate. To stabilise enterprise relationships, pay must be thought to be 'fair', but it can never be demonstrated to be 'fair' in any economic sense, except perhaps by unsatisfactory appeals to a model of the pricing system involving remote and mechanistic equilibrating tendencies conjured from highly unrealistic assumptions. Because the market process is deficient, it becomes impossible to specify 'co-operation', in economic terms alone, in any way which can side-step the moral dimensions of industrial government and ownership. The characteristics of 'co-operation'—quite apart from the fact that what may be functional to the organisation may be dysfunctional to the individual—are bound up with the nature of the *work process* itself: communal identification, reciprocating information flows, the avoidance of unilaterally designed or imposed aids, and the sharing of responsibility and results. So except by introducing a prescriptive content, in *social* terms, into the concept of 'co-operation' in the enterprise, it cannot become operational. And it is this problem which Cole spots, and attempts to solve by urging that 'out of the bargaining trade union must grow the producing Guild'.

Unlike some of his fellow Guildsmen, Cole tended to accept nationalisation as a practical phase in which labour would begin the gradual process of democratising industry. The impact of bureaucracy would stimulate the demand for internal control, and would pull in technicians and managers, leading to the emergence of strong National Guilds. Out of the equilibrium of joint control power will slip into the hands of the workers: nationalisation is only dangerous in proportion as trade unionism is weak. Yet he also insists that workers' control—in both nationalised and private sectors— could not come about unless the *unions* wanted it, and that it had to develop from within the collective bargaining system. It cannot grow from outside. On this logic, the tendency for nationalisation from 1945 to 1970 to avoid *major* experiments in industrial democracy, even in the re-nationalised steel industry, would be partly explicable in terms of the weakness of trade union structure and attitudes.

In the chapter titled 'State Ownership and Control', the time scale becomes a mixture of immediate strategy and millennial vision, precariously phased on the gradual tactics of 'encroaching control'. Joint control is seen as a means and not an end. By 'joint control' Cole, in 1917, implies the development of effective job regulation through transitional social machinery, and not the Whitley idea of joint industrial wage-negotiating bodies which came to dominate collective bargaining doctrine right up to the close of the 1960's. Where Cole may be criticised is not so much in his analysis, as in expecting too much from the Trade Unions too soon. He himself realised that there is a sense in which a transition period of divided control with capitalism is inevitable', and predicted that 'Labour must pass through the stage of joint machinery for the control of production before it can assume complete control'.

The modern Guild theorist might argue it is only now, when the tripartite approach to industrial relations policy raises problems of co-ordinating overall objectives with enterprise behaviour, that the mixed economy has reached the transition stage of shared power. Both political doctrine and industrial practice now appear to be converging upon the idea that the present system may be reasonably interpreted as a series of transitional steps towards workers' control. The Labour Party, for fifty years intrinsically hostile to the case for industrial democracy, has finally endorsed it. The special 1968 statement, *Industrial Democracy*, starts from the principle that 'the growth of industrial democracy must be based on the general and effective recognition of the *right* of workers to organisation, representation and participation in major matters affecting their working lives.'[1] Within industry, the current evolution of collective bargaining anticipates a progressive process of participation within the plant, through the framework of procedures laid down by joint rules. Productivity agreements, for

[1] Suspicion of Guild Socialism, however, still colours this significant document. It goes on to say that, 'The aim of this approach would be to extend democracy in industry, not by evolving new and complex (and perhaps alien) structures, but by gradually increasing involvement in a development of existing machinery—which is already known and used because it deals with fundamental questions like pay and conditions. It would encourage a movement towards participation in democratic procedures; a natural evolution rather than an attempt to conjure democracy out of the air.'

example, have created bodies charged with the specific functions of joint determination over a wide range of factors affecting enterprise behaviour and worker welfare. Even management has come to appreciate that the psycho-socio-technical environment—which includes within its umbrella the claims of workers to become fully functioning human beings—is a key to the integration of the individual and the organisation.[1] The traditional notion of 'managerial prerogatives', which Cole attacks so fiercely, has been eroded by the growth of shop steward power under full employment. There is a general recognition that the bottom of our two-tier system of industrial negotiation is perhaps more important than the top. The new realism, the new humanisation of industrial values, the development of new procedures, and the fanning-out of the bargaining range comprise a process amenable to long-term social goals. It is here that modern Guild theory imparts a directional sense.

It may be thought that this is interpreting the current evidence too selectively. There is, indeed, a 'modern' school of thought upon industrial relations: which argues that it is the joint authorship of the industrial rules, rather than the procedures and sanctions available for their interpretation, which characterises collective bargaining. It follows that the bargaining process does not exclude third-party interests. Collective bargaining boils down to an activity, producing social costs or benefits, which involves power relationships between conflicting groups in the formulation of jointly agreed rules for regulating behaviour. But there is no *inevitable* incompatibility

[1] See Chris Argyris, *Interpersonal Competence and Organizational Effectiveness* (Tavistock, 1962).

between this analysis and the theoretical structure of Guild Socialism. The Guild theorist, as Cole explains in the chapter 'National Guilds and the Consumer', frankly admits the function of a third party, to introduce a 'consistency pattern' into industrial relationships, so that individual interests do not seriously conflict with the overall social interest. Guild theory does not differ greatly, from the 'modern' school of thought, upon *fundamentals*. It differs upon the *way* in which third-party interests should be introduced, by insisting that social responsibility should be created through an entirely new relationship—between the Guilds and the State. Social responsibility, in this sense, carries a double connotation. It means that industry should become more responsible to the community. But it also means that industry should become more responsible to human beings valued as ends in themselves.

The ultimate test of Guild theory, forged in the fading light of laissez-faire society, lies in its adaptability to present-day circumstances. To avoid confronting the embedded problems of distribution—the distribution of income, property and power—society has turned temporarily towards growth, efficiency and technology as an escape from social reconstruction. These 'economic' objectives, apparently above the fray of conflicting values, carry a spurious primacy because they narrow down to threatened national survival in a competitive world. But their social quality is negligible, since ultimately such preferences stem from, and appeal to, the passing value systems belonging to an acquisitive society. The process may become increasingly self-destructive: pressures for fundamental economic change, unregistered on a system which stifles worker consent, understanding and participation, tend to fail the social test. The mushrooming of large-scale organisation, the hidden locations of decision-making powers, the destruction of face-to-face relationships, breed explosive social crisis at the maximum; or, at the minimum, a despairing mood that the social system is 'out of control'. The objections to a present-day application of Guild *theory* have become far less formidable than they once seemed.

Some of the objections mustered against workers' control are as naïve and unrealistic as the Guild ideals were once thought to be. The weakest objection may be summarised as the 'plain man's view': industrial democracy 'runs against the grain of human nature'; workers are incapable of governing themselves; they have neither the inclination, the education nor the talents. This view, however, rests upon a long-exploded assumption—still commonplace in bar-room conversation—that 'human nature' is constant, that it is an entity, that it is easily perceived, and that it is a simple attribute belonging solely to isolated individuals. As William Morris acidly reminds us, in *News from Nowhere*, 'human nature' cannot be analysed without the social context and the opportunities denied or offered by it: 'What human nature? The human nature of paupers, of slaves, of slave-holders, or the human nature of wealthy free men? Which? Come tell me that!' The trouble with the 'plain man's view' is precisely that man has a *social* personality: individual 'human natures' interact between themselves and with their social environment; individuals internalise the values inherent in their immediate social context; 'individual personality' is not a simple attribute open to casual observation but a complexity for the impersonal and objective appraisal of the psychologist and sociologist. Social education is just as much concerned with changing human perceptions as with increasing human skill and knowledge.

The weakness in the 'plain man's view', which denies opportunity by denying human potentiality, is that it embraces an authoritarian value system which is *socially* derived from the self-justification of old-style management. It reflects the nineteenth-century idea that the worker is 'morally deficient'. In the twentieth century, just as society has discovered that mass unemployment was not the fault of the individual worker but the fault of the system, so society is discovering that the under-employment of social skills is not the moral deficiency of the individual but the fault of a system which acknowledges democracy in political affairs while denying democracy in industrial affairs.

An equally flimsy objection to the Guild ideal is that, since it falls into the trap of fostering bureaucracy via democracy, it cannot be seriously considered as an alternative to the existing system of industrial autocracy. But this argument falls to the wayside since it depends upon double standards. Few advocates would go on to suggest that, since political democracy itself is vulnerable to the same danger, *political* democracy must be rejected, although most are more than willing to reject industrial democracy on these very grounds. The argument contains a half-truth: democratic institutions are imperfect, and are prey to oligarchic and bureaucratic demoralisation. The inner strength of the Guild ideal, however, flows from its concrete focus upon the omnipresent danger of bureaucracy in political and social structures. Whatever the quarrels over the

institutional blueprints of Guild Socialism, one is
forced to recognise that they are designed to subdue
this danger by the decentralisation of power and the
creation of a system of checks and balances. The Guild
system is not a perfect one. But the true touchstone is
whether it is more just and less imperfect than the
current system of government in industry.

The traditional objections to the Guild programme
from the Collectivists are stronger, but they now carry
less weight: the programme presupposes an unrealistic
cohesion in Trade Union structure and attitudes.[1] It
remains true that there is no Trade Union movement
with a collective purpose, only a collection of Trade
Unions with sectional interests. But it is also true that,
in the last few years, unions have begun to seek *common*
objectives in an economy committed to economic
growth and stability. The reshaping of union structures
has been perceptibly moving nearer towards the original
Guild concepts of 'industrial unionism'.[2] The arguments
long deployed against 'industrial unionism' have been
so familiar that it is easy to overlook the modern trends
towards the concept of industrial self-identification. It
is easy to pick holes in the concept of an 'industry',
where boundaries are blurred by international operations, multi-product enterprises and occupational
spread. Nevertheless, the concept has now been seeded
through the new commitment to economic planning:
for instance, industrial self-identification through the
industrial 'neddies' and the industrial training boards is
now being reflected backwards into the Trade Union
movement.

[1] Branko Pribicevic, *The Shop Stewards' Movement and Workers'
Control* (Blackwell, 1959).
[2] See the TUC special reports on the proceedings of the 1969 post-
Donovan union conferences on collective bargaining.

A more serious obstacle to the operational *feasibility* of Guilds arises from the problems of investment and pricing criteria. These bristle with difficulties, as society has seen in the case of the nationalised sector,[1] and there are many theoretical problems in achieving the appropriate 'efficiency fit' for the Guild system. But this should not blind society to the *existing* irrationalities in private investment and pricing decisions. It is this phenomenon which has produced the continuous demand for planning and economic reform.

The theoretical problems of the Guild Utopian economy will belong to the economic theorist.[2] He will readily admit that, in our real life economy, Pareto-optimality is not a useful criterion and that competitive equilibrium is devoid of data content. However, he is less ready to generalise about an abstract future economy whose resources are not under State or private ownership. The real intellectual task, for those students of political economy who are dedicated to social reform, is to develop Utopian economic theory now: to a stage where it matches the insights and achievements of Utopian social theory.

JOHN CORINA

St. Peter's College, Oxford

[1] See *Reports from the Select Committee on Nationalised Industries* (1965–8).

[2] See M. L. Burstein, *Economic Theory. Equilibrium and Change* (Wiley, 1968).

CHAPTER I

THE NATURE OF THE STATE

I

IT has often been said that, if men would only agree
upon the definition of the terms they use, they would
have nothing left to quarrel about. This is probably
true ; but it is the less important because the definition
of terms is the last point on which men are ever likely
to agree. If I begin this book with a definition, it is
because that definition will plunge me at once into
controversy, and furnish the readiest opportunity of
explaining my general position.

What is a State ? A State is nothing more or less
than the political machinery of government in a
community.

The civilised world of to-day consists of a number
of politically independent and sovereign communities,
of which many have other communities dependent
upon them. Each independent community expresses
itself in its relations to the others through its machinery
of government, *i.e.* through the State. Each independent community, and most of the dependent
communities, use their States also for many internal
acts affecting the relations of individuals and groups
one to another and to the whole. States are thus
governmental institutions existing to express common

purposes and undertake common actions on behalf of communities.

In every community there are many forms and instances of common action in which the State has no part. Within each community, and often extending into several communities, there are innumerable forms of association which are no part of the State. The sum total of organised corporate action in the community is far greater than the action undertaken by the State, the degree in which it is greater depending upon the extent to which co-operation prevails in the community, and on the sphere of action marked out for itself by the State within the community.

For two different things two names are needed. When I have to refer to the organised machinery of government, national and local, I shall speak of 'the State.' When, on the other hand, I have to refer to the whole complex of institutions for common action in the community, I shall speak of 'Society.' State, Churches, the Labour Movement—these and many other institutions are included in the term 'Society.' But both the State, or governmental machine, and Society, the complex of communal institutions, are distinct from the community itself, which stands behind them and sustains them. Society is the mechanism of the communal will ; but that will resides only in the community itself.

Here already are all the materials of a logomachy. All these special associations, I shall be told, are just as much a part of the State as the Government itself ; for the State is the community, and there is no difference between them. Such an argument takes my breath away ; but it is with this facile identification of the community and the State that the advocates of State

Sovereignty throw dust in the public's eyes. The answer to it is simple. If the State is the community, and the community the State, why all this pother about the sphere of State action ? Why advocate or oppose State Socialism, since it is manifest that, however our industry may be organised, it is the State that organises it ? Why denounce the Trades Disputes Act—are not the Trade Unions a part of the State ? Why do the Majority and Minority of the Poor Law Commission thus furiously rage together—is not even the Charity Organisation Society a part, and no mean part, of the State ?

Surely these questions suffice to show how fatal it is to use a vital word in two different senses. The State seems to be the community, and can plausibly be put forward as the community, simply because it does claim to be the supreme representative of the community, and because it does at present hold a position of such power as to make its influence in the community superior to that of any other association. But all this is merely a question of fact. The fact that the State claims to be the community, and in fact exercises the greatest part of the community's power, does nothing to prove that the State is rightfully the community, or its sole representative, or that it has an absolute claim upon the individual's loyalty and service.

Our definition has carried us a certain distance. We have seen that the State is different from the community, and that it is not the only institution in the community. That being established, we can repeat our original question in a new form.

What is the real nature of that governmental machine which we have agreed to call ' the State ' ? The question will certainly give rise to an interesting variety

of answers. The Anarchist will tell us that the State
is the protector of property, and that with the passing
of Capitalism the need for the State, and the State
itself, will disappear. The Philosophic Radical will
tell us that the State exists to remove the hindrances
to the good life, and, in doing so, to promote the
greatest happiness of the greatest number. The
Collectivist will hold out the ideal of a State democratically controlled organising the whole national life in the
common interest. Lastly, the Idealist philosophers will
maintain that the State is the supreme expression of
the national consciousness, and that in it alone is the
will of the individual fully realised.

But suppose none of these answers satisfies us—
suppose we say that they are not definitions at all,
but descriptions of what their makers believe that the
State does or might do—where then shall we seek
for a better answer and a truer definition ? We
have maintained that the State is a machine : let
us take the machine to pieces and see of what it is
made.

At different times and in different places, the State
has assumed many forms ; and its actual character
has always borne a close relation to the social structure
of the community in which it has existed. Feudal
communities found expression in feudal States, or
rather created feudal States to be their expression.
In the same way, modern capitalism has created the
capitalist State, and the States of to-day faithfully
reflect the social and economic structure of the communities in which they exist. Wealth dominates
them, as wealth dominates the social life of to-day ;
beginnings of democracy modify their capitalist character, as the social autocracy of capitalism is already

challenged and modified by the beginnings of social democracy.

The real action of the State in any time or place is, then, determined by the distribution of power in the community. Political power is in itself nothing : it is important not for itself, but as the expression of social power. This social power may assume many forms—military, ecclesiastical, agrarian, economic, industrial—but, under modern conditions, it is inevitably in the main economic and industrial in character. Whatever may have held good in other times, it is true of our own that economic power is the key to political power, and that those who control the means of production are able, by means of that control, to dominate the State.

Nor is their power dependent on an actual organisation of the machinery of State in their interest. However the State may be organised, and whatever parliamentary system may exist, economic dominance will find its expression in political dominance. It is a commonplace that Great Britain to-day is an oligarchy equipped with democratic, or partially democratic, political institutions. The fact that these institutions are largely democratic in form does not make them democratic in practice, because the power of capitalism stands behind the State. Capitalism controls the funds of the great parties, and thereby controls their policies : Capitalism controls the press, and thereby twists and deforms public opinion to its own ends : and, even if these expedients fail, no Government dares to run seriously counter to the wishes and interests of the great economic magnates.

I do not say that this domination of capitalism is absolute. Small things can be done, and small reforms secured, against its will ; but it cannot be seriously threatened by political means. In politics, democracy can nibble, but it may not bite ; and it will not be able to bite until the balance of economic power has been so changed as to threaten the economic dominance of capitalism. Then, maybe, politics will become a real battle-ground instead of an arena of sham fights ; but the power of the disputants will be still the economic power which stands at their back.

The external forms of State organisation, therefore, do not serve, under existing conditions, to determine the real character of the State ; for, whatever these forms may be, its real character is determined from without, by the interplay of economic forces. These actual forms are none the less important for our purpose, and are the real subject matter of this chapter. While there exists a conflict between social classes, whether in industry or elsewhere, the State machinery will be warped to express the results of that conflict ; but, given a community in which no such class-struggle exists, what would be the character of the State ? What, in fact, would be the character and form of the Socialist State ?

The State in its evolution has assumed many forms as well as expressed many social powers. The feudal State was territorial in its basis, and, in so far as it was representative, represented territorial landowners. With the decay of feudalism, the territorial basis of the State was weakened, though it survives faintly to our own time in some rural constituencies, which continue faithfully to send the local landowner to Parliament. Largely, however, the old territorial State passed away before modern times, and was replaced by an oligarchy of wealth divorced from local service. The rotten borough, of course, was the supreme expression of this delocalised oligarchy.

The beginnings of democracy in the State are also the beginnings of a new territorialism. The House of Lords, once the most purely territorial of assemblies, has almost wholly lost that character, and is now a mere survival. The House of Commons, on the other hand, is still territorial in its basis, in that its members are elected by, and sit for, geographical constituencies. It is true that under present conditions this geographical character is more apparent than real : the member elected for a particular constituency is often merely a ' carpet-bagger,' the nominee of one of the parties, supported in his candidature out of national party funds, and wholly unconnected with the constituency which elects him. Even Labour and Socialist representation is by no means innocent of the ' carpet-bag ' ; for the big national Trade Union may send its parliamentary nominee to a constituency much as the organisers of the capitalist parties would send theirs.

Nevertheless, it may safely be affirmed, as a broad generalisation, that the State, in so far as it is democratic, is also territorial. The Collectivist clearly recognises this fact when he puts forward his demand for nationalisation as a demand that industry shall be controlled by the consumer. For ' consumer ' has, in the main, a geographical meaning. The interest which binds men together as consumers is a local interest, whether it be the common interest that finds expression in the Co-operative Store or in Municipal Trading, or the wider common interest that is found in the Co-operative Wholesale Society or in national ownership and control of industry.

If, then, we would discover the true nature of the

State and its relation to the individual and to other forms of association in a democratic Society, we must treat it as a geographical organisation, in which men are represented on a basis of neighbourhood or inhabitancy. In the lesser organs of State power, *i.e.* in Local Government, this geographical basis is clearly realised ; but it is not so often seen that the principle of organisation is essentially the same in a democratic national Parliament as in a municipality.

As a territorial or geographical association, the State is clearly marked out as the instrument for the execution of those purposes which men have in common by reason of ' neighbourhood.' It is easiest to make plain the meaning of this principle by taking first the case of a municipal body. That body represents all the citizens as enjoyers in common of the land, housing, amenities and social character of the city. The municipal council is therefore, or would be if it were democratic, the proper body to deal with those public matters which, broadly speaking, affect all the citizens equally and in the same way, that is, affect them as citizens. It has not the same *prima facie* qualification for dealing with those matters which affect the citizens in different ways, according as they happen to be bakers or tramwaymen, Protestants or Catholics. The municipal council represents the individuals who inhabit the city as ' users ' or ' enjoyers ' in common, and is qualified to legislate on matters of ' use ' and ' enjoyment ' ; but if we would represent individuals as bakers or tramwaymen, Protestants or Catholics, we must seek other forms of organisation in which these things are made the basis of representation.

The case is the same with the national State. Parliament does, in so far as it is democratic, represent men as 'users' or 'enjoyers' in common, this time on a national instead of a local basis. It is therefore qualified to deal with matters of national 'use' or 'enjoyment'; but it is not equally qualified in those matters which affect men differently according as they are miners or railwaymen, Catholics or Protestants.

The theory of State Sovereignty falls to the ground, if this view of the fundamental nature of the State is correct. State Sovereignty, if the phrase has any meaning at all, implies, not indeed that the State ought to interfere in every sphere of human action, but that the State has ultimately a right to do so. It regards the State as the representative of the community in the fullest sense, and as the superior both of the individual 'subject' and of every other form of association. It regards the State as the full and complete representative of the individual, whereas, if the view just put forward is correct, the State only represents the individual in his particular aspect of 'neighbour,' 'user' and 'enjoyer.' The advocates of State Sovereignty, if they do not regard the State as being the community, do at least regard it as 'sustaining the person of the community,' whereas our whole view is that the person of the community cannot truly be sustained by any single form of organisation.

This difference of view appears most distinctly when we survey the differing views taken by various schools of thought concerning the nature of associations other than the State, and their relation to the State. A controversy, mediaeval in its origin, but revived in modern times, has centred round this question, and has derived topical interest in our own day and from our special point of view, because it has arisen in an acute form in connection with the legal position of Trade Unionism. The Osborne decision, which rendered illegal the use of Trade Union funds for political purposes, was based upon a totally wrong conception of the nature of Trade Unionism. Special legislation accordingly had to be passed to restore to the Unions even a modified freedom in this respect.

The real principle at issue was greatly more important than the important special point involved. The judges, in giving their decision, were really affirming their view that Trade Union rights are purely the creation of statute law and that Trade Unions themselves are artificial bodies created by statute to perform certain functions. Some opponents of the Osborne decision, on the other hand, expressed the view that a Trade Union is not a creature of statute law, but a natural form of human association, and therefore capable of growth and the assumption of new purposes. In short, there was really, on the one side, the view that all the rights and powers of other forms of association are derived from the State, and, on the other side, the view that these rights and powers belong to such associations by virtue of their nature and the purposes for which they exist.

Let us now try to apply the view which we have taken of the State's real nature to this particular case. Trade Unions are associations based on the ' vocational ' principle. They seek to group together in one association all those persons who are co-operating in making a particular kind of thing or rendering a particular kind of service. In the common phrase, they are associations of ' producers,' using ' production ' in the widest sense. The State, on the other hand, we have decided to regard as an association of ' users ' or ' enjoyers,' of ' consumers,' in the common phrase.

If this view is right, we cannot regard Trade Unions as deriving their rights, including the right to exist, from the State. Associations of producers and consumers alike may be said, in a sense, to derive these rights from the community ; but we cannot conceive of an association of producers deriving its right to exist from an association of ' users.'

Our view, then, of the nature and rights of vocational and other forms of association is profoundly modified by the view we have taken of the nature of the State. We now see such associations as natural expressions and instruments of the purposes which certain groups of individuals have in common, just as we see the State, both in national and in local government, as the natural expression and instrument of other purposes which the same individuals have in common when they are grouped in another way. Similarly, our whole view of the relation of the State to other forms of association is profoundly modified, and we come to see the State, not as the ' divine ' and universally sovereign representative of the community, but as one among a number of forms of association in which men are grouped according to the purposes which they have in common. Men produce in common, and all sorts of association, from the mediaeval guild to the modern trust and the modern Trade Union, spring from their need to co-operate in production : they use and enjoy in common, and out of their need for common action and protection in their use and enjoyment spring the long series of States, the various phases of co-operation, the increasing developments of local government. They hold views in common, and out of their common opinions spring propagandist and doctrinaire associations of every sort : they believe in

common, and out of their need for fellowship and
worship spring churches, connections and covenants.

In all this diversity of human association, the State
can claim an important place, but not a solitary
grandeur. States exist for the execution of that very
important class of collective actions which affect all
the members of the communities in which they exist
equally and in the same way. For other classes of
action, in respect of which men fall into different
groups, other forms of association are needed, and
these forms of association are no less sovereign in their
sphere than the State in its sphere. There is no
universal Sovereign in the community, because the
individuals who compose that community cannot be
fully represented by any form of association. For
different purposes, they fall into different groups, and
only in the action and inter-action of these groups
does Sovereignty exist. Even so, it is an incomplete
Sovereignty ; for all the groups, which together make
up Society, are imperfectly representative of that
General Will which resides in the community alone.

This may seem to be a highly generalised view of
social organisation, and one which will not bear application to concrete problems. Of that, the reader will
be able to judge better at the end of this book ; for
the following chapters are, in the main, an attempt
to apply it. It is admitted, at the outset, that it does
not fully apply, and cannot be fully applied, to Society
as it exists to-day, because at every turn we are met
to-day by the conflict between economic classes for
the control of the machinery of social organisation.
But, in framing any far-reaching policy for the future,
we must have in mind, not only the Society of to-day,
but the logical development of that Society along

democratic lines, and, in particular, when we discuss the nature of any piece of social machinery, we must endeavour to see it both as it is, warped by class conflict, and as it would be if there were no class conflict in the community. In this chapter, while we have not been able to eliminate wholly consideration of the State as it is, we have been considering mainly the State as it would be in a democratic community immune from class conflict. We have seen that, in such a Society, the theory of State Sovereignty would be no more defensible than it is to-day, because the purification of the State would serve only to emphasise its real character as a geographical or territorial association of neighbours, users or enjoyers, and would make clear the limitations of its functions by opening the way for the full and free growth of other forms of association.

II

Having sketched in general my view of the true function of the State in a democratic community, let me endeavour to state my view more concretely, with reference to the particular theory of industrial organisation which I have in mind.

To every actual social system corresponds a theory of social relations. Rousseau's conception of the General Will greatly affected Revolutionary France ; the ideas of Bentham and Mill did much to mould the social legislation of industrial Great Britain. Every people, in fact, gets the social philosophy it deserves, and every social system in part throws up, and is in part thrown up by, an equivalent social theory. Guildsmen, therefore, cannot afford to neglect social theories, which are the stuff of which revolutions are made.

State Sovereignty is the theoretical equivalent of Collectivist practice : Guild Socialism, in its turn, must face anew the problem of ultimate social obligation, and must work out for itself a new theory.

I do not deny, as indeed, no one can deny if he desires to call himself either National Guildsman or Guild Socialist, that industry is not everything, and that industrial democracy cannot be truly national unless it is responsible in some sense to the community as a whole. What I do most emphatically deny is that this ultimate court of appeal is the State, in any sense in which the term is ordinarily understood. Of course, if by ' State ' is meant merely any ultimate body, there is no more to be said : in this sense everyone who is not an Anarchist is an advocate of State Sovereignty. But if the sovereignty of the State means the sovereignty of Parliament with its subordinate local bodies, then I maintain that it is utterly inconsistent with the principle on which Guild Socialism rests.

Parliament, Municipal and County Councils, School Boards, Boards of Guardians and the like, in fact, the whole complex machine which we call the State, are territorial associations, elected on a territorial basis by all the persons recognised as citizens who live within a definite locality. One and all, they are based upon the fact of living together, even if some relics of a different system survive, or if the territorial basis has become purely nominal, as in the House of Lords.

The bond between persons who live together is, in its material aspect, the fact that they are users or consumers in common of commodities and services. Parks, roads, houses, water and many other ' public utilities ' are consumed in common by all the dwellers within such and such an area. The sovereignty of the territorial association therefore means the sovereignty of the consumer—a fact which is continually recognised and acclaimed by Collectivists.

The Guild idea, as applied to industry, is in essence a denial of the industrial sovereignty of the organised consumers, that is, of territorial associations. It repudiates the industrial sovereignty of Parliament. But this does not mean either that it rejects the idea of communal sovereignty, or that it finds its sovereign within the Guilds themselves.

Anarchism set out to destroy State Sovereignty without replacing it : Syndicalism denied the sovereignty of the State only to enthrone the General Confederation of Labour in its stead. Guild Socialists, recognising that a purely industrial sovereign is no advance on a purely political sovereign, must create a political theory to fit the Guild idea.

Collectivism, we have seen, is the practical equivalent of State Sovereignty. It is not generally realised how completely Syndicalism is an inversion of Collectivism. The one asserts the absolute sovereignty of the consumers, of the territorial association : the other the sovereignty, no less absolute, of the producers, of the professional associations. Criticised for leaving out the producers, Collectivists will ask what it matters, since producers and consumers are, or would be in a Socialist Society, the same people ; criticised for neglecting the consumers, Syndicalists make precisely the same reply.

Guild Socialists recognise that neither the territorial nor the professional grouping is by itself enough ; that certain common requirements are best fulfilled by the former and certain others by the latter ; in short, that each grouping has its function and that neither is completely and universally sovereign. They see that the Guild, the grouping of all workers engaged in the same industry, is the body best fitted to execute certain purposes of a national character, and accordingly they assert that the National Guild is a necessary articulation of the national consciousness.

Similarly, they recognise that all the dwellers in a single area, the consumers in common of certain services and commodities, can best further their own and the nation's interest by joining together and forming a body to see to the supply of these services. They hold that the economic relationship between man and man only finds full expression when producers and consumers alike are organised—when the producer and the consumer negotiate on equal terms.

At the first stage, then, Guild Socialists postulate a double organisation—the National Industrial Guild on the side of the producers, and the Municipal Council on the side of the consumers. And clearly above the various municipal bodies there is, on the consumers' side, Parliament, the supreme territorial association.

It is at this point that Guild Socialists may easily be tempted to go wrong. While everyone visualises Parliament as the supreme territorial body, are we all equally clear on the industrial side? Too many people seem to think all along of the Guilds as a multiplicity—of each separate Guild as receiving its charter from Parliament, and dealing thereafter directly and finally with Parliament. That is certainly not my conception of the Guild system. Just as I visualise the smaller territorial associations unified in the great territorial association of Parliament, so I conceive that the various Guilds will be unified in a central Guild Congress, which will be the supreme industrial body,

standing to the people as producers in the same relation
as Parliament will stand to the people as consumers.
To deny State Sovereignty in industry is not to reduce
industry to a mere multiplicity of warring Guilds ; it
is to confront Parliament with an industrial body
which has an equal claim to be representative of the
nation as a whole. Neither Parliament nor the Guild
Congress can claim to be ultimately sovereign : the one
is the supreme territorial association, the other the
supreme professional association. In the one, because
it is primarily concerned with consumption, government is in the hands of the consumers ; in the other,
where the main business is that of production, the
producers hold sway.

But, as a recent critic of Guild Socialism has pointed
out, this separation of functions, which is fundamental
to the Guild system, does not solve the problem. The
nation is in all its aspects so interdependent, production
and consumption are so inextricably intertwined, that
no mere abstract separation of functions can form a
basis for a theory of the modern community. The
problem cannot, I admit, be left where it stands : if
the old Sovereign of Collectivism and the rival Sovereign of Syndicalism are alike dethroned, it remains for
Guild Socialists to affirm a new and positive theory of
sovereignty.

I can deal with the matter here only very briefly,
and solely in its industrial aspect. Where a single
Guild has a quarrel with Parliament, as I conceive it
may well have, surely the final decision of such a quarrel
ought to rest with a body representative of all the
organised consumers and all the organised producers.
The ultimate sovereignty in matters industrial would
seem properly to belong to some joint body representa-

tive equally of Parliament and of the Guild Congress. Otherwise, the scales must be weighted unfairly in favour of either consumers or producers. But if, on such questions, there is an appeal from Parliament and from the Guild Congress to a body more representative than either of them, the theories of State Sovereignty and Guild Congress Sovereignty must clearly be abandoned, and we must look for our ultimate sanction to some body on which not merely all the citizens, but all the citizens in their various social activities, are represented. Functional associations must be recognised as necessary expressions of the national life, and the State must be recognised as merely a functional association—' elder brother,' ' primus inter pares.' The new social philosophy which this changed conception of sovereignty implies has not yet been worked out ; but if Guild Socialists would avoid tripping continually over their own and other writers' terminology they would do well to lose no time in discovering and formulating clearly a theory con-consistent with the Guild idea and with the social structure they set out to create.

III

Our conceptions of government and social organisation depend inevitably upon our outlook on life. The power of a group advocating any particular type of social organisation depends upon the extent to which its members have, fundamentally, the same outlook on life.

The system of National Guilds appeals to me first of all as a balance of powers. Guildsmen have always recognised, and drawn a distinction between, two forms

of social power, economic and political. Economic
power, they hold, precedes political power. The social
class which at any time holds the economic power will
hold the political power also, and will be dispossessed
in the political sphere only by a new class which is able
to overthrow it in the economic sphere.

The first question which National Guildsmen have
to face, in adopting this position, and, at the same time,
holding to their double theory of social organisation, is
whether the very nature of the distinction which they
draw between economic and political power does not
result in obliterating the difference between them. This
is the fundamental character of the criticism urged
against them by Syndicalists and Marxian Industrial
Unionists. " You agree with us," such critics will
say, " that the State is only a pale reflexion of the
economic structure of Society. Why, then, seek to
preserve this mere mechanical device of capitalism
when the conditions which created it have ceased to
exist ? "

It is not enough for Guildsmen, or, at least, it does
not seem to me to be enough, to reply that reflexions
may have their uses, and that, if capitalistic industrialism has turned the State to its own ends, democratic
industrialism, in the day of its triumph, may with good
effect do the same. This is an answer, and perhaps a
sufficient answer ; but it is not, I am convinced, the
right answer for Guildsmen to make. For I am not
convinced that the State must be, under all social
conditions, merely a pale reflexion of the economic
structure of Society—at least, in any sense which
would preclude equality of power between them on
many issues.

In countries given over to capitalist industrialism,

the State is controlled by the industrial capitalists. That is a true description of things as they are, and it is clear that things can be changed only by means of a re-distribution of economic power. But, when this re-distribution has taken place and National Guilds are in being, will it still be true that economic power precedes political power ?

In our interpretation of history, the evolution of Society is seen as a long series of struggles between social classes for the possession of economic power. We envisage National Guilds, as Marx envisaged his conception of Socialism, as the culmination and completion of this long process. We do not doubt that development will continue after National Guilds have been brought into being ; but development will assume new forms. The class-struggle will be over, and the ' social class ' will be a thing of the past. Under these new conditions, will the old relation between economic and political power remain unchanged ? Is it not rather true that the existing relation arises out of, and depends upon, the class-struggle, so that with the ceasing of the class-struggle it, too, will cease to exist ? The contrast between economic and political power has only a strained application to those primitive conditions which preceded an acute division of classes : the strain will be altogether too great if we try to apply it to conditions in which there are no distinctions of class.

What, then, will be the relation between economic and political power under the Guilds ? A relation, I think, of equality—equality upon which the poise and vitality of Guild Society fundamentally depend. For, to me at least, the balance of power is the underlying principle of the Guilds and any departure from it would be destructive of their essential character. Let me explain more precisely what I mean.

We have disputed, time and again, about the Sovereignty of the State, and its application to Guild philosophy ; but we have often conceived the problem rather in a negative than in a positive way. Sometimes we have started with the Guilds as a positive system, and have tried to see in what respects we desire to limit their authority by State intervention, or by the assigning of certain functions to the State rather than to the Guilds. At other times, we have started from the side of the State, and considered in what respects we desire to see its power limited or its functions curtailed. What we have seldom done is to consider at the same time the positive character of both the State and the Guilds, so as to focus at once the whole problem of the relation between them.

This, however, is what we must try to do when we attempt, not to define the limits of State or Guild action, but to lay bare the basic principle of National Guilds. The fundamental reason for the preservation, in a democratic Society, of both the industrial and the political forms of social organisation is, it seems to me, that only by dividing the vast power now wielded by industrial capitalism can the individual hope to be free. The objection is not simply to the concentration of so vast a power in the present hands, but to its concentration anywhere at all. If the individual is not to be a mere pigmy in the hands of a colossal social organism, there must be such a division of social powers as will preserve individual freedom by balancing one social organism so nicely against another that the individual may still count. If the individual is not to be merely an insignificant part of a Society in which his personality is absorbed, Society must be divided in such a way as to make the individual the link between its autonomous but interdependent parts.

This is what the system of National Guilds achieves. It divides social authority equally between the economic and the political organisation, and, in so doing, it preserves the integrity of the individual, who has rights and duties in both the economic and the political spheres.

I contend, then, that the balance of economic and political power is the fundamental principle of National Guilds, and that, if that goes, the security for individual freedom goes with it. I know there are some who contend that the preservation of such a balance is impossible, and some who contend that no such balance is desirable. I want, for the moment, to come back to those who contend that it could not be preserved.

They are of two kinds—those who hold that economic power will still precede political power, and that the Guilds will necessarily outweigh the State, and those who hold that, in a democratic Society, the balance will shift, and, the conflict of classes being over, the State will outweigh the Guilds. To the latter I would reply that, even apart from class conflict, the economic, or, rather, industrial, bond will remain more intense than the political, and that its greater intensity will be enough to balance the wider ' spread ' or extension of the political bond. To the former a rather longer reply must be given. Every individual under the Guilds will not be a member of a Guild ; but every individual, we may expect, will be a member of some form of association based on social service rendered—a productive association in the widest sense of the word. Similarly, it goes without saying that every individual

will be a member of the State, and probably of other
associations of ' users,' ' consumers,' or ' enjoyers.' It
is certainly true in any form of Society that the ' enjoyment ' of things produced depends upon production ;
but it does not follow that the power of the productive
association precedes or determines that of the association of ' enjoyers.' It does follow when one class owns
and controls the means of production that it must, to
all intents and purposes, own and control everything
else ; but it does not follow that, when producer and
' enjoyer ' are the same, the productive association will
dominate the association of ' enjoyers.' The greater
intensity of the productive association is an intensity
of each Guild, or producing group, within itself : it is
not a single undifferentiated intensity of the whole body
of producers, and in becoming one and uniform in the
Guild Congress it must also become less intense. The
unity of the ' enjoyers ' association, on the other hand,
is practically indivisible : not so intense in its nature,
it is of about the same intensity at the point of contact.
In other words, the greater solidarity and uniformity of
the State about compensates for the closer attachment
which the individual may be expected to feel to his
Guild. The Guilds will be many, the State one ; and
State unity will counterbalance Guild corporatism.

I do not deny that there is a danger in both directions,
or that, when National Guilds are in being, the balance
may be upset, and the essential character of the system
destroyed. That will, indeed, be the ever-present peril
against which it will be the function of guildsmanship
to guard. All I am concerned to deny is that there is
anything in the nature of the Guild system which makes
the balance unattainable or incapable of preservation.
Far from that, National Guilds seem to me to offer the

only reasonable prospect of a balance of powers, and that is the fundamental reason why, in the name of individual freedom, I call myself National Guildsman.

IV

The governing principle of the American constitution is that of the separation of the three powers—legislative, executive and judicial. Nor is this only a theoretical principle ; for, in the main, the separation holds good in practice. The principle of our own government, on the other hand, is the combination of these powers. In theory, and practice, the judicial power, owing to the absence of a formal constitution, is subordinated to the legislature. In theory the executive is subordinate to the legislature, though it would be truer to say that in practice the legislature is increasingly subordinate to the executive. Whether we look to principle or to practice, it is at any rate true that with us legislature and executive are not two powers fundamentally distinct, but one power internally differentiated. The effect of this upon our working political theory is obvious. Legislature and executive may conduct internal struggles for mastery one against the other ; but in relation to the mass of the people they present a united front. Representative government is exalted by them into a principle which practically carries with it the exclusion of the represented from an effective share in government. The separation of powers, as theorists have often pointed out, ensures a recognition of the principle that sovereignty resides outside both legislature and executive : their combination readily results in the acceptance of the representative institution as sovereign.

When we speak of State Sovereignty, we may have at the back of our minds the idea that this sovereignty belongs to the whole people ; but we are thinking always of its exercise by the State as a complex of institutions—in a ' democratic ' country, of representative institutions. If the national institutions are in effect combined in a single machine, we think of sovereignty as exercised by this machine, even if it belongs of right not to the machine, but to the people behind it. State Sovereignty, in the sense of governmental Sovereignty, therefore finds its only natural and complete expression in a system under which the powers of government are united in the hands of a single authority. The overweening claim of the State machine to the absolute allegiance of the citizen, called in this connection the ' subject,' is only possible under a system in which governmental authority is unified under a ' Prince,' whether that prince be a despot or a representative institution.

This has led some opponents of State Sovereignty to look favourably upon the division of powers between an independent legislature, executive and judiciary. But, in the case of the first two, which under modern conditions constitute the real problem, it is at once apparent that no such division is possible or desirable. The struggle for parliamentary government, which must be recognised as at least a phase in the European form of the struggle for political freedom, has centred round the demand of the legislature for control of the executive. If it has not secured that, it has at least welded the two into a single power, preserving their internal distinctness, but rendering them incapable of disintegration.

Nor is this to be regretted. A democratic country

must be governed mainly by legislation, and those bodies in it which are legislative in character must preponderate. This is not true of a federal government such as that of the United States, though it is slowly becoming more true as America is drawn more into world politics ; but it is true to a great extent of the States which constitute the Union. It is indeed only the federal character of the United States that makes the separation of powers workable. A Society like our own must bind closely together the legislature and the executive, because with the laws in constant change legislation and administration lose their distinct character. There can for us be no solution of the problem of State Sovereignty by a division of legislative and executive power.

How, then, are we to realise, for such a Society, the benefits of the separation of powers ? How are we to re-affirm popular sovereignty, and, in so doing, re-establish the individual in his fundamental rights ? The main business of government for us is the making and modification of laws which serve as the basis of administration. If this seems a commonplace, it must be remembered that it would not seem so in all places or in all times. We live under a reign of national law, and this seems to involve the unification of the making and administering of law under a single ultimate authority.

We must, then, seek our division of powers by the light of a new principle. We must recognise that the control of legislation and administration cannot be divorced, and, if we are to find a cleavage at all, we must make a new cut. In fact, we must separate the powers of government not horizontally, but vertically. Every important act of government, or at least every internal act, passes through the successive stages of legislation and administration. The old doctrine of the separation of powers is based on the principle of a division by stages : the legislative stage is to be divorced from the stage of administration. The new doctrine must be that of division by function : the type, purpose and subject-matter of the problem, and not the stage at which it has arrived, must determine what authority is to deal with it.

This involves a new conception of the nature and relationship of legislation and administration. Many writers have remarked the tendency of recent political changes to devolve administrative functions upon bodies standing outside the State machine, or only loosely connected with it. But no such tendency has shown itself in the strict sphere of legislation, and there the State has preserved its sole competence. It has devolved administrative power ; but the devolution has been accomplished by the grant of the State, and has been subject to recall by a sovereign Parliament. It has been a method of convenience, and not a recognition of a new principle.

Nevertheless, it is a beginning, which the close connection between legislation and administration under modern conditions renders doubly valuable. It is not a recognition of a new principle, but it does open the door to such recognition. It is, in fact, the first step in a division according to function not only of administrative, but also of legislative, competence.

For nothing less than this the new theorists of the division of powers must stand. The Guildsman must claim for the Guilds, not only administrative, but also legislative functions. Their law must be as sovereign in the industrial sphere, exercised through the Guild Congress, as the law of the State must be sovereign in the political sphere. And, while laws are enforced at all, it must be no less enforceable. Where now the State passes a Factory Act, or a Coal Mines Regulation Act, the Guild Congress of the future will pass such Acts, and its power of enforcing them will be the same as that of the State.

This leads at once to a new conception of the judiciary, which in this country now hovers between independence and dependence on the State. Attention is often drawn, in connection with the separation of powers, to the position of the Supreme Court of the United States ; but the independence of the Supreme Court is based on the existence of a written constitution, which the legislature has no power to alter without an appeal to the people. Apart from that, the American Federal Courts merely apply and administer federal law, as the British courts apply and administer British law. In principle, they are subordinate to the legislature.

What, then, will be the position of the judiciary under the Guilds ? It will have two sets of laws to administer—State law and Guild law, each valid within its sphere, and co-ordinated, where need arises, by the Joint Congress of the Guilds and the State. It is not desirable to divide the judiciary, as it is desirable to divide legislation and administration, because the judiciary is concerned, not with policy, but with interpretation of policy already decided.

Guild theory involves, then, the division of the ' legislative-executive power ' according to function between the State and the Guilds ; but it preserves the integrity of the judiciary, making it an appendage neither of the State nor of the Guilds, but of the two combined.

The arguments for a balance of powers between the State and the Guilds were set out in a previous section of this chapter.   In this section I have attempted to show how this balance would work out constitutionally. It involves a revolution in our theory of government ; but it also provides the only means of realising in practice what has been clear in theory to many political students—a separation of powers which will be effective against the absolutist claim of modern legislative assemblies.   A balance of power is essential if individual freedom is preserved ; but no balance is possible unless it follows the natural division of powers in the Society of to-day.   Politics and economics afford the only possible line of division, and between them the power of legislation and administration can only be divided on the basis of function.

CHAPTER II

No movement can be dangerous unless it is a movement of ideas. Often as those whose ideals are high have failed because they have not kept their powder dry, it is certain that no amount of dry powder will make a revolution succeed without ideals. Constructive idealism is not only the driving force of every great uprising ; it is also the bulwark against reaction.

If, then, Trade Unionism is to be the revolutionary power of the future, it will become so only by virtue of the idealism that inspires it. While it remains merely materialistic, it will not stand a dog's chance of changing the capitalist system into something better. Socialists, therefore, when they put their trust in organised Labour, are expressing their belief that Trade Unionism means something more than the desire of its members for greater material comfort.

The old-fashioned attitude towards Trade Unionism is summed up in the text-book definition : " A Trade Union is a continuous association of wage-earners for the purpose of maintaining or improving the conditions of their employment." At first sight, this seems a fair enough description ; for certainly in the past the Unions have been mainly concerned with this aspect of ' collective bargaining.' The definition is indeed an adequate account of Trade Unionism as it was conceived by the ' Old Unionists ' themselves. Historically, the primary function of the Unions has been to maintain the price of the labour-commodity within the capitalist system.

When Socialism first became strong in England, the Unions were still reformist to the last degree. It is not too much to say that, crossed in early youth in its love of revolution, Labour had taken the vow of celibacy, and refused to mate with any idealistic movement. The revolutionary Unionism of the time of Robert Owen moved prematurely out to battle, and suffered ignominious defeat : to those who survived its downfall, the only possible course seemed to be that of saving the relics of the Trade Union army by turning it into a sort of civil guard—by abandoning every form of militancy and confining its activities, wherever possible, to peaceful negotiation with the employers. All thought of ending capitalism was banished from the Trade Union world ; and every suggestion of political bias was repudiated. The Unions accepted a frankly reformist position : sliding-scale agreements and arbitration boards came to represent the height of their ambition.

It was not unnatural, therefore, that the early Socialists, including most of the prominent members of the old Social Democratic Federation, regarded the Unions as too hopelessly reactionary to be of any assistance in achieving the Socialist Commonwealth. The result of this natural mistake was, however, none the less disastrous. English Socialism, as it grew up, remained a doctrine almost wholly political in character : on the industrial side, its last word concerning the future organisation of production was nationalisation.

Meanwhile, largely under the influence of the spreading Socialist ideas, the Unions themselves began to change. The Dock Strike of 1889 was, of course, the first great visible sign of the new spirit ; for it meant nothing less than the dawn of a new class-consciousness. Trade Unionism could thereafter no longer mean only the corporate egoism of the skilled tradesmen ; the unskilled workers came to take their place along with their fellows in the battle for industrial freedom. This change of spirit is even now far from complete ; but it was certain from this point that the substitution of class-consciousness for trade-consciousness in the Trade Union world was only a matter of time.

The growth of the new spirit marks the lost opportunity of Socialism. Then was the time for political Socialism to make itself complete by including the idea of self-government in industry, by recognising the Trade Unions as the future masters of production. Their failure to do this meant a set-back of a quarter of a century to the Socialist cause. The events which culminated in the Dock Strike were not, indeed, without their effect upon Socialism, since they led directly to the foundation of the Independent Labour Party.[1] But the I.L.P., instead of declaring for the true industrial democracy, chose a purely political programme gleaned half from the Fabians and half from the S.D.F. Though they owed their being to an industrial revolt, Keir Hardie and his friends still utterly failed to understand its meaning. They had not grasped the true function of Trade Unionism, and they remained sceptical of its ultimate value.

When, however, a few more years had elapsed, and there still seemed no signs of the conversion of the bulk of the working-classes, the Socialists at last realised

---

[1] See p. 259.

the futility of ignoring the Unions. Their next step
was accordingly the creation of the Labour Party, a
federation of Trade Unions and Socialist Societies.
But here their failure was no less remarkable. Driven
by the logic of facts to see the necessity of Trade
Union support, they wholly failed to see more than
this, or to understand how their appeal ought to be
made. Instead of enlarging their theory on the
industrial side, and recognising the Unions as entitled
to the control of industry, they endeavoured to collar
Trade Unionism in support of their own political programme. By this move, which reflects equal discredit
on the commonsense of both parties, they gained a
great accession of immediate strength ; but at the
same time they lost a great opportunity, and sowed
the seed of their own weakness in the future. Instead
of trying to inspire the Unions with an industrial
idealism, they attempted to make them purely political
idealists and to pour the political wine into the industrial bottle. The result was inevitable ; the Trade
Unions did not become idealistic, and the composite
political body in which the Socialists chose to merge
their identity was not only utterly without ideals, but
also very soon emasculated the idealism of its Socialist
wing. The final result we know : it is a Labour Party
of which Capitalism has long lost all fear.

Human nature, however, came to the rescue. While
the recognised leaders of Trade Unionism in too many
cases frittered away their strength in politics—which,
necessary as it may be, is not their job—the rank and
file were being slowly fired by the new idealism which
the Socialists had failed to understand. Half-uncon-
sciously, the revolt against despotism in the workshop
began to take form, and the workers began to realise

that there could be no end to their subordination until they themselves were masters of their own industries. The conduct of the nationalised services, too, made them feel that the management of industry by State departments, though, generally extended, it might result in a fairer distribution of income, could never by itself answer their demand for industrial freedom. Syndicalism, or at any rate doctrines tinged with Syndicalism, began to take root, and, when the industrial unrest took form, it was found to be not merely a demand for higher wages, but an insurgence against tyranny and an aspiration towards industrial self-government.

This new spirit grew up within the Trade Unions, and to a great extent outside Socialism, simply because Socialists had no imagination. But, growing up in this way, it was inevitably one-sided and incomplete. It was a purely industrial doctrine, when the need was for a doctrine at once industrial and political. It is the business of Socialists to-day to achieve what should have been achieved at the time of the Dock Strike twenty-five years ago, and to make a synthesis of the twin idealisms of Socialism and Trade Unionism. The working out of the new Socialism should be the main business of all those who know the value of ideals, and desire to bring about a social revolt imbued with constructive idealism.

In the Society of to-day the State is a coercive power, existing for the protection of private property, and merely reflecting, in its subservience to Capitalism, the economic class-structure of the modern world. The Trade Unions are to-day merely associations of wage-earners, combining in face of exploitation to make the conditions of their servitude less burdensome. Out of these two—out of the Capitalist State and the Trade Union of wage-earners—what vision of the future Society can we Socialists conjure up ?

Realising rightly that the structure of our industrial Society finds its natural and inevitable expression in the class-struggle, and preoccupied ceaselessly with the demands of our everyday warfare with Capitalism, we are too apt, despite our will to regenerate Society, to regard the present characteristics of the State and the Unions as fixed and unalterable. Some regard the State as essentially the expression of Capitalism, and hold that with the rise of the worker to power, the State and all its functions will disappear automatically. This is Anarchism, to which one kind of Syndicalism approximates. Others, again, regard the Trade Union as essentially a bargaining body which, with the passing of Capitalism, will have fulfilled its purpose, and will at once cease to exist or become of very minor importance. This is the attitude of pure State Socialism— of collectivist theory, as it has been commonly misunderstood, both in Great Britain and abroad.

Both these views rest on false assumptions. One side presupposes that the State must be always much as it is to-day ; the other assumes that its narrow conception of the function of the Trade Union under Capitalism includes all the functions the Unions ever could, or ought to, assume. Both views are one-sided in that they accept the possibility of transforming one of the two bodies in question, and deny the possibility of transforming the other. But nothing is more certain than that both State and Trade Union, if they are to form the foundation of a worthy Society, must be radically altered and penetrated by a new spirit.

A stable community, recognising the rights and personality of all sections of consumers and producers alike, can only be secured if both the State and the Trade Unions take on new functions, and are invested with control in their respective spheres. Collectivism which is not supplemented by strong Trade Unions will be merely State bureaucracy on a colossal scale ; Trade Unions not confronted by a strong and democratised State might well be no less tyrannous than a supreme State unchecked by any complementary association.

The proper sphere of the industrial organisation is the control of production and of the producer's side of exchange : its function is industrial in the widest sense, and includes such matters as directly concern the producer as a producer—in his work, the most important and serviceable part of his daily life. It has no claim to decide ' political ' questions : for its right rests upon the fact that it stands for the producer, and that the producers ought to exercise direct control over production.

The proper sphere of the State in relation to industry is the expression of those common needs and desires which belong to men as consumers or users of the products of industry. It has no claim to decide producers' questions or to exercise direct control over production ; for its right rests upon the fact that it stands for the consumers, and that the consumers ought to control the division of the national product, or the division of income in the community.

Industry, in the widest sense, is a matter of both production and use. The product has to be produced, and it has to be determined who shall have the right to consume it. On the one hand, the decision of the character and use of the product is clearly a matter primarily for the user : on the other, the conditions under which work is carried on so vitally and directly concern the various sections of organised producers that they cannot afford to let the control of those conditions remain in the hands of outsiders. The old Collectivist claimed everything for the democratic community, and maintained that the workers would find their grievances adequately ventilated and their interests thoroughly safeguarded by means of a reformed Parliament under democratic control. He looked forward to a future Society in which the State and the Municipalities would employ all the workers much as they now employ men in the post office, the Government dockyards, or on the tramways, with the difference that the goodwill of the whole body of consumers would secure for the worker decent wages, hours and conditions of labour. The new Syndicalist claims everything for the organised workers ; he would have them so organise as to secure the monopoly of their labour, and supplement this first principle of economic power by the provision of economic resource, and then he would have them, by direct action, oust the Capitalist from the control of industry, and enter themselves into complete possession of the means of production and distribution.

There is in this more than a clash of policies ; there is a clash of fundamental ideas. The Collectivist, immersed in the daily struggle of the worker for a living wage, has thought only of distribution. High wages under State control have been the sum of his ambition ; he has dismissed, as artists, dreamers, or idealists, those who, like William Morris, have contended that no less fundamental is the question of production—the problem of giving to the workers responsibility and control, in short, freedom to express their personality in the work which is their way of serving the community. The problem of Socialist theory in the present is the reconciliation of these two points of view ; for either, alone, is impotent to form the framework of a noble ideal. Political democracy must be completed by democracy in the workshop ; industrial democracy must realise that, in denying the State, it is falling back into a tryanny of industrialism. If, instead of condemning Syndicalism unheard, the Socialist would endeavour to grasp this, its central idea, and harmonise it with his own ideal of political justice, Collectivism and Syndicalism would stand forth as, in essentials, not opposing forces, but indispensable and complementary ideas.

A close analysis of the Syndicalist demand points the way to the only real solution. That absolute ownership of the means of production by the Unions to which some Syndicalists look forward is but a perversion and exaggeration of a just demand. The workers ought to control the normal conduct of industry; but they ought not to regulate the price of commodities at will, to dictate to the consumer what he shall consume, or, in short, to exploit the community as the individual profiteer exploits it to-day.

What, then, is the solution ? Surely it lies in a division of functions between the State as the representative of the organised consumers and the Trade Unions, or bodies arising out of them through industrial Unionism, as the representatives of the organised producers.

These bodies we call National Guilds, in order both to link them up with the tradition of the Middle Ages and to distinguish them from that tradition. We, who call ourselves National Guildsmen, look forward to a community in which production will be organised through democratic associations of all the workers in each industry, linked up in a body representing all workers in all industries. On the other hand, we look forward to a democratisation of the State and of local government, and to a sharing of industrial control between producers and consumers. The State should own the means of production : the Guild should control the work of production. In some such partnership as this, and neither in pure Collectivism nor in pure Syndicalism, lies the solution of the problem of industrial control.

Naturally, such a suggestion needs far more elaborate working out than can be given here, and, in particular, much must be left for decision in the future as the practical problems arise. We cannot hope to work out a full and definite scheme of partnership in advance ; but we have everything to gain by realising, even in broad outline, what kind of Society we actually desire to create. We need at the same time to satisfy the producers' demand for responsibility and self-government, and to meet the consumers' just claim to an equitable division of the national income, and to a full provision of the goods and services which he justly requires.

Some sort of partnership, then, must come about ; but there is a notable tendency nowadays for persons to adopt the phrase without intending to bring any effective partnership into being. The partnership, to be worth anything, must be a partnership of equals, not the revocable concession of a benignant and superior State, and, to make it real, the Guilds must be in a position to bargain on equal terms with the State. The conditions upon which the producers consent to serve, and the community to accept their service, must be determined by negotiation between the Guilds and the State. The Guild must preserve the right and the economic resource to withdraw its labour ; the State must rely, to check unjust demands, on its equal voice in the decision of points of difference, and on the organised opinion of the community as a whole. As a last resort the preservation of equality between the two types of organisation involves the possibility of a deadlock ; but it is almost impossible to imagine such a deadlock arising in an equalitarian Society.

I have stated my ideal very baldly, because it has already been stated well and fully elsewhere, and I do not desire to go over again the ground which others have covered. I must, however, state briefly the fundamental moral case both against Socialism as it is usually conceived and in favour of the ideal for which I am contending.

What, I want to ask, is the fundamental evil in our modern Society which we should set out to abolish ?

There are two possible answers to that question, and I am sure that very many well-meaning people would make the wrong one. They would answer POVERTY, when they ought to answer SLAVERY. Face to face every day with the shameful contrasts of riches and destitution, high dividends and low wages, and pain-fully conscious of the futility of trying to adjust the balance by means of charity, private or public, they would answer unhesitatingly that they stand for the ABOLITION OF POVERTY.

Well and good ! On that issue every Socialist is with them. But their answer to my question is none the less wrong.

Poverty is the symptom : slavery the disease. The extremes of riches and destitution follow inevitably upon the extremes of license and bondage. The many are not enslaved because they are poor, they are poor because they are enslaved. Yet Socialists have all too often fixed their eyes upon the material misery of the poor without realising that it rests upon the spiritual degradation of the slave.

I say they have not realised this, although they have never ceased to proclaim that there is a difference between social reform and Socialism, although they have always professed to stand for the overthrow of the capitalist system. For who among our evolutionary Socialists can explain wherein this difference consists, and who of our revolutionists understands what is meant by the overthrow of Capitalism ?

It is easy to understand how Socialists have come so to insist upon the fact of poverty. Not one of them, at least until he has eaten of the forbidden fruit of office in the political Garden of Eden, but is moved by an intense conviction that our civilisation is beyond measure degrading and immoral. His first object, then, is to make others see that he is right. What more natural than to exhibit, before the eyes of all men, the open sore of physical misery ? Even the least imaginative can see the evils of poverty, and the majority are supposed to lack imagination. We, therefore, confront the world with the incontrovertible fact that the few are rich and the many poor. The idea that the fundamental aim of Socialism is the abolition of poverty begins in an *argumentum ad hominem.*

I have not time to describe the effect of this attitude on the practice of Socialists in the political field. I can only say, in a few words, why I believe it to have been disastrous. Our preoccupation with poverty is the cause of our long wanderings in the valley of the shadow of reformism : it is the cause of that dragging of Labour into a Liberal alliance which has wrecked every chance of successful political action for a generation to come. There are too many to whom Socialism has come to mean a steeper graduation of the income-tax, the nationalisation of mines and railways and the break-up of the poor law, together with a shadowy something behind all these to which they can give neither name nor substance. The very avidity with which we clung, like drowning men, to the somewhat bulky straw of the Minority Report was a clear indication of our bankruptcy in the realm of ideas. To many of us, that very adroit and necessary adjunct to the capitalist system seemed the crowning expression of the constructive Socialism of our day. Our generation was seeking for a sign ; but there was no sign given it save the sign of the prophet Jonah. And Jonah, if my memory serves, was a minor prophet.

The biblical Jonah once had the fortune to be swallowed by a whale. In our days, the tables have been turned, and, instead of the Labour movement swallowing its Jonah, Jonah has swallowed the Labour movement.

Inspired by the idea that poverty is the root evil, Socialists have tried to heal the ills of Society by an attempt to redistribute income. In this attempt, it will be admitted that they have hitherto met with no success. The gulf between rich and poor has not grown an inch narrower ; it has even appreciably widened. It is the conviction of Guild-Socialists that the gulf will never be bridged, as long as the social problem is regarded as pre-eminently a question of distribution.

Idle rich and unemployed poor apart, every individual has two functions in the economic sphere—he is both a producer and a consumer of goods and services. Socialists, in seeking a basis on which to build their ideal Society, have alternated between these two aspects of human activity. The Fourierists, the Christian Socialists and the Communists, with their ideals of the phalangstery, the self governing workshop, and the free Commune, built—and built imperfectly—upon man the producer. Collectivism, on the other hand, which includes most modern schools of Socialism, builds upon man the consumer. It is our business to decide which, if either, of them is right.

It is the pride of the practical social reformer that he deals with ' the average man in his average moments.' He repudiates, as high falutin nonsense, every attempt to erect a new social order on a basis of idealism ; he is vigilantly distrustful of human nature, human initiative and human freedom ; and he finds his ideal in a paternal governmentalism tempered by a preferably not too real democratic control. To minds of such a temper, Collectivism has an irresistible appeal. The idea that the State is not only supreme in the last resort, but also a capable jack of all trades, offers to the bureaucrat a wide field for petty tyranny. In the State of to-day, in which democratic control through Parliament is little better than a farce, the Collectivist State would be the Earthly Paradise of bureaucracy.

The Socialist in most cases admits this, but declares that it could be corrected if Parliament were demo-

cratised. The ' conquest of political power ' becomes
the Alpha and Omega of his political method : all his
cheques are postdated to the Greek Kalends of the
first Socialist Government. Is, then, his ideal of the
democratic control of industry through Parliament an
ideal worthy of the energy which is expended in its
furtherance ?

The crying need of our days is the need for freedom.
Machinery and Capitalism between them have made
the worker a mere serf, with no interest in the product
of his own labour beyond the inadequate wage which
he secures by it. The Collectivist State would only
make his position better by securing him a better wage,
even if we assume that Collectivism can ever acquire
the driving power to put its ideas into practice : in
other respects it would leave the weaker essentially as
he is now—a wage-slave, subject to the will of a master
imposed on him from without. However democratically
minded Parliament might be, it would none the less
remain, for the worker in any industry, a purely
external force, imposing its commands from outside
and from above. The postal workers are no more
free while the Post Office is managed by a State department than Trade Unionists would be free if their Executive Committees were appointed by His Majesty's
Minister of Labour.

The picture I have drawn, it may be said, neglects
an essential factor—Trade Unionism. The Collectivist
relies upon the organised bargaining power of the worker
to correct the evils of bureaucracy ; he looks forward
to a time when, in every State department and in every
municipality, the right of the Unions to speak on behalf
of their members will be fully recognised. As Mr. and
Mrs. Webb, the Sir and Lady Oracle of the Socialist

movement, laid down in the ' classic ' final chapter of *Industrial Democracy*,[1] Trade Unions, so far from becoming unnecessary in the Socialist State, will find there only their full development. Strong enough to resist bureaucracy, they will embody that industrial freedom which the worker demands as his right.

When Syndicalism first became a recognised force in this country, there was a regular scurry among the back-numbers to drink again of the invigorating draughts of *Industrial Democracy*. The famous final chapter was constantly quoted to prove that there was really nothing new in the essential parts of Syndicalism, and that Socialists had all along recognised the importance of Trade Unionism. The cobwebby solution that is no solution at all was called to the aid of the reaction : and it was proposed to find, in *Industrial Democracy*, a *via media* which should satisfy the Syndicalists without violating the worn-out phrases of the Collectivists. Needless to say, such a solution has pleased none save its authors ; but a discussion of it is the shortest way to the heart of the problem.

The Collectivist is prepared to recognise Trade Unionism under a Collectivist régime. But he is not prepared to trust Trade Unionism, or to entrust it with the conduct of industry. He does not believe in industrial self-government ; his ' industrial democracy ' embodies only the right of the workers to manage their Trade Unions, and not their right to control industry. The National Guildsman, on the other hand, bases his social philosophy on the idea of function. In the industrial sphere, he desires not the recognition of Trade Unions by a Collectivist State, but the recognition of a democratic State by National Guilds controlling industry in the common interest.

[1] See p. 259.

Those of us whose hopes of working-class emancipation are centred round the Trade Unions must be specially anxious to-day. When the war broke out Trade Unionism was passing through a critical period of transition, and it is just at such times that external shocks are most dangerous. Weary of their long struggle to secure ' reforms,' weary of trying at least to raise wages enough to meet the rise in prices ; weary, in fact, of failure, or successes so small as to amount to failure, the Unions were beginning to take a wider view and to adopt more revolutionary aims. Mere collective bargaining with the employers would, they were beginning to feel, lead them nowhere ; mere political reforms only gilded the chains with which they were bound. Beyond these men began to seek some better way of overthrowing Capitalism and of introducing into industry a free and democratic system.

The first effect of this change of attitude was seen in the more militant tactics adopted by the Unions. The transport strikes of 1911 and the miners' strike of 1912, little as they achieved in comparison with the task in prospect, served as stimulants throughout the world of Labour. The Dublin strike and the London building dispute quickened the imaginations thus aroused and set men thinking about the future of Trade Unionism.[1] If there were comparatively few Syndicalists, Syndicalist and Industrial Unionist ideas were having a wide influence throughout the movement, while the new doctrine of National Guilds was slowly leavening some of the best elements in the Trade Union world. In short, wherever the Unions were awake, the thoughts of their members were taking a new direction, and growing bodies of Trade Unionists were

[1] See p. 260.

demanding the control of industry by the workers themselves.

This idea of the control of industry, which was forced to the front by the coming of Syndicalism in its French and American forms, is not new, but is a revival of the first ideas of working-class combinations. It represents a return, after a long sojourn in the wilderness of materialism and reform, to the idealism of the early revolutionaries. But this time the idealism is clothed not only with a fundamentally right philosophy, but also with a practical policy. The new revolutionaries know that only by means of Trade Unionism can Capitalism be transformed, and they know also by what methods the revolution can be accomplished. They aim at the consolidation of Trade Union forces, because beyond the Trade Union lies the Guild.

Out of the Trade Unionism of to-day must rise a Greater Unionism, in which craft shall be no longer divided from craft, nor industry from industry. Industrial Unionism lies next on the road to freedom, and Industrial Unionism means not only ' One Industry, One Union, One Card,' but the linking-up of all industries into one great army of labour.

But even this great army will achieve no final victory in the war that really matters unless it has behind it the driving force of a great constructive idea. This idea Guild Socialism fully supplies. The workers cannot be free unless industry is managed and organised by the workers themselves in the interests of the whole community. The Trade Union, which has been till now a bargaining force, disputing with the employer about the conditions of labour, must become a controlling force, an industrial republic. In

short, out of the bargaining Trade Union must grow the
producing Guild.

In the Middle Ages, before the dark ages of Capitalism
descended on the world, industry was organised in
guilds. Each town was then more or less isolated and
self-sufficient, and within each town was a system of
guilds, each carrying on production in its own trade.
These guilds were indeed associations of small masters,
but in the period when the guilds flourished there was
no hard-and-fast line between master and man, and
the journeyman in due course normally became a
master. The mediaeval guilds, existing in an undemocratic society, were indeed themselves always to some
extent undemocratic ; and, as Capitalism began to take
root, inequality grew more marked and the guild system gradually dissolved. Our age has its own needs ;
and the guilds which Guild Socialists desire to see
established will be in many ways unlike those of the
mediaeval period ; but both are alike in this, that they
involve the control of industry by the workers themselves.

In the earlier half of the last century there flourished
a society, animated, no doubt, by the best intentions,
which called itself ' The Society for the Diffusion of
Useful Knowledge.' It was the aim of this body,
which had a most influential backing among capitalists,
politicians and University professors, to demonstrate
to the working class the benefits which they had
received from the introduction of machinery and the
growth of the industrial system. In its pamphlets,
which were widely circulated, it pointed to the immense
increase in the supply of material commodities which
machinery had made possible, and to the consequent
greater prosperity of the whole community. It also

demonstrated to the workers the appointed functions of capital and labour in the industrial system, and the laws of political economy which finally determined their relative positions. Having done this, it paused satisfied, and thanked God that things were as they were.

It is as a disturber of this commercial complacency that William Morris takes a foremost place among democratic writers. As poet and craftsman alike, he found his impulse to self-expression thwarted by commercialism ; he opened his eyes and saw around him the products of commercialism, and knew that they were not good. He strove, in a commercial world, to make beautiful things that were not commercial ; but, though he made beautiful things and made them a commercial success, he was not satisfied. He desired to make beautiful things for the people ; but he found that the people had neither money to buy, nor taste to value, what he made. The more he sold his wares to the few rich, the more conscious he became that under commercialism there could be for the many no beauty and no appreciation of beauty.

Thus it was that Morris passed from Art to Socialism, because he saw that under Capitalism there could be no art and no happiness for the great majority. As an artist, he based his Socialism upon art, as each of us who is a Socialist must base it upon that in life which he knows best and values most. For commercialism is a blight which kills every fine flower of civilised life.

Morris's conception of art was a great and wide conception. Art was not for him a mere external decoration of things made : it was the vital principle that inspires all real making. He did not mean by art merely pictures, sculpture, poetry, music, or ' arts and crafts ' ; he meant the making of all things that can be made well or ill, beautifully or without regard to beauty. He held that all true art springs from the life of the people, and that, where their life is good, art will flourish naturally—that, where life is base, art can never flourish. He saw clearly that, so long as men remained in thrall to the industrial system, there could be no good art and no good life for the mass of the people.

Perhaps he did not see so clearly the way out—that was less his business. What he did was to put clearly before the world the baseness and iniquity of industrialism, and its polluting effect on civilisation despite the increase of material wealth. That was enough for a man to do, and Morris did it well and thoroughly.

Himself above all a craftsman with a joy in the labour of his hand and brain, Morris could not rest content with a world in which this joy in labour, to him the greatest thing in life, was denied to all but a few. He was by nature a maker of things, but the age in which he lived forced him to divert more and more of his energies into the making of trouble. Many people are puzzled at first to find in him at once ' the happiest of poets,' as Mr. W. B. Yeats called him, and a preacher of militant Socialism. They fail at first to reconcile the quiet beauty of his poetry and his romances of his printed books and his decorations, with the idea of a revolt against anything. Yet the very qualities that went to the making of these things also made Morris a Socialist. He wanted passionately that the things men had to make should be worth making—' a joy to the maker and the user.'

It is unfortunate that so many people, especially in

the Labour movement, know Morris only, or mainly, as the author of *News from Nowhere*. They will get a far clearer idea of his view of life from his books of lectures, such as *Hopes and Fears for Art*, in which he set out clearly his conception of the relation of art to the social system. They will find there the patriot who loves his own country without hating or despising others, and loves it for what it is in itself and not for its position in the race of nations. They will find the believer not only in a popular art, but in an art springing directly from the free life of a free nation. Or, in the *Dream of John Ball*, they will find still more clearly spoken the message of a free England, in which men can be happy because their lives are worth while, and they count as comrades and not merely as ' hands ' in a profit-making system. Or, of his verse, let them turn to *The Pilgrims of Hope*, one of the greatest of modern epics, unfinished as it is. There again they will find the hope of a better world arising through the striving and willing of the common people upon the wreckage of the old world. When they know these, they will be better able to understand *News from Nowhere*, and it will seem to them less a vision of a far-off and even impossible Utopia than an expression of Morris's firm faith in the ultimate value of human happiness.

I have dwelt thus upon the Socialism of William Morris because I feel that he, more than any other prophet of revolution, is of the same blood as National Guildsmen. Freedom for self-expression, freedom at work as well as at leisure, freedom to serve as well as to enjoy—that is the guiding principle of his work and of his life. That, too, is the guiding principle of National Guilds. We can only destroy the tyranny of machinery—which is not the same as destroying machinery itself—by giving into the hands of the workers the control of their life and work, by freeing them to choose whether they will make well or ill, whether they will do the work of slaves or of free men. All our efforts must be turned in that direction : in our immediate measures we must strive to pave the way for the coming free alliance of producers and consumers.

This is indeed a doctrine directly in opposition to the political tendencies of our time. For to-day we are moving at a headlong pace in the direction of a 'national' control of the lives of men which is in fact national only in the sense that it serves the interests of the dominant class in the nation. Already many of the Socialists who have been the most enthusiastic advocates of State action are standing aghast at the application of their principles to an undemocratic Society. The greatest of all dangers is the ' Selfridge ' State, so loudly heralded these twenty years by Mr. ' Callisthenes ' Webb. The workers must be free and self-governing in the industrial sphere, or all their struggle for emancipation will have been in vain. If we had to choose between Syndicalism and Collectivism, it would be the duty and the impulse of every good man to choose Syndicalism, despite the dangers it involves. For Syndicalism at least aims high, even though it fails to ensure that production shall actually be carried on, as it desires, in the general interest. Syndicalism is the infirmity of noble minds : Collectivism is at best only the sordid dream of a business man with a conscience. Fortunately, we have not to choose between these two : for in the Guild idea Socialism and Syndicalism are reconciled. To it Collectivism will yield if only all lovers of freedom will rally round the banner, for it has a message for them especially such as no other school of Socialism has had. Out of the Trade Union shall grow the Guild ; and in the Guild alone is freedom for the worker and a release from the ever-present tyranny of modern industrialism.

CHAPTER III

THE RE-ORGANISATION OF TRADE UNIONISM

THE events of the war[1] have shown clearly to all the world, as nothing else could have done, the potential strength and the actual weakness of Labour. To intelligent Trade Unionists all over the country they have brought home the need for a drastic re-organisation of the machinery of the Trade Union movement. More and more, the younger workers are seeing that no mere piecemeal adaptation of the old Trade Unionism will meet the case : what is wanted is a new policy and a thorough reconstruction.

Those who hold this view are not blind to the enormous difficulties that are in the way. We are a conservative race, and our conservatism is exaggerated in our institutions. The structure of the Labour movement has been erected piecemeal and without a deliberate plan, and in the good old way we should vastly prefer still to proceed. But the moral of recent events is too plain to be ignored. The machinery of Trade Unionism is giving way under the pressure of new circumstances, and nothing short of drastic re-organisation can save it from collapse.

There are at least two groups of events that are a clear sign of the crisis in Trade Unionism. Beginning before the war, but continuing without interruption

[1] See p. 260.

54

during the war, the struggle between Craft Unionism and Industrial Unionism has done much to undermine the old order. The National Union of Railwaymen stands not only for a new conception of Trade Union structure, but also for a new policy. It is the ' new model ' of twentieth century Trade Unionism as surely as the Amalgamated Society of Engineers was the ' new model ' of 1850.

Secondly, within the Unions themselves, we have the growing conflict between the leaders and the rank and file. This conflict finds expression in many different ways ; but by far the most significant are the various rank and file movements centred in the workshop which have sprung up in many of the largest engineering districts. When Mr. Arthur Henderson and Mr. Lloyd George accuse the Clyde Workers' Committee of being ' in revolt against Trade Unionism,'[1] they mean simply that the shop stewards who compose the Committee have a new conception of Trade Union action which they desire to substitute for the conception of Mr. Arthur Henderson and his fellows, and in pursuance of which they are driven to take unconstitutional action and to set the officials of their Unions at defiance.[2] There is a real conflict of policy and purpose between the old school of Labour leaders and the new school of ' rank and filers,' and, whatever the issue may be, this conflict is likely to cause drastic internal changes in the Trade Union movement.

The third problem has to do neither with the relations between particular Unions nor with the internal government of the Unions, but with the general co-ordination of Trade Union activities. The war has brought clearly into the light of day the general disorganisation of the army of Labour and the absence of any authority

[1] See p. 260.   [2] See p. 260.

able either to speak for Labour as a whole or to reconcile and co-ordinate the separate policies of the various
sections. This weakness is especially clear in relation
to the formulating of Labour policy for the period
after the war, most particularly the demands to be
made in connection with the Government pledges to
restore Trade Union conditions. It seems to be no body's
business, or at any rate not to be within any body's
power, to do so much as attempt to bring together
and reconcile the conflicting sections of Labour opinion,
or to provide a common policy for the skilled, the unskilled and the women Trade Unionists.

Our programme, therefore, of Trade Union re-
organisation will fall mainly under three heads. We
shall have to see what changes are necessary, first, in
respect of the structure of the Trade Union movement ;
secondly, in respect of its internal organisation and
government ; and thirdly, in respect of the better co-
ordination and solidarity of the whole army of Labour.

I do not propose to go over again the ground already
covered with some fullness in an earlier book of mine,[1]
but merely to summarise the various problems and to
suggest possible solutions, particularly in view of more
recent developments of Trade Union action and
theory. These developments have not altered the
views suggested in that book ; but they have in some
respects materially added to and supplemented them.
A short summary of the situation as I now envisage
it will probably serve better than anything else to
bring home the need for a thorough everhauling of
the whole Trade Union movement.

In theory, the great bulk of active Trade Unionists
seem to agree that drastic changes are required. Put

[1] *The World of Labour*. Third edition. 1917. G. Bell & Sons.

the case for amalgamation, or the case for internal re-organisation, or the case for working-class solidarity before any big meeting of Trade Unionists, and they will cordially and heartily agree. But ask these same Trade Unionists to take the steps necessary to give effect to these ideas, and a very large proportion of them will draw back or remain apathetic. At once difficulties will suggest themselves ; at once the whole force of Labour's conservatism will array itself on the side of reaction. A movement that has grown as old as our Trade Union movement without any thorough overhauling has naturally gathered much moss, and the picturesque appearance which this moss presents seems to be regarded as a sufficient reason for not clearing it away. Moreover, like all movements, Trade Unionism tends to develop into a vested interest. The official too often regards his job as a gilt-edged security, and his members as his private property. The member, especially in the Craft Union, is apt to look on all amalgamators and advocates of better organisation as sinister plotters with designs on the friendly benefits to which his contributions entitle him. These, and other similar causes, hinder the re-organisation of Trade Unionism on more efficient lines, and cause the advocates of solidarity, after a while, to give up the task in despair.

How far has the war been able to shake Trade Unionism out of its lethargy, and how far are after-war conditions likely to stir it still more ? On the answer to these questions largely depends our hope of re-organisation and of advance. It is certain that the events of the war, and especially the industrial changes which have resulted from the war, have awakened among Trade Unionists a quite unprecedented amount of intellectual activity. In every district up and down the country men have been trying to get a clearer view of Trade Union purpose and method. Circles have been formed for the study of Trade Union problems : special committees of enquiry have been started by Trades Councils and Trade Union branches : the workers have realised more clearly than of old the need for education and enlightenment. These things will certainly produce their effect. Members of different Trade Unions and industries have been brought closer together, and have come to realise, not only each other's point of view, but the point of view that is common to them all. There is, then, hope that, if the need is clearly realised, and the remedy clearly set forth, the Trade Union movement will rise to the occasion, and re-adjust its machinery to meet the new conditions. If it does not, it is safe to prophesy that what it fails to bring about by voluntary re-adjustment will emerge in the long run out of devastating internal conflict.

TRADE UNION STRUCTURE.—No one who has any claim to speak with authority in the Trade Union world now questions the need for amalgamation of Trade Unions on the most extensive scale that is possible. Every one agrees that the continued existence of eleven hundred odd distinct Unions is both absurd and disastrous, and agrees in theory that the number ought to be drastically reduced. But every one is not agreed on the form which amalgamation ought to take, and still less is every one willing to make the mutual concessions by which alone amalgamation can be brought about.

Broadly speaking, there are two conflicting theories of Trade Union structure. One party believes that skilled and unskilled should be organised in separate societies, and regards Trade Unionism mainly from the point of view of the skilled craftsman, who desires to protect his standard of life not only against the employer, but also against the unskilled workers below him. This is the Craft Unionist position. Curiously and yet naturally this position finds allies among the unskilled, who hold that by organising apart they can protect their interests against the skilled workers as well as against the employers, whereas if skilled and unskilled are organised together they hold that the skilled interest will inevitably triumph.

On the other side are ranged those who believe that skilled and unskilled should be organised in the same Unions, and regard Trade Unionism mainly from the point of view of the class struggle. On this view, the differences between sections of the working class are fatal to the advancement of that class and of the community, and such differences, which can be only secondary, should be harmonised inside a common organisation built on a class basis. This is the Industrial Unionist position ; but it belongs also to certain other types of Union which are not strictly ' industrial ' in structure.

These two theories lead to two differing forms of Trade Union organisation. Craft Unionism groups in the same organisation all workers who are doing the same kind of work or who are engaged upon the same process—all weavers, all carpenters, all clerks, all labourers. Industrial Unionism, on the other hand, groups in the same organisation all workers who are co-operating in producing the same product or type of product—all workers in or about mines, on or about railways, all engineering and shipyard workers, all building workers, etc.

This is a very rough statement of the rival theories, and there are numerous complications when we try to apply it in practice. For instance, either form of organisation may be broad or narrow. A Union may be confined to a single craft or industry, or several kindred crafts or industries may be grouped together in a single Union. In such cases, broad may fall out with narrow, and yet broad and narrow may combine to do battle with Unions of the opposite type.

Roughly, however, despite complications, the distinction holds. Above the countless subordinate types of Trade Union organisation stand out the two main types—crafts and industrial, and between these two the battle rages.

There are two main arguments, either in itself sufficient, in favour of Industrial Unionism. But both these arguments hold good only on an initial assumption.

The first argument is that Industrial Unionism provides the stronger force to use against the capitalist. Advocates of Industrial Unionism always point out that against the mass formation of Capitalism a mass formation of Labour is needed, that Craft Unionism has not the strength to combat the vast aggregations of Capital, that it leads essentially to dissension in the workers' ranks, that it enables the employer to play off one set of workers against another, and so to strengthen the capitalist organisation of industry. These arguments are overwhelming in force if, but only if, Trade Unionism is regarded as a class-movement based upon the class-struggle. If it is not, may not the skilled worker be right to fear alliance with the man further down, and may he not see more hope for himself in holding the unskilled worker under, and thereby preserving his own monopoly of labour ? May he not be right, I mean, if, and only if, there is no class-struggle ?

Jack London in *The Iron Heel* and H. G. Wells in *The Sleeper Awakes* have both envisaged a state of Society in which Capitalism has triumphed for the time by buying over the skilled workers to its side, and with their help exploiting the unskilled the more securely and completely.[1] Far be it from me to say that this, or anything like it, is in the mind of the Craft Unionist to-day ; but it is, I feel, the logical outcome of Craft Unionism. If the skilled workman so much needs protection from the man beneath him that they cannot organise together against Capitalism, is it so long a step for him to ally himself with Capitalism, and to sell his class for security and better conditions under Capitalism ?

I do not for a moment suggest that any Craft Union would do this, though I do suggest that some capitalist will play for it in the period of reconstruction after the war. They will come to the skilled Trade Unions with specious proposals that offer immediate advantages to the craftsman, and in return for these advantages they will endeavour to bring the skilled Unions over to Capitalism, to achieve a ' National Alliance of Employers and the Better Class of Employed,' and so to make easier the path of exploitation. I do not suggest that there is any danger of such offers being accepted, if they are understood ; but I do suggest that the sooner we abandon Craft Unionism the safer we shall be.

We must base our Trade Union organisation firmly upon the class-struggle : we must so organise as to promote the unity of the whole working class. Does not that mean that we must move constantly in the direction of Industrial Unionism ?

[1] See p. 261.

The first argument in favour of Industrial Unionism, then, is this. It alone is consistent with the class-struggle : it alone is true to the principle of democracy and fraternity.

The second argument is no less fundamental, and it again rests on an assumption. If the purpose of Trade Unionism is merely protective, if it exists only to maintain or improve conditions of employment within the wage-system, then there is no case for one form of organisation rather than another. We can decide as expediency may suggest. But if the purpose of Trade Unionism is a bigger and a finer thing than the mere protection of the material interests of its members ; if, in fact, Trade Unionists have set before themselves the positive aim of winning, through their Unions, self-government in industry, there can be no doubt about the right structure. Clearly, Craft Unions, based on process and not on product, cannot make any effective claim to control industry. Only an Industrial Union, embracing the whole personnel of an industry, can assume control over that industry.

It is, no doubt, natural that, in the past, Trade Unionists have thought more of the immediate effect of their organisation in maintaining or improving conditions than of the provision of a constructive alternative to the existing system. This is not true of the advanced sections in the Labour movement to-day. Some of them at least see that their effective-ness depends on the possession of a constructive alternative ; but there are still some who are impatient of theories about the future organisation of Society. Such men feel that it is their first business to attack and overthrow Capitalism, and that, till our industrial system lies in ruins, it is hopeless to think of detailed methods of reconstruction. This is certainly a short-sighted view, and it is of the greatest significance that the Guild idea is now taking hold of the workers with growing strength and rapidity. For, when once they grasp the central dogma of National Guilds, they will see that along with the work of destruction must go a process of building up, and that the new Society must be developed by the workers themselves out of the materials which the capitalist system affords.

Guildsmen, at any rate, are in no danger of failing to understand this. They agree with the Syndicalists in recognising that the Trade Union is the germ of that body which will in the fullness of time assume the conduct of industry. It is important that they should go further, and see clearly that the success of their efforts depends on the development of Trade Union structure in the near future. Guild Socialists cannot afford to dismiss this question of structure as being merely a problem for experts in industrial action. It does matter, from the point of view of economic reconstruction, no less than from that of efficiency in the class-struggle, that Industrial Unionism should triumph as quickly as possible.

Collectivists who pretend to be more or less sympathetic to Guild Socialism always plead that enlarged powers should be given to the Trade Union under Socialism as an ' organ of criticism.' They maintain that the Unions, so far from losing their importance, will remain powerful, and will receive large powers of representation and consultation from the Socialist State. In short, they dream of industry run by a series of State departments which concede to the Unions, as bargaining bodies, complete recognition. But, in their vision of the future Society, the Trade

Union remains, so far as control is concerned, always external, advisory, critical. It never assumes control, and leaves to the State the function of advising, criticising and bargaining as an external body.

It is not necessary or relevant here to expose the futility of the Collectivist view. What is important now is to point out that either of the two possible bases of Trade Union organisation might conceivably suffice under Collectivism, though even here the ' industrial ' basis is, from a fighting point of view, by far the more efficient. For the Guild Socialist there is no such choice. He looks forward to a state of Society in which the actual conduct of industry will belong to the Guilds, and he sees clearly that this will come about, not through the voluntary concession of such powers by the State, and still less through the ' setting-up of Guilds by the State,' but as the result of the persistent demands of the Trade Unions themselves. Only by the impetus of their own intelligence and economic power can the workers pass from the era of collective bargaining to the era of collective control, to Guild Socialism from the wage system.

If, then, the workers are to demand control from the State or from the employers, they must build up an organisation capable of assuming control. Clearly such a body must be ' industrial ' in structure. All workers in or about mines must be in the Miners' Union, the whole personnel of the cotton mills must be in the Union of the Cotton Industry. A body consisting of clerks or mechanics or labourers drawn from a number of different industries can never demand or assume the conduct of industry. It can secure recognition, but not control. A Postal Workers' Union or a Railway

Union, on the other hand, can both demand and secure producers' control.

This is no doubt why not a few Collectivists—many of whom are less fools than bureaucrats—have an exceeding tenderness for the principle of Craft Unionism. They are wont to dwell lovingly on the nature of the bond which binds fellow-craftsmen together ; and, when they are driven from the advocacy of old-fashioned Craft Unionism by its obvious impotence in face of modern Capitalism, they fall back upon a ' greater occupational unionism,' which unites several kindred crafts in one Union, but preserves intact the occupational or ' craft ' principle.

One instance will explain this. Advocates of amalgamation on an industrial basis often have thrown in their faces the *Amalgamated* Society of Engineers, and we are told either that this is amalgamation of the right sort, or that the A.S.E. has failed to eliminate such ' craft ' Unions as the Patternmakers, the Coremakers, and the Ironfounders from the engineering trades, and that, therefore, ' craft ' Unionism is right and amalgamation wrong. Whichever is said, the answer is obvious. The A.S.E. is not an *industrial* but an *occupational* amalgamation. It includes men of a number of skilled crafts ; but it has never aimed at organising every worker in the engineering industry.[1]

It is, therefore, not at present a body capable of assuming any great measure of industrial control, though it may prove to be the nucleus of such a body. But it could only become capable of control by becoming a complete Industrial Union.

The structure of Trade Unionism, then, must be industrial, if it is either to serve its purpose of fighting Capitalism, or to take on its newer and higher function

[1] See p. 261.

of control.　Out of Craft Unionism, however widely its net is spread, can come only bureaucracy tempered by recognition : Industrial Unionism will not only serve as an instrument in the war against the wage-system, but will also prepare the workers, while they are engaged in the struggle, for the period of direct industrial control which awaits them at its end.

I have dealt with the problem of structure briefly and without any attempt to face the obvious difficulties, because I wish here to paint in very broad outline the steps necessary for a re-organisation of Trade Union methods and policy.　We have seen now, first, that amalgamation of Unions is urgently needed, and secondly, that amalgamation ought to follow ' industrial ' lines.　We must now turn to the problem of internal government.

Long before the war, difficulties between the leaders and the rank and file were a familiar feature of Trade Union politics.　Moreover, the situation in this respect was steadily worsening as the rank and file movement grew stronger.　The war has served very greatly to intensify the old differences, and there is no doubt that, as soon as the burden of war is removed, there will be warm times for certain Trade Union leaders. The industrial truce and the suspension of normal movements directed against employers through constitutional Trade Union channels have driven the rank and file to some extent to take matters into their own hands.　Unofficial movements have grown up, and unconstitutional action has been taken only to be discountenanced by the officials and executives of the Unions concerned.　Many hard things have been said of officials, and, on their side, the officials have not only said many hard things of the rank and file, but also become less democratic and more prone to insist on their right to power. This tendency has been aggravated by circumstances : the Government and the Press have not wearied of appealing to the nice, good, well-behaved leaders against the naughty rank and file, and the leaders have been encouraged in the belief that it is for them to command, and for their members to obey.

> ' I am a blesséd Glendoveer:
> 'Tis mine to speak, and yours to hear.'

There are Glendoveers and to spare in the Labour movement, and the powers that be take great delight in calling them ' blesséd.' In fact, as we have prussianised our national life, we have, to the measure of our power, prussianised Trade Unionism. But, since it has not been possible to do the job with any completeness, the result has been the creation of a truly formidable movement of revolt.

Let us take two instances of this tendency. Realising the need for centralised control, the railwaymen before the war placed full power over trade movements in the hands of their executive. At once came a reaction towards more democratic control. First, the general meeting of delegates managed to get control of big questions of policy, and subsequently to amend the rules so as to recognise its right to control. Secondly, the District Councils, which are explicitly barred by the rules from taking any share in the formulation of policy, have in fact been the motive power in every forward movement during the war period. They have pushed the executive and the officials ; they have largely controlled the general meetings ; and now, they are playing the foremost part in the formulation of N.U.R. policy.[1] Thus the rank and file organisation

[1] See p. 261.

has, in this case, established its control over the official machinery of the Union.

The second instance is that of the various Workers' and Shop Stewards' Committees which have sprung up in a number of engineering centres, notably the Clyde and Sheffield. These committees are probably the most significant of all the developments of latter-day Trade Unionism, and the problem which they raise is one which calls urgently for solution.

Active Trade Unionists have long lamented the lack of interest among their fellows in Trade Union branch meetings. The branch meetings are usually, except on the occasion of some general forward movement, ill-attended, and serve in the main only as places at which contributions can be paid. The members of the branch have in common one with another their membership of the same trade or industry ; but, apart from general trade questions, they have few commor pre-occupations or problems. They work, as a rule, for various employers, and the employees of a single firm are scattered in a large number of distinct Unions and branches. In fact, in most cases, the Trade Union branch is based not on the workshop, but on the private residence. The Gorton branch of a Union will consist not of the men who work in Gorton, but of the men who live there : those who work in Gorton, but live elsewhere, will be scattered far and wide in other branches.

It has long been the practice of certain Trade Unions, in certain districts, to appoint shop stewards to look after the interests of their members in the workshops. In a good number of cases, there have also been formed, either by the Unions or spontaneously, shop committees with the same object. Wherever such organisation in the worshop has been strong, it has undoubtedly helped to make Trade Unionism a more vigorous and aggressive, if also a more unruly, force. In the last two years the workshop movement has received a great impetus. Not only have more and more districts been setting up shop stewards and workshop committees : there has also been a tendency for the shop stewards from all the shops in the district to come together in a Central Committee, and for this committee to arrogate to itself very considerable powers.

For instance, the Clyde strike of February 1915 was the work of an *ad hoc* organisation, the Central Labour Withdrawal Committee. About the middle of 1915, this body adopted its present title of the Clyde Workers' Committee.[1] It is, in the main, a committee of shop stewards, drawn from all engineering and shipbuilding Unions, and representing a very large proportion of the Clyde establishments. A similar committee, no less strong, exists in Sheffield, and there are similar organisations in many of the larger districts.

Now, these committees are both hopeful and dangerous. They are hopeful in that they have clearly found a method of organisation that is far more effective and stimulating than the older Trade Union methods : but they are also dangerous in that, by usurping the powers and functions of the recognised local machinery of the Unions, they throw Trade Unionism out of gear, and cause a deal of energy to be wasted in friction between the officials and the rank and file.

The true basis of Trade Unionism is in the workshop, and failure to realise this is responsible for much of the weakness of Trade Unionism to-day. The workshop affords a natural unit which is a direct stimulus to self-assertion and control by the rank and file. Organisation that is based upon the workshop runs the best

[1] See p. 261.

chance of being democratic, and of conforming to the
principle that authority should rest, to the greatest
possible extent, in the hands of the governed. This
will fail to recommend it to those Trade Union leaders
who resent every sign of activity among the rank and
file as a slight upon their personal capacity for government, and who desire, in the true fashion of parlia-
mentarians, to subordinate both the people and the
legislature to the executive. But with their opinion
we are not concerned. More conscious democracy is
needed in the Trade Union movement, and this organisation based on the workshop does at least help to
provide.

If the workshop is the right unit for Trade Union
organisation, surely the moral is plain. Colossal waste
of energy is involved where the workers have to build
up an unconstitutional workshop organisation outside
the recognised local machinery of the Trade Unions.
Take the present position on the Clyde. There are in
the Clyde area several hundred Trade Union branches
connected with the engineering and shipbuilding
industry. The vast majority of these are based, not
on any particular works or workshop, but on the
habitancy of their members. Above them come a
considerable number of District Committees of various
Unions, consisting of delegates from branches. Then
come several allied trades committees and the District
Committee of the Engineering and Shipbuilding Trades'
Federation. This is the official and constitutional
machinery. On the other hand, there are in most
shops shop stewards, elected by the men in the shop,
but ratified by their own Unions; sometimes there
are shop committees also; and there is over these
the unofficial Clyde Workers' Committee, which is

usually in conflict with the two most powerful official
bodies, the Engineering and Shipbuilding Trades'
Federation and the District Committee of the Amalgamated Society of Engineers.

It is not difficult to realise that this machinery
involves a very great deal of unnecessary duplication.
I am speaking now, not of the senseless sectionalism
and overlapping between Union and Union or the
crying need for amalgamation, but of the duplication
of the branch and the district committee on the one
hand, and the shop stewards and their joint committee
on the other. Would it not be the best way out of the
difficulty to sweep away this duplication by altering
the basis of Trade Union organisation.

Instead of the ' residence ' branch, let us have the
' works ' branch. Let large works be split, where
necessary, into more than one branch, and small works
be combined into a single branch ; but let the general
principle of organisation be that of the ' works ' branch.
Then the shop stewards will become the branch officials,
and the shop stewards' committee the branch committee.
The District Committee, consisting as now of delegates
from branches, will then consist, as the unofficial
committees do to-day, of the leading shop stewards
drawn from the shop branches. The unofficial
workshop movement will have been taken up into,
and made a part of, the official machinery of Trade
Unionism.

Should we be better off if this came to pass ? I
think we should, for two reasons. In the first place,
the rank and file would be far better equipped for
taking into their own hands the direction of policy,
and for controlling and guiding their leaders ; and,
in the second place, the Trade Union movement would

have received a new orientation in the direction of control.

It is certain that, where workshop organisation is strongest, the Trade Union demand for the control of industry is also strongest. The natural striking point for Trade Unionism is the workshop, and it is in the workshop that the most advanced demands will be formulated, and by workshop action that the greatest concessions will be secured. If we want Trade Unionism to develop a positive and constructive policy, it is in and through the workshop that we must organise ; for there alone will constructive demands be made.

The present organisation of Trade Unionism was suited to the movement in its negative and critical stage. But as soon as Trade Unionists set before themselves the object of supplanting the employer in the control of industry, they must take the works as their basis of organisation, and strain every nerve to win in the workshop and the works a direct control of production.

I am here concerned with this policy only in so far as it suggests structural and governmental changes in Trade Union organisation. The changes I have outlined above seem to me to be the smallest that can avert calamity in the Trade Union world. Unless they are made, officials are doomed to get more and more out of touch with the rank and file, the official machinery of Trade Unionism is bound to find itself confronted with stronger and stronger unofficial machinery based on the workshop, and a vast amount of the energy which ought to be directed to the winning of control by the Trade Unions will inevitably be dissipated in internal conflict. If we would avert these things, we must overcome our conservatism, and have the courage to attempt a drastic reconstruction of Trade Unionism.

I have dwelt at length upon this question, because it seems to me at the moment the most important of the many questions of internal policy that confront the Trade Union movement to-day. I can only deal more briefly with other changes that are hardly less urgently required. We have seen that amalgamation on ' industrial ' lines is an essential step in the direction of control. But we must not imagine that amalgamation is simply a matter of taking a number of Unions and throwing them into one, or a mere absorption of small Unions by large ones. Amalgamation both necessitates and makes easier large changes in internal organisation. For instance, there could be no better opportunity for a change in the basis of the Trade Union branch from ' residence ' to ' works ' than an amalgamation of Unions, which would enable a new constitution to be drafted to suit the new conditions. Again, amalgamation must make provision, wherever possible, for the representation, within an industrial Union, of crafts, sections and departments. It must safeguard, and provide means of expression for, sectional interests within the amalgamation which expresses the solidarity of the whole industry.[1] Yet again, the Industrial Union, by reason both of its size and complexity and of its class structure, calls for more elastic and democratic methods of government than have hitherto prevailed.

The problem of legislative and executive power in the Trade Union movement has always been one of considerable difficulty. Every Union has its Executive

[1] See *The World of Labour*, Ch. VIII., for a fuller treatment of this and the following points.

Council, which is, under the rules, the supreme executive authority ; and every Union has also. some higher authority, more of a legislative character, for the making of rules. Rules, however, deal mainly with internal matters, and the most important part of a Union's work is concerned with its external relations, negotiations and settlements with employers, or with the State. Of recent years, there has been a growing struggle for the control of these questions of policy between executives and delegate meetings. Old-fashioned Trade Unionism generally solved the difficulty by the use of the referendum ; but the weakness of the referendum, except where a very simple and definite question can be submitted, is now generally realised. The old problem therefore recurs with renewed intensity.

The miners settle all important issues of policy by means of large and representative delegate meetings. The railwaymen at first vested final power of settlement in the hands of their Executive ; but almost at once they took this power away and placed it in the hands of their General Meeting of representatives. Among the engineers, while the districts enjoy considerable autonomy in local movements, the supreme control of policy rests upon the Executive.[1] Here interesting developments have taken place during the war ; for, without constitutional sanction, the Executive have twice called National Conferences and thrown upon them the onus of taking difficult and detailed decisions which could not have been dealt with by referendum.

These developments point clearly in the direction

[1] Subject to possible interference by a Delegate Meeting of a somewhat unrepresentative character.

of an enlarged use of representative meetings for the decision of important issues of policy. There is a very great advantage in getting such matters dealt with and settled by men coming directly from the workshops, who will be able to go back and report fully to their fellows what they have done and why they have done it. Only by some such method can the Executive and the Head Office be kept closely in touch with feeling in the districts, or the districts be made aware of the exact nature of the problems with which the Executive and the Head Office have to deal.

We must, if we would fit Trade Unionism for the new tasks which lie before it, make the machinery of the Unions more democratic, and adjust it more thoroughly to the new conditions. If the employers are learning the lesson that obsolete machinery in the workshop does not pay, it is time that Trade Unionists learnt that it does not pay in the Labour movement either.

So far we have been speaking only of the structure and government of individual Trade Unions. It remains to say something of the co-ordination of the whole army of Labour. We have seen that the Industrial Union possesses this enormous advantage over the Craft Union, that it does express in miniature the class structure of Society. It does bring skilled and unskilled together in one organisation, and thereby go far to destroy snobbishness and exclusiveness within the working class. But even Industrial Unionism is not without its perils, especially in view of the immediate economic situation. May not the workers in a particular industry see the prospect of greater immediate advantage to themselves by combining with their employers to exploit the consumer than by combining with their fellow-workers in other industries

to fight against Capitalism ?   I have no great belief in
the reality of this danger ; but it is as well to face it,
such as it is. Especially under a Tariff system, will
not the interest of the workers be enlisted on the side
of the employers in securing preferential treatment for
their industry ?   This, at least, I should regard as an
argument rather against Tariff Reform than against
Industrial Unionism.   And, in any case, I do not
think the danger is made greater by Industrial Unionism.   The gravest danger, as I have said, appears to
be that of an alliance between skilled workers and
employers ; and the coming of Industrial Unionism
would certainly serve to remove this danger.

It will, however, be agreed that it is not enough to
amalgamate Unions by industries, or even to create
blackleg-proof Unions in each industry.   There is also
the problem of the unification and co-ordination of
the whole force of Labour.   The events of the war
have brought out very clearly the fact that there is
no body which can really claim to represent Labour
as a whole or to direct Labour policy.   They have
also shown no less clearly the need for some such
body.

We have now a number of bodies which serve, more
or less, to co-ordinate Labour activities.   First, there
is the Trades Union Congress, an annual gathering of
most of the principal Unions, primarily official in
character, meeting for one week in every year, and
always clogged with futile and detailed resolutions of
minor importance.   The Congress elects annually its
executive, the Parliamentary Committee, consisting
entirely of officials, and meeting monthly during the
year.   Secondly, there is the Labour Party, a federation of Trade Unions, Trade Councils and Local Labour

Parties, Socialist Societies and one or two miscellaneous
bodies. This too holds an annual conference, and has
an Executive Committee corresponding to the Parliamentary Committee of the Trades Union Congress.
Thirdly, there is a Joint Board, representing the two
Committees, which takes action on matters affecting
the movement as a whole.

In addition to these, there are certain *ad hoc* bodies,
which have sprung up during the war period. These
are, first, the War Emergency Workers'[1] National Committee, which includes both the above and also many
other bodies, Trade Unions, Co-operative bodies,
Women's Societies, Socialist Societies, etc., and secondly,
the Joint Labour Committee on After-War Problems,
which represents the Trades Union Congress, the
Labour Party, the General Federation of Trade Unions,
and the War Emergency Workers' National Committee.

There is, then, no lack of machinery : the trouble is
in quality rather than quantity. For none of these
bodies has really any power or authority, either in
external or in internal policy. They cannot bind the
Unions in dealing with the employers or the State ;
and they cannot harmonise with any authority internal differences within the Labour movement. Under
present conditions, this is certainly fortunate for
Labour ; for the Trades Union Congress and the
Labour Party are at present dominated by the old
ideas of Trade Unionism. The dominance of the
official element, the ruthless use of the block vote,
the congestion of business and the manipulation of
the platform combine to secure reactionary decisions.
In the quarrel between Craft and Industrial Unionism
the Trades Union Congress is on the side of the crafts-

[1] See p. 261.

men . the Labour Party is dominated by the big
Unions, which desire to make it rather a federation of
trades than a class organisation. Merely to increase
the powers of the central bodies will not, then, achieve
the end in view ; what is wanted is a change in their
composition and outlook, a destruction of the block
vote and the card vote, the re-admission of the Trades
Councils to the Trades Union Congress, a freer rank
and file delegation from the Unions—above all, freedom
for the individual chosen by his fellows to represent
them at the Congress or Conference to cast his vote
freely as a representative, and not as a mere delegate
of the Union as a whole.

At present, before the Trades Union Congress or
the Labour Party Conference meets, there are in many
cases separate meetings of the delegates from the
various industries—miners, cotton operatives, transport workers, engineers. At these meetings, the agenda
is discussed and the attitude of the group decided
upon. Thereafter, however narrow the majority may
have been, the whole voting strength of the group is
not infrequently cast on the side of the majority. For
instance, the miners may have decided by a small
majority to support a particular resolution : if subsequently this resolution comes up for a card vote, the
whole 600,000 votes of the miners will be cast in its
favour.

This distorting mirror of Trade Union opinion is an
unmitigated nuisance. It robs the Congress proceedings of all real interest : it makes the individual delegate
a mere voting machine, and impels him to regard the
Congress more as an annual outing than as a serious
conference on urgent problems. Not till this and
similar abuses have been swept away can we set about

the building of a real central authority for the Labour movement.

Centralisation is needed not only nationally, but also locally. The Trade Union branches in a town or district to-day are far too isolated, and have far too few points of contact or opportunities for interchange of feeling and opinion. The Trades Councils have been ostracised by the Trades Union Congress, deprived of industrial functions, and starved for money. Only with the coming of a political Labour movement have they found any encouragement or opportunity for effective action. One of the most urgent problems of the day is the direction of the activity and energy of the Trades Councils into effective industrial channels. They are in many ways the soundest part of the Labour movement, the most imbued with the class spirit and the most accessible to new ideas. It is criminal to allow their energy and initiative to run to waste.

What, then, should be the function of the Trades Councils in a re-organised Trade Union movement? First of all, they should serve as the centres of Labour propaganda and education. They should make Trade Unionists, and, having done this, they should make good and enlightened Trade Unionists. The Trades Councils should be linked up closely with the educational side of the Trade Union movement, with the Workers' Educational Association and with the Labour Colleges. They should run, in connection with these bodies, classes on industrial and kindred subjects, and they should serve to bring together into one fellowship the whole Trade Union life of their district. Secondly, they should be given new industrial functions. The control of the Labour Exchanges, either wholly or jointly with the employers, should pass into their hands, and they should assume a share in the control of the provision for and against unemployment. Local féderations of Trade Unions should be linked up with the Trades Councils ; they should be kept fully informed of all local movements, and should serve as centres for information about and research into local industrial conditions. Moreover, the waste and overlapping involved in the separate existence, in many towns, of Trades Councils and Local Labour Parties should be done away with, and there should be one body with two distinct wings, or aspects of activity.

Clearly, if the Trades Councils are to fulfil these functions, they must have money. They will need buildings of their own to serve as centres for the whole Labour life of their district, for meetings, demonstrations, conferences, concerts, plays and all other aspects of the industrial, political, educational, research and social work of the Labour movement. Whence, then, is this money to come ? Clearly, it can come only out of Trade Union contributions. Every Trade Union should insist that all its branches shall affiliate to the local Trades Councils, and Councils should be formed wherever they do not exist. Then it should be made possible for branch contributions to the Trades Councils to be increased, in order that the local life of Trade Unionism might be made more vigorous and more class-conscious.

No doubt, there will be many to whom these hopes of Trade Union re-organisation will appear as dreams unlikely of fulfilment. I reply that the only hope for Trade Unionism lies in a recovery of its power and will to dream dreams—and to fulfil them. Trade Unionism has got into a rut : it has become no less conservative than the institutions which it is its mission to destroy and to supplant. The things we need most in the Trade Union movement to-day are not even the big structural changes which I have endeavoured to outline, but faith and idealism and mutual trust—not in leaders, but of the rank and file in themselves. If we can get these, or even get a strong minority imbued with these, the changes in machinery will be easily brought about.

It is often said that what the Trade Union movement needs most is intelligent and clear-sighted leadership. This is both true and untrue. It is not mainly upon great national leaders that the future of Labour depends, but on local and workshop leaders, upon the intelligent minority among the rank and file. We need a policy and a method of organisation which will make the Trade Union movement the best possible training ground for such men—which will at once keep them in the most direct contact with the mass of Trade Unionists, and give them responsible work to do which will call for all their intelligence and all their force of character. There are great obstacles to overcome. We have to draw these men from industry, and industry under present conditions is organised by Capitalism to provide not intelligence and self-reliance, but servility and automatism. Only through their own organisations can the workers hope to counteract this tyranny of industrialism : and the method clearly prescribed for them is that of a progressive invasion of capitalist control of industry, a progressive wresting of the right to make decisions from Capitalism and a vesting of it in the workers themselves, a progressive atrophy of Capitalism corresponding to a development of function and opportunity and power for the proletariat. This is the true line of advance ; and this policy Trade

Unionism must pursue, not only in its dealings with employers and with the State, but also in refashioning its own organisation. New functions call for new methods and new machinery ; but above all, they call for new men. Trade Unionism must become again a democratic movement, basing itself upon the workshop, and finding in the workshop the source and replenishment of its power. And, in proportion as the workshop is made the centre of Trade Union life, these other things will be added unto it—new functions, new methods, new machinery and new men.

CHAPTER IV

THE ABOLITION OF THE WAGE-SYSTEM

I. PAY AND WAGES

WE are all familiar with those critics of the economics of National Guilds who protest that the difference between ' pay ' and ' wages ' is purely nominal, and refuse to recognise ' the abolition of the wage-system ' as a reasonable or practicable aim. Always, they tell us, there will have to be some form of payment for service rendered, or for citizenship, and to them it makes no difference whether this is called ' wages ' or something else. National Guildsmen are inevitably impatient of such critics ; because, in their minds, the abolition of the wage-system is present as the economic postulate of National Guilds. They do not mean by ' wages ' merely ' some form of payment ' : they mean a quite definite form of payment which is an economic postulate of capitalism. In speaking of the wage-system, they are speaking of the system under which labour is bought and sold in the labour market as an article of commerce. In demanding the abolition of wagery, they are repudiating utterly the idea that labour is a commodity, or that it ought to be bought and sold for what it will fetch in a ' labour market.' By ' wage,' they mean the price paid for labour as a commodity, and for this method of payment they wish to substitute another and a better method.

National Guildsmen have always recognised that there is more than one alternative to the wage-system. In general, they have contrasted chattel-slavery, wage-slavery, and National Guilds, and, with special reference to the propaganda of nationalisation, they have pointed to the danger that the wage-system might continue under State Socialism, and the State continue to buy its labour as a commodity. Just as the labour of postal or tramway workers is treated as a commodity to-day, even though their employer be a Government department or a local authority, the labour of all workers might be so treated under a universal régime of Collectivism. It might, or, again, it might not. The omnipotent State *might* decree the abolition of rent, interest, and profits, and thereafter pay its employees on some basis other than the wage-system—perhaps equality. Or, again, it might not. There is no assurance that State Socialism would abolish the wage-system : indeed, there is every probability that it would not. For it would not strike directly at the wage-system, which is the root of the whole tyranny of capitalism ; and only a direct blow at the root is likely to avail.

There are four distinguishing marks of the wage-system upon which National Guildsmen are accustomed to fix their attention. Let me set them out clearly in the simplest terms.

1. The wage-system abstracts ' labour ' from the labourer, so that the one can be bought and sold without the other.

2. Consequently, wages are paid to the wage-worker only when it is profitable to the capitalist to employ his labour.

3. The wage-worker, in return for his wage, surrenders all control over the organisation of production.

4. The wage-worker, in return for his wage, surrenders all claim upon the product of his labour.

If the wage-system is to be abolished, all these four marks of degraded status must be removed. National Guilds, then, must assure to the worker, at least, the following things :

1. Recognition and payment as a human being, and not merely as the mortal tenement of so much labour power for which an efficient demand exists.

2. Consequently, payment in employment and in unemployment, in sickness and in health alike.

3. Control of the organisation of production in co-operation with his fellows.

4. A claim upon the product of his work, also exercised in co-operation with his fellows.

These four claims I propose to analyse in what follows ; but, first, let me try to clear away what seem to be real misunderstandings in the way of the acceptance of our economics—misunderstandings which come partly of terminology, and partly of the illustrations which we employ.

We are fond of saying that in the Army men's sense of service is heightened because they receive not wages, but pay. But, in fact, the conditions of service in the Army are, as we all know, very far from removing the disabilities of labour. Our Army is a class Army, in which the private has no effective share in the organisation of the Service. Nor has he any share in the disposition of the spoils of victory ; for these are apportioned by a secret class diplomacy. His ' pay ' may not be determined accurately by the state of the labour market ; but there is no doubt that the prevailing standards of wage payment have a very great influence in determining its amount, especially with regard to separation allowances and the variation of pay and allowances between grades and ranks of the Service. Only in one of the four respects we have mentioned does he differ *toto cœlo* from the wage-earner, and that is in that he is paid alike in employment and temporary unemployment, in sickness, short of discharge, and in health. National Guildsmen, therefore, use the example of the soldier in order to emphasise one of the four great iniquities of the wage-system ; but they do not, therefore, imply that the soldier's condition is that of an economic or social paradise. Indeed, they explicitly affirm that this feature of the soldier's service, wherein it differs from the wage-system, is found also in chattel-slavery.

This point is emphasised here, because it is one in respect of which National Guildsmen are often mis-understood. Both in the case of the Army, and in the parallel case of the Panama Canal, our arguments have been assailed on the ground that the discipline in these cases is more autocratic and the subordination of the worker proportionately more complete than under the unmodified wage-system. This is perfectly true ; but it does not alter the fact that in these cases one of the four great disabilities of the worker has been removed without a return to chattel-slavery. At the same time, it serves to emphasise the danger of mistaking the abolition of one factor in the wage-system for the abolition of the system itself. There is, as we shall see, a real peril that the abolition of one factor apart from the others may in effect bring with it a virtual return of chattel-slavery.

Under chattel-slavery, two of the four iniquities of

the wage-system did not exist. Labour was not
abstracted from the labourer, and, consequently,
employment was not abstracted from unemployment.
Let us profit by reflection upon this fact. We must
demand, and that firmly, the removal, not of one or
two or three of the four disabilities, but of them all.
And, if we are to make our demand effective, we must
have to our hands the means.

II. LABOUR AND THE LABOURER

I have so far done little more than repeat, with a few
cautions, the classic diagnosis of wage-slavery advanced
by National Guildsmen. I want now to turn to the
examination of the first of the four diseases which
afflict the industrial system, and to the remedies
proposed. It is the essence of wage-slavery that it
abstracts labour from the labourer, and countenances
traffic in labour while it no longer permits traffic in men.

There was a time when this abstraction seemed to
those who fought to bring it about the realisation of
human freedom and equality. No longer, they proudly
proclaimed, could man be treated as a commodity,
devoid of rights, to be bought and sold in the market
for a price, and to be owned and controlled absolutely
by his lord and buyer. The world put away chattel-
slavery as an unclean thing, and in name made all men
equal before the law. But it did not make the law
itself equal before men ; nor could it make men equal
before capital.

To chattel-slavery, therefore, succeeded ' the economy of wages,' forerunner of the ' economy of
high wages.' The employing class easily reconciled
itself to the loss of ownership over men, when it found

the hiring of their labour a cheaper and more efficient instrument for the making of profits. The landlord readily acquiesced in the emancipation of the serf when he saw that thereby he escaped the responsibilities of landholding, and gained his freedom to exploit his land at will. In short, under chattel-slavery and serfdom the ownership of capital and of labour was in the same hands ; for the rich man effectively owned both land and capital, labour and the labourer. The wage-system has changed all that by divorcing the ownership of labour and capital ; for it has left capital in the hands of the few, and has made of the many a class that possesses nothing save its own labour.

Fundamentally, then, in its economic aspect the change to wage-slavery is a change from integration to disintegration ; a division between two classes of the ownership of the means of life. The effect of this disintegration was at once not simply to divorce the ownership of men from the ownership of commodities, but to divorce the majority of men from the labour embodied in them. Under chattel-slavery, the owner bought a man entire ; under the wage-system, he buys merely so much or so long of a man's labour.

This once seemed a great advance, and in many ways was an advance. But so far as industry was concerned, it was a set-back as well as an advance. It constituted a recognition of the fact that all men have rights as men, and that no man ought to be, in the absolute sense, lord of another ; but it also effectively prevented those whose rights were thus recognised from exercising their most important right, the free disposition of their service. We must not minimise the importance of the step taken by the abolition of chattel-slavery ; but we must also fully recognise how far progress has been thwarted by the separation of the ownership of labour from the ownership of capital.

Some who recognise this are too fond of describing the revolution wrought by the abolition of chattel-slavery purely as a division between the labourer and his labour. It is even more profoundly a division of ownership, a disintegration of industry, which is at the same time a step towards a new integration. They who own both capital and the labourer exercise an indisputable control over both : they who own only labour must sell their labour to the owners of capital : they who own capital continue to control, though not to own, the labourers. There is, therefore, no way out of the wage-system by a mere re-uniting of labour and the labourer ; the only way out is for the labourer to secure control of capital as well as labour.

Thus far the arguments of National Guildsmen are practically identical with those of the Distributivists and of Mr. Belloc.[1] They begin to diverge when the words ' ownership ' and ' control ' come to be more closely examined. Mr. Belloc looks to a distribution of capital among the owners of labour : National Guildsmen continue to insist on the need for collective ownership of capital by the State. What bearing have our reflections upon these two views ?

I must divide my answer into two parts, the first relating to the complete system of National Guilds which I have in view, and the second to the period of transition to that system. Why do I maintain that National Guilds will serve to realise economic freedom if they will not give to the individual owner of labour any direct ownership of capital ? I do so because they will give him, with his fellow-citizens, a collective ownership and control of capital, which will

[1] See p. 262.

be one guarantee of his exercise of his right of ownership and control of labour. That is to say, National Guilds imply a democratic State.

There may be some to whom this seems, at first sight, an admission of the Collectivist case. Surely, I shall be told, this is an admission that a democratisation of the State can bring about industrial freedom. The verbal truth of such a statement, I, at least, have never denied ; for precisely what National Guildsmen have held is that democratisation of the State is impossible except by a frontal attack upon the wage-system itself. Everything, therefore, turns upon the period of transition, and the means to be adopted in destroying the wage-system.

The operation of the wage-system has caused both labour and capital to pass from an individual to a ' joint stock ' exercise of ownership. Both profits and wages still pass ultimately to the individual, but their control has been transferred to companies, syndicates and rings, on the one hand, and to Trade Unions on the other, in all the principal industries. The problem of transition, therefore, cannot be regarded in terms of the individual, but must be regarded in terms of the combine. It seems to me the main fallacy of the Distributivists that they refuse to envisage the period of transition in terms of human aggregates. Even if the individual distribution of ownership were the end, it could not be the means or the method of destroying the wage-system.

The real problem, then, is that of the nature of Trade Union intervention in industry. Must that intervention take the form of demanding an ever-increasing share in the ownership of capital, or can it be content with assuming a complete control in addition to its present ownership of labour ? What we have said above seems to indicate that it cannot stop short of a demand for the ownership and control of capital.

We have said above that, under National Guilds, this ownership would not be exercised by the Guilds but by the State. But National Guildsmen, of course, do not recognise the State of to-day as a body capable of exercising ownership on behalf of the community. We are, therefore, driven back, in relation to immediate policy, upon a further question. How far, in the transition period, can the ownership of capital which the workers must have be achieved by means of the State, or how far must the workers themselves provisionally assume ownership in order to create a democratic State to which they may transfer it ?

The answer would seem to be this. The first and most important task for the workers is that of perfecting and completing their control of labour, which will, at the same time, place in their hands the power of conquering and democratising the State ; but if at any point it becomes necessary for the control of labour that they should assume any measure of ownership or control of capital, they should not hesitate to fight for this also in the industrial field.

The exact implications of this view are not, perhaps, immediately clear. It means no less than this ; that at some time before the wage-system is ended, it may become necessary for Labour to take a hand in the running of industry, and to accept what is sometimes called ' a common responsibility with capitalism.' There may come a time when, owing to Labour pressure, capitalism and the capitalist State are no longer strong enough to control industry alone, and, at the same time, the workers are not strong enough to assume

complete control. Then may come the offer of partnership, envisaged long ago by the authors of *National
Guilds*. In such case, what could Labour do but
accept a sort of partnership, with a firm intention of
dissolving it as soon as the requisite strength had
been attained ?

This way clearly lies a danger ; but the danger is less
in the suggestion itself than in the possibility of its
acceptance as an immediate plan of campaign. For it
is certain that the time for such a partnership is not yet
It could be acceptable only when the fabric of capitalism
had been undermined by the perfection by the workers
of their control over labour ; and it could be assumed
only upon terms of, at least, full equality. Nothing
less than half can be good enough to balance the danger
involved for Labour in a joint responsibility with
capitalism. But the day of such equality of Labour
has by no means arrived ; and it will arrive only if the
workers concentrate for the present upon the perfecting
of their control over their labour, by a constant extension of their power and authority in mine, railway,
factory and workshop. The extension of control over
labour is for the immediate future the true path for
Labour to pursue.

Lest I seem to have digressed idly and in vain
from my starting point, let me try to sum up in a few
sentences the general purport of these reflections.
Chattel-slavery combined the ownership of capital and
of the labourer in the hands of the few. Wage-slavery
divorced these two forms of ownership, and thereby
also divorced labour from the labourer. The wage-
system must end with a re-integration, with the placing
in the hands of all of both capital and labour. In
order to bring this about, the wage-earning class

must assume control of capital. This control, under
National Guilds, will be exercised collectively, through
the State ; but, as the State can be democratised only
by the growth of Labour's industrial power, the workers
must be prepared, if necessary, to assume, through
their Trade Unions, a half share in the ownership of
capital, as a step in the direction of National Guilds.
They must not, however, accept any joint responsibility
with capitalism in return for less than a half share in
ownership, and the day for such a share is not yet.
For the present, therefore, the task of the workers is
to concentrate on increasing and perfecting their
control of their labour, which is the basis of their
industrial power.

III. Security

The inevitable result of the divorce of the ownership
of labour and capital has been the loss of security by
the wage-earner. Speaking broadly, the slave was
secure ; his job was continuous, and his master was
obliged to maintain him in employment and in unemployment, in sickness and in health. This security,
which was a security without rights based upon the
denial of freedom, the wage-system swept away. For
an actual security based upon bondage it substituted
a no less actual insecurity based upon an incomplete
personal freedom. Our problem to-day is that of
re-establishing security without re-instituting virtual
chattel-slavery.

In the Tudor period, when the migration of workers
from agriculture to the factories threatened to deprive
the landowner of the means of tilling the land, legislation was enacted to prevent the workers from moving

freely. Without a security at all comparable to the security of chattel-slavery, the worker was tied to his employer.[1] In our own time, the passage of the Munitions Act placed for a time many workers in a similar position. The employer could refuse his employee a leaving certificate, and so prevent him from getting work elsewhere, and, at the same time, withhold from him both work and wages. Even now, though this abuse has been modified, the worker who is subject to the Munitions Act is virtually tied to his employer, receiving in return security of employment. The War Munition Volunteer and the Army Reserve Munition Worker are even tied, not to a particular employer, but to any employer to whom the Government may send them. Under such conditions, the worker recovers the security of chattel-slavery ; but he does so at the sacrifice even of the limited freedom to choose his employer which the wage-system has hitherto allowed.

One of the objects which National Guildsmen must attain in destroying the wage-system is the re-establishment of security ; but they must beware lest, in seeking this, they succeed only in riveting the chains more firmly upon the working-class. This is the peril that lurks in some of the projects for the re-establishment of security which are now being put forward in the name of reconstruction.

The proposals fall into two classes. On the one hand, it is suggested that the State should assume the responsibility for security of employment or for maintenance in unemployment on behalf of the whole working-class. On the other hand, it is suggested that the maintenance of the worker in employment and unemployment alike should become a direct charge

[1] See p. 262.

upon industry itself. And these proposals are applied
to periods of sickness as well as to unemployment.

Within restricted spheres, both principles are operative at the present time. On the one hand, we have
the State administration of Health and Unemployment
Insurance, and a certain amount of State relief of
unemployment under the Unemployed Workmen Act :
on the other, we have the employers' contributions
under the Insurance Act,[1] and, what is by far a purer
case, the Employers' Liability Act and the Workmen's
Compensation Act. Moreover, in the Insurance Act we
have a mixed principle, which makes the employer to
some extent an agent of the State and an intermediary
between the State and the workman.

It is, however, generally recognised that none of
these measures constitutes an establishment of security,
and active propaganda is proceeding in respect of the
two rival methods. The advocates of State action
desire the complete assumption by the State of the
liability for the provision against and for unemployment, on a non-contributory principle—that is, out of
revenue raised by taxation. To this it is objected by
employer and workman alike that it would immensely
increase the element of bureaucratic control over
industry, and by workmen, in addition, that it would
place Labour as completely in the hands of the State
as it is now placed there by the Munitions Act and the
Military Service Acts. The saner advocates of State
action reply that the remedy lies in placing the administration of Employment Exchanges and of the provision
for and against unemployment, not in the hands of State
officials, but in the hands of employers and workmen
jointly. Here, again, objection is taken on the ground
that this would involve the expenditure of money

[1] See p. 262.

raised by public taxation by bodies not publicly responsible, or, at least, not publicly controlled. This is, indeed, a serious objection, because it will probably shipwreck the scheme. If ' public money ' is to be expended, Parliament and the Treasury will insist on controlling the expenditure of it. If this happens, we at once find ourselves back under the domination of bureaucracy.

We shall be better able to meet this difficulty if we first look at the opposing solution of the problem. By the opponents of State control, among whom National Guildsmen, as advocates of industrial autonomy, most naturally find their place, it is urged that the way out of the difficulty is for industry itself to assume the burden. Nor is this put forward as a mere expedient; for it is clear that National Guilds must afford security by assuming responsibility for the Guild members in employment and in unemployment, in sickness and in health.

This suggestion at present lacks precision ; but it seems to assume roughly this form. Each industry, it is proposed, should assume the responsibility for its whole personnel, in bad and good trade alike. The unemployed, and probably the sick also, should be a charge upon the industry, and should be maintained out of its product. To the capitalist, it is pointed out, this principle already applies : he, at any rate, can be maintained by the industry, whether he is well or ill, working or idle. It applies, further, to the management, and, to a considerable extent, to the salaried staff. Why should it not apply to the workers also ? Would it not, indeed, be a most important step in the recognition of industrial democracy that the workers' right to full maintenance out of the product of their industry should be securely established ?

The peril of this suggestion clearly lies in the fact that we are as yet very far off the establishment of National Guilds. To make unemployment and sickness a charge on the Guilds is one thing ; to make them a charge on industry, as it is now constituted, is clearly quite another, and might easily involve the placing of the worker in a more complete subordination to capitalism than ever. If he who pays the piper calls the tune, there is evidently a danger that capitalism, in assuming the responsibility for the worker in sickness and unemployment, might also virtually assume ownership of the worker. In that case, we might have made a breach in the wage-system ; but we should have substituted for it a new form of chattel-slavery.

There seem to me to be insuperable objections both to the complete assumption by the State of the provision for and against unemployment, and to an assumption of the same responsibility by capitalism. It is, how-ever, evident that somehow this responsibility must be assumed, and that Labour is not in a position, and cannot fairly be asked, to assume it. There seem to be two further alternatives which we have not yet considered.

First, there is the ' Ghent system ' of unemployment insurance, by which the State subsidises Trade Unions to the extent of a proportion of their expenditure on unemployment benefit.[1] This system already occupies a subordinate position in the scheme established under the Insurance Act, one of its defects lying in the State's insistence on a fairly large element of control in return for its subsidy. But there is a more serious defect ; for it makes the amount of State assistance depend upon the amount spent by the Trade Unions on voluntary unemployment insurance. This both rules out those

[1] See p. 263.

classes of workers who cannot afford to insure themselves at all, or adequately, at their own expense, and is, besides, unfair in that it places a large part of the cost of insurance upon the shoulders of the wage-earner. It is not, and cannot be made, a universal scheme of maintenance in times of unemployment, and, what is more important, it is wholly ineffective in furthering the decasualisation of labour.

This should be one of the first objects for National Guildsmen ; for casual labour is one of the greatest obstacles to blackleg-proof industrial organisation. Can we not, then, devise means of getting round the objections to the assumption by industry of the burden of unemployment ? Clearly, if the burden is placed upon industry, those who control industry will have every incentive for making it as light as possible.

This brings me to the remaining alternative, which is the control of maintenance benefits in sickness and unemployment by the Trade Unions, the cost being borne by a levy upon industry exacted under authority of an Act of Parliament. Let an Act be passed setting up for each industry a statutory body representing employers and Trade Unions, with power to levy a rate upon all the firms in the industry in proportion to the numbers employed by them. Let the payment of benefits from this fund be placed absolutely in the hands of the Trade Unions, and let Parliament have no control either of the amount of the levy or of its expenditure. This would be a clear step in the direction of industrial autonomy.

This, however, would not solve the whole problem ; for industry is not yet decasualised, and there are many workers, and not a few employers, who cannot be assigned definitely to any industry. For these there would have to be a general body, on which, from the Labour side, the General Labour Unions would be strongly represented, and this body would levy a general rate on all employers employing such unallotted labour.

To these bodies, and to a Central body co-ordinating them all, should also pass the control of the Labour Exchanges, and of any other industrial agencies set up by the State for dealing with questions of employment.[1]

That there are perils in this scheme, as there are perils in all forms of co-operation between employers and Trade Unions, cannot be denied. But, under capitalism, we are, perforce, driven to choose between evils. We have the choice between bureaucratic State control and a limited co-operation with the employers for particular purposes, and it seems natural that advocates of National Guilds should prefer the second alternative to the first. Those who dwell upon the danger seem to hold that the effect of co-operation with the employers will inevitably be that Labour will fall in love with capitalism. Is it not far more likely that a taste of control will produce a taste for control? National Guildsmen have never believed that the new Society can spring full grown from the old, like Athene from the head of Zeus. The new conditions must germinate within the old, by the gradual assumption by Labour of functions which are now the preserves of the employers. Before Labour can control, it must learn how to control; and this it will do only by actual

---

[1] I have stated this proposal dogmatically; but I do not at all desire to be dogmatic about it. I throw it out as a suggestion, of which I am myself far from certain, in the hope that it may at least serve to provoke discussion. For a further treatment of the point, I may refer the reader to *Guild Principles in Peace and War*, by Mr. S. G. Hobson, with whom the proposal originated.

experience of control. For this experience, we must be prepared to risk much ; and the risk in such a scheme as this does not seem to me to be great.

The danger that is real in the preaching of security lies in schemes that would have the effect of tying the workers more closely to a particular employer. We have already experience of the effects of such security in the Royal Dockyards, and wherever the prospect of a pension ties the workman to his job. For this reason, there must be no attempt to deal with the problem of security in relation to the particular workshop. The workman must get security, not as an employee of such and such a factory, but as a member of the industry in which he works. This is the path of industrial autonomy ; and, if this is followed, it will be a long step towards the abolition of the wage-system, though it will not by itself abolish that system. Ultimately, the complete control of employment and unemployment, and complete responsibility for the workers in sickness and in health, must pass to the Guilds ; but the most we can hope for at present is a system in which the workers' right to security is recognised, and in which, without any sacrifice of freedom, he plays a controlling part in the administration of the means to that security.

IV. THE CONTROL OF PRODUCTION

The democratic government of the factory by those engaged in it would be the plainest sign of a change in industry. But it would not by itself destroy the wage-system. The employer might hand the management of his factory over absolutely to the workers employed in it, or even to the Trade Union of their industry : he might ' salary ' the Trade Union, where he now salaries a manager. And, having done all this, he might conceivably continue much where he is to-day—he might go on buying and selling commodities or stocks and shares, and he might still draw from the community his toll of rent, interest and profits. Having won the control of the factory, the workers would only have democratised the management ; they would not have overthrown the wage-system, or socialised industry itself.

Yet again, therefore, in writing of a particular part of our policy, I have to lay stress upon its essential incompleteness when it is viewed in isolation from the rest. Having done this, I can safely go on to point out wherein it is of fundamental importance, without fear of being supposed to regard the part as greater than the whole.

The control of production is important both as an end and as a means. It is an essential part of that system of industrial self-government which I desire to see established, and it is an essential means to the establishment of that self-government.

There is no need to waste words in showing that the control of production is a part of the end ; for that follows naturally, and inevitably, from the whole idea of industrial freedom upon which the Guild system rests. The *idée maîtresse* of National Guilds is industrial self-government, and, clearly, that idea must find a primary expression in the democratic control of the productive process. Control of the factory by the workers employed in it is the corner-stone of the whole edifice of National Guilds.

So important a part of the end is very naturally also not the least important of the means. National Guilds become realisable in proportion as the producers, through their democratic organisations, fit themselves to replace the capitalist or the bureaucrat, and do actually replace him—in proportion as they become capable of controlling that which he now controls, and do actually control it. Now, capitalists to-day enjoy rent, interest and profits by virtue of their control over two spheres of industrial activity, production and exchange. The former, which is the control of the productive processes, is the subject of this section ; the latter, which is the control of the raw material and the finished product, will be dealt with in the next section of this chapter.

In both spheres, capitalist control is largely exercised through others. These others are the management, sometimes pure salary-earners, sometimes also profit-sharers on commission, or share-holders in the business. At present, these managers, of all grades from foremen up to the great managing directors of huge combines, are the servants of the capitalist class, who do their bidding, and maintain in their interest the autocratic control of industry.

The industrial organisation of Labour is primarily a workshop organisation, deriving its strength from the monopoly of labour which it is able to establish in the workshop. In proportion as the workshop life of Trade Unionism is vigorous, Trade Unionism itself is strong. This fact has many morals with regard to the internal organisation of the Trade Unions ; but these I have no space to point out now. What I desire to make plain at the moment that, since it is in the workshops that Trade Unionism is strong, it is in the workshops that Labour must begin its great offensive. And, in this sphere, the problem for Labour is that of detaching the salariat from its dependence on capitalism, and attaching it as an ally to Trade Unionism.

National Guildsmen have often pointed out how this process can begin—by the strengthening of Trade Union organisation in the workshop, by a closer and closer relating of Trade Union machinery to the organised life of the workshop, and by the gradual winning over from capitalism of the grades of supervision and management, beginning with the wresting by Labour from its enemies of the right to choose and control foremen and superiors in every industry.

This progressive invasion of capitalist autocracy in the workshops, the factory, and the mine has long been placed in the forefront of the propaganda of National Guilds. It is sometimes objected to it by Collectivists and others that it does nothing to strike at the basis of rent, interest and profits, and, indeed, that this is a fundamental weakness of the whole immediate policy of National Guildsmen. It is this argument which I desire to answer.

A class that becomes atrophied is doomed to decay. The power of any class in any stage of human society rests ultimately upon the performance of functions. These functions may be socially useful or anti-social : an anti-social function may be just as good an instrument of survival as a social function. But as soon as a class is left without functions, the decay of its power and prestige can be only a matter of time. It was the deprivation of the *noblesse* of France of all social functions that made possible the overthrow of the *ancien régime* ; and we, in our day and generation, shall succeed in overthrowing industrial capitalism only if we first make it socially functionless.

This means that, before capitalism can be overthrown, there must be wrested from it both its control of production and its control of exchange. This done, the abolition of its claim to rent, interest and profits will follow as a matter of course.

The obvious striking point for labour to-day is the workshop. The assumption by the Trade Unions of workshop control would not destroy rent, interest and profits, but it would be a shrewd blow struck at the roots from which they spring. This is its fundamental import for Labour at the present time.

The method by which the Trade Unions are to assume control of the workshop and the productive processes are matters of keen debate among National Guildsmen ; but the foregoing principles can hardly be called in question. Let us try to see now what follows from them in the way of ' next steps.'

The first question that arises is whether, at any stage, Labour ought to assume any form of *joint* control with capitalism over the workshop, or any joint responsibility for its conduct. Joint control in any real sense is clearly impossible. Labour cannot be expected, with the wage-system practically unimpaired, to become responsible for the carrying on of capitalist industry. Labour is the aggressor in its strife with capitalism, and aims at the complete overthrow and supersession of capitalism. It cannot, therefore, in any real sense, become responsible for a system which it desires to end. But there is, I think, a sense in which a transition period of divided control with capitalism is inevitable.

Let us take the analogy of a subject race—India, let us say—that seeks to achieve self-government and emancipate itself from its conquerors, but has no immediate hope of complete independence, and might have serious difficulty in governing itself if it had such hope. The position of India in relation to Great Britain offers, indeed, many fruitful analogies to the position of Labour in relation to capitalism. The Indian is driven to seek emancipation through a gradual extension of his share in the functions of government. Moreover, he is driven, in the early stages of the movement towards self-government, to assume a measure of joint control over Government. The Indian Legislative Councils to-day represent a balance between official and non-official elements ; they are a sort of joint committee in which the governors and the governed meet for consultation, and in which the governed have an opportunity of criticising their governors. As some schools of Indian Nationalists have freely pointed out, this method has its dangers, and many Nationalists who have entered the Councils as critics, have been more or less completely absorbed by the governmental machine. But there are few, save catastrophic revolutionists, who doubt that the India Councils Act of 1909, and similar reform measures, do tend in the direction of self-government. The Nationalist movement, by this measure of participation, does not sacrifice its power, its independence, or its rights of agitation and criticism.

I believe that there must be a somewhat similar stage in the evolution of industrial self-government, and that Labour must pass through the stage of joint machinery for the control of production before it can assume complete control. The question is whether, in assuming partial control, Labour runs the risk of sacrificing its independence, and so blocking the way to a further advance.

Our judgment upon this question depends finally

upon our judgment of the Trade Union movement and of human nature. Do we, or do we not, believe that the Trade Union movement has so little capacity for idealism and self-government, or that human nature is so easily satisfied and so gullible that the exercise of a little power will be enough to still unrest and smother discontent ? I do not. Individuals may, and will, fall by the wayside, and be lost to the movement ; but the movement itself will go on, gathering in appetite and swallow as it feeds. A taste of control will engender a taste for control.

But, as I have said, the assumption of new functions by Trade Unionism will not only develop new desires and capacities among Trade Unionists—it will also place a new strain upon the Trade Union movement. New men will have to be found, and new machinery will have to be devised. I believe that one method of search will serve to find both. We must make the works the unit of Trade Union organisation, and afford to the Trade Unionist in the works his training in government.

From Trade Union control in the workshop, backed by a strong natural organisation of Trade Unionism, will follow an extension of Trade Unionism over the management. The capitalist will be gradually ousted from his dictatorship in the control of production, and with the atrophy of one of his two primary functions will go a shifting in the balance of economic power and a weakening of the wage-system. We must now turn to the other primary function of capitalism—the control of the product.

V. THE CONTROL OF THE PRODUCT

I come now to what is, I confess, by far the most difficult of the tasks which Labour must accomplish if a free Society is to replace the wage-system. It will not be easy for Labour to secure control of production ; but it will be far more difficult for it to secure control of the product.

Capitalism has two primary functions—the control of the processes of production and the control of exchange. The first is exercised by its control of the workshop. This brings it into a direct and constant contact with the worker, and we have seen that the main object of Labour at present should be to oust the capitalist from this sphere of control by the use of its industrial power. This, however, as we saw, might be accomplished without the destruction of capitalism, and with only a bare breach in the wage-system itself. For, if capitalism retained its control of the product, it could still draw its toll of rent, interest and profits. The worker would have a freer workshop life ; but even the organisation of the workshop would remain subordinate to the economic requirements of capitalism.

Capitalist control of the product has three principal aspects. It is expressed in the financial system by which the great investors and syndicates regulate the flow of capital ; in the control of raw materials— buying ; and in the control of the finished product— selling. Investing, buying and selling, even more than producing, does capitalism lay waste Society.

This fact, I take it, is in the minds of ' National Guildsmen ' when they say that " economic power precedes and dominates industrial, no less than political, power." Our problem, then, is to accomplish a democratisation and Guildisation of investment, purchase and sale, as well as of production.

We are, perhaps, too apt to think of ' capitalism ' and ' the employer ' as synonymous, and upon this mistake to build erroneous conclusions. In fact, the individuals whom we lump together as the ' capitalists,' or the ' employing class,' fall into at least three distinct groups, though, of course, these groups are closely connected, and it is often impossible to say to which of them a particular individual should be assigned.

First, there are the great capitalists, or owners of money power. Sometimes these capitalists confine their operations to a single industry, sometimes their operations extend over many industries, sometimes they are pure financiers, whose relation to industry is indirect, sometimes they are merchants, whose whole business is buying and selling.

Secondly, there are the smaller employers, capitalists too, but not powers in the financial sphere. These men are mainly producers, or smaller merchants, managing, as a rule, their own businesses, and striving to extract a profit for themselves.

Thirdly, there are managing directors, associated with big businesses, industrial, commercial or financial, but not themselves owning any great share in the capital which they manipulate.

The economic world is increasingly dominated by the first of these classes. The financier, with capital to invest, is the supreme power behind the capitalist throne. In industry, where large-scale production is the rule, the great industrialist increasingly dominates the smaller employer : where small-scale production continues, as in the woollen industry, the merchant is supreme, and constantly subordinates the interests of the producing employers to his own.

We often proclaim that the State is a capitalist State. It is, in fact, a ' big business ' State, dominated by the capitalists of the first group, the financiers and the great industrialists. The big business has not, as Marx thought it would, crushed out the small ; but more and more it dominates and controls it.

Our own is not the first epoch in which Society has followed this course of evolution. The breakdown of the Mediaeval Guilds was mainly due to the rise of a merchant class possessed of capital. This class received into itself, and into alliance with itself, the greater producing employers : the smaller employers it ground down and overwhelmed. It did not necessarily destroy or absorb them ; but it turned them from master-craftsmen into dependent producers.

Labour, then, in seeking to destroy the capitalist control of production, has to deal with the first group of capitalists, the financiers and the great lords of industry. These are not, from our point of view, two groups, but one group, though they have many external differences which lead to friction among them-selves. It is a sign of the times that Lord Rhondda, not content with coal, or even coal and iron, should be acquiring ' interests ' in the most various types of enterprise.

In seeking to control production, the method for Labour is clear. By the development of Trade Union organisation it can look to the winning of control in the workshop and the works. But what is to be its method of winning control over the product—over investment, buying and selling ?

Some will answer simply, ' The State.' But, every

day, the State is passing more completely under the control of those very persons whose power we are seeking to destroy. The State may, on occasion, be ruthless in its dealings with the mere employer ; it is not ruthless in dealing with the great industrial and financial potentates. For to these potentates our rulers owe their rule ; and to-day these potentates are themselves, in many cases, our rulers.

During the war, the State has immensely increased its control over industry. It has controlled the employer, particularly the small employer : it has become a merchant, while safeguarding the profits of merchants. Some Guildsmen welcome these developments of State control. Trade Unionism, they hold, cannot hope to control buying and selling by means of its industrial power : we must, therefore, look to the State to assume the *rôle* of banker, financier and merchant, while Labour is developing its control of production.

This clearly means nothing less than State Capitalism, the concentration of the functions of investment, purchase of raw materials, and, to some extent, sale of products in the hands of a State dominated by the profiteering interest. What hope has Labour that it will be able, if this comes about, to secure the abolition of the wage-system by securing democratic control of the product ?

On the other hand, if we reject this line of development, what is our alternative ? There are Guildsmen who seem to think that, if only Labour can get control of production, all other things will swiftly and automatically be added unto it. There are two sufficient reasons why this is not the case.

First, as economic power now dominates industrial

power among the employers themselves, it *might* continue to dominate industrial power, even if this were transferred to Labour. I say it ' might,' for reasons which will appear later.

Secondly, we cannot ensure the downfall of capitalism except by rendering it socially functionless. This we can only do by robbing it of its control of exchange, as well as of its control of production.

We must, then, if we are to overthrow the wage-system, find means of striking directly at the capitalist control of exchange, and of securing for Labour a control of the product.

I think the course is clear, though tortuous. The action of the proletariat striving for emancipation assumes three main forms. Of these, two—industrial action and political action—are evolutionary in character ; the third, insurrection or the General Strike, is catastrophic. Let us examine the function of these three in Labour's advance towards control of the product.

Industrial action, as we have seen, will result in an increased control over production. This, however, will not by itself end the wage-system, or destroy capitalism's control of the product. At the same time, it will undoubtedly cause a breach in the system, and that breach cannot be entirely confined to the workshop and the works. The final control of the product will still, no doubt, rest with the big capitalists ; but Labour will establish at least a measure of control over purchase and sale, though not over investment. Pressed by Labour from one side and by finance on the other, the ordinary employer will yield something to each, and Labour will secure, by industrial action, a certain limited measure of control over the product.

Industrial organisation and action will have the further effect of stimulating and vitalising political action. The character and the effect of political action are inevitably determined and conditioned by the economic strength of the actors, and industrial strength is, in this relation, a very important element in economic strength. As, then, Labour advances in industrial power, it will be possible for it to use the State for the purpose of depriving capitalism of its second economic function—the control of exchange. Such political action by Labour is likely to be most effective in the sphere of finance and investment, rather than in buying and selling of industrial products. By taxation, and by the control of banking, and of home and foreign investments, the State will be able to strike at the economic power of capitalism.

It may be held by many Guildsmen that this is mere self-delusion, and that political power cannot, even with industrial power behind it, be used for the destruction of economic power. They may be right ; but I do not think that their case is proved. Even if the State only assumes the control of exchange in the interests of capitalism, it will run a serious risk of leaving the capitalist classes without economic function. It is my contention that without economic function, social or anti-social, they cannot long sustain their economic power.

Let us suppose for a moment that the Jeremiahs are right in denying the possibility of destroying the economic power of capitalism by any combination of industrial and political action. There remains the weapon of catastrophic action, envisaged generally in the shape of the General Strike. We will imagine the masses endowed with dominant industrial power, controlling production through a blackleg-proof Trade Union organisation, possibly holding political power as well, but unable by any constitutional means at their disposal to shake off the economic power of capitalism. Surely, under such circumstances, the remedy of the catastrophic General Strike could not fail ; for there is one power which precedes all others, and that is man-power, the organised determination of human wills.

The General Strike, then, or its equivalent, may be the last stage of the march of Society towards industrial freedom. But clearly catastrophic action can only be based upon long preparation and upon actual achievement of an evolutionary character. The more we are inclined to foresee catastrophic action as the last stage of the coming social revolution, the more prepared must we be for the evolutionary steps which alone can pave the way for the great catastrophe. It may be true that the wage-system can be destroyed only by a frontal attack upon the economic power of capitalism in the spheres of commerce and finance ; but it is no less clear that the way to such an attack lies over the front line of Capitalism—the control of pro-duction. We come back, therefore, to the view that for the moment Labour's task is to concentrate on industrial action and organisation.

Standing alone, this statement may be misleading. Since the only method for Labour is that of making Capitalism socially functionless, it must aim, wherever possible, in destroying or taking over the functions of capitalism. Investment, the final seat of capitalist authority, it cannot effectively touch till the last stages are reached ; but it must and should, as its basic industrial power increases, stretch out its hands to control, as far as it can, both purchase and sale. Before it can attack the capitalist as financier, it will have to attack him not only as producer, but also as merchant. This point needs further development.

VI. Purchase, Sale and Investment

The producing employer is necessarily not only a producer, but also to some extent a buyer and seller. He has to buy his raw materials, and he has to market his wares. His functions in this respect differ widely from industry to industry, and from individual to individual. In many cases, the great producer assures his supply of material by extending his control over basic and subsidiary industries other than that in which he is directly engaged. On the other hand, many producing employers are virtually no more than tributaries of the big merchants, or of the big producers, to whom practically the whole of their wares are consigned, or from whom they draw their materials.

The rising power of labour is fundamentally a workshop power, and it is in the workshop that Labour will first acquire control. But workshop control, or at least works control, cannot be exercised without intervention in buying and selling. A works could not continue to produce for long if a state of war raged between one party exclusively in control of its productive departments, and another in exclusive control of its office. If, then, Labour is to exercise works control, it will be driven to take into consideration and under control purchase and sale.

Clearly, this problem assumed different forms according to the nature of the works concerned. If the business is one in which the producing capitalist is, in fact, independent, and has a large measure of control

over purchase and sale, Labour will find itself up
against the whole force of Capitalism at its strongest
point. If, on the other hand, the works is one in which
the employer is a mere dependent on the merchant
or the great industrialist, one of two things will happen.
Either the dependent employer will be pushed out
altogether, and the big capitalists will assume direct
control, or else the dependent employer may be forced
into the ranks of Labour. The same considerations
apply to the smaller employer, who, though not
actually dependent, is potentially so, because he has
not the force to stand up to the big business, as soon
as it desires to engulf him.

The small employer is usually his own manager, and,
as such, is performing, well or ill, a useful industrial
function. He has, therefore, as a manager, a legitimate
place in the economy of National Guilds, and the
natural course would be for Trade Unionism to absorb
him along with the dependent salariat. Unfortunately,
he is, in many cases, a small hereditary capitalist, and
a bad manager who would not be a desirable adjunct
to Labour's forces. The probability is that, as Labour
reaches the stage of works control, the class of small
employers will split into three. Some, including many
of the best, will be retained by the big capitalists as
their high salariat ; some will be driven out ; and some
will come over to Labour as elected managers, subject
to Trade Union control.

In any case, whether the employer originally confronted be large or small, dependent or independent,
Labour will sooner or later find itself confronted with
' big business.' It will have nominal control of the
workshops, and, in some cases, of the works as well ;
but it will find itself, as the smaller employers are

finding themselves to-day, still subject to the dominion of the big industrialists and merchants, who control the raw materials of industry, and the disposal of the finished product.

We saw in the last article the three weapons, industrial, political and catastrophic, which Labour can use, and their general application to the ending of wage-slavery. I want now to look more closely at the possible uses of the evolutionary means during the period of transition. Can Labour really use its industrial power to secure not only control of production, but also control of the product?

Just as, in the workshop, I believe that in some cases a share in control without sacrifice of independence will have to be assumed before complete control can be won, so I believe that complete control of the workshop and the works will make possible and involve a share in the control of purchase and sale. The point of doubt seems to me to be not whether such control will be, or ought to be, assumed, but what form it will, or ought to, take.

The danger is that of profit-sharing, a danger present in all schemes of (joint control), whether in workshop or business. It is the fear of profit-sharing establishing a common solidarity between Labour and Capitalism that leads some National Guildsmen to oppose, at all stages, all forms of ' joint control.' I agree with them concerning the dangers of profit-sharing at any stage ; but I cannot see how this ought to lead to opposition to all control-sharing. Sooner or later, the capitalists will ' try on ' profit-sharing, when they find that they can no longer resist the Labour demand for control. Labour must take the control and reject the profit-sharing, and must be prepared to take a limited control if it cannot yet secure complete control. There is no essential connection between control-sharing and profit-sharing.

We come next to the State ? What ought to be our attitude, as National Guildsmen, towards the assumption by the State of economic control ? I am speaking now not of State control of production, which I deal with in a later chapter, nor of State control of finance, which I shall deal with later, but of State control of purchase and sale.

During the war, the State has been the greatest merchant. It has bought and sold on a huge scale, and its operations have included every stage of the commodity from the raw material to the finished article. If it has been very tender to the merchants and the industrialists where profits are concerned, it has certainly usurped many of their functions, and reduced many an industrialist temporarily to the position of a mere manager. Some people hold strongly that this tendency ought to be encouraged and perpetuated, and that as the Trade Unions assume from below the control of production, the State should assume from above the control of the product, until ultimately the two meet, and the employer is eliminated or, rather, ground to powder between the upper and the nether millstone. I cannot quite take this view, because I regard the State of to-day as so clearly the *alter ego* of the big capitalists.

In defining the Guildsman's attitude to nationalisation, I take the view that a change from one form of Capitalism to another is not in itself the Guildsman's concern, though he is concerned indirectly in the effects of the change on Capitalism.[1] I there point out the

[1] See Ch. VII.

advantages, from a Guild standpoint, of unified management, and of the greater responsibility of the State. These arguments, I think, hold, but hold less strongly, when we are speaking of the State, not as producer, but as merchant. For clearly, in this case, there is not the same direct advantage to the workers in confronting a unified management as in the industrial field.

If, however, my forecast of the steps towards control is correct, there will be a time when the advantage will count. If it is true that, as Labour wins control over production, it will find its control thwarted, because it will still be confronted with Capitalism in possession of the control of the product, so that the controller of the product will come to be the next object of Labour's assault, then it follows that the arguments which we apply to State control of production can be applied at a later stage to State control of the product. In neither case will the fact that the State assumes control do anything to end Capitalism : in neither case should it deter Labour from making, with all its force, the demand for control—of the product, as well as of production.

National Guildsmen are, then, in much the same neutral position towards State control of buying and selling as towards nationalisation of production. We are free to advocate or to oppose it in any case, according as the particular effects seem likely to be good or bad from our point of view. In any case, we shall agree that State control will not end Capitalism, and is not, in the long run, compatible with National Guilds. Of this, however, there is more to be said.

Under a system of National Guilds, how much control over the product would Guildsmen demand,

and how much would they place within the province
of a democratised State ? That is the last question
I shall ask in this chapter ; but I cannot answer it
until I have dealt more fully with another point—
the question of investment.

It is a commonplace that, of the product of industry,
some is consumed and some saved. Wages being of
necessity mostly consumed, the main source of saving
is profits. Saved profits form the fund out of which
capital is replenished by investment. The proportion
of the product consumed and saved, apart from the
reserve funds of companies, is determined by the
individual choice of the recipients of profits.

Now, if Labour were to succeed in making an industry
unprofitable to the capitalist by raising wages through
the industrial power of a blackleg-proof organisation,
capital would not leave the industry, because it could
not ; but new capital would not flow in. New capital,
however, is essential to the conduct of an industry.
Either, then, Labour cannot get at profits through
its industrial power, while the existing system continues,
or Labour must find a new source for the supply of
capital. This, under the wage-system, it cannot do.
Industrial action alone cannot destroy profits, or even
lower them, unless it can overthrow the whole capitalist
system. This, we have seen, cannot be done purely
by industrial power.

Is political action likely to be more successful ? I do
not think so. The assumption of the financial functions
of Capitalism by the State, even in the interests of
the capitalist classes, would, indeed, do more than
anything else to atrophy the capitalists ; but for
that very reason it can happen only through an
egregious capitalist blunder. I should welcome the

nationalisation of banking and finance ; but I do not
expect them to happen.

We come back, then, here again, to the view that
apart from capitalist blunders, a catastrophe will be
necessary to end the wage-system. Only the man-
power of an awakened people can defeat the economic
power of a clever Capitalism. If, indeed, the great
capitalists were to blunder by adopting complete State
control in their own interests, and so allowing their own
class to be atrophied, catastrophe might be avoided, and
triumph would certainly be easier. We cannot,
however, afford to count on capitalist blunders, even
if we think them possible. The idle rich class is not
dangerous : the busy rich class emphatically is.

VII. After Wagery

It is one thing to prescribe a method, and another to
define an ideal. We have seen that, in order to end
the wage-system, Labour must assume control not
only of production, but also of the product. We have
endeavoured to analyse the wage-system into its
components, and to devise means for its dissolution.
We have now to ask what, if we succeeded, would be
the claims of National Guilds to control ? Would they
claim control both of production and of the product,
and, if so, would their claim be an exclusive claim ?

It is clear, I think, that the claim would be to both
forms of control ; but that, in one case at least, it would
not be exclusive. The control of the product is the
stronghold of Capitalism, because upon it profiteering
mainly depends. The whole conception of profiteering
being alien to National Guilds, what measure of control
over the product should the Guilds demand ?

We can, again, conveniently divide our answer under
the three heads of purchase, sale and investment. How
far would the Guilds claim control of raw material ?
How far would they claim control of the finished
article ? And how far would they claim control of
the flow of capital ? In all these cases, I think their
control would be shared in varying measure with other
bodies, and principally with the State.

Control of raw materials may mean much or little.
It may mean the procuring by various methods of
supplies from abroad ; it may mean the securing of a
controlling interest in another home industry producing
the raw materials required ; or it may mean merely
the purchase of raw material from an independent
body. Two of these seem to me to be natural and
inevitable Guild functions, while the second would only
arise in the form of close relations and agreements
between interdependent Guilds. The purchase of raw
materials from abroad might, indeed, in not a few
cases, be centralised in the hands of all the Guilds
jointly ; but that does not make it any the less a
Guild matter.

The disposal of the finished product offers more
difficulty, since upon this the profits of the capitalist
are based. In this connection, we have to answer
two questions. First, would the Guilds market their
own products ; and, secondly, what would become of
the payment made for those products ?

The second point may be taken first. We have seen
that the whole idea of production for profit is alien to
the system of National Guilds. The Guilds, then, will
clearly not sell for the profit of their members. The
income of the Guild member will not be determined by
the amount which he is able to extract from the

consumer of his product. This being so, one or both
of two things must happen. Either the price of
products must be regulated by some authority external
to the particular Guild that is producing or selling
them, or there must be a system of levy or taxation
on Guild incomes which will skim off any surplus that
might otherwise take the form of profit. I shall deal
with this question more fully elsewhere : here I desire
only to emphasise the fact that a Guild conducting sale
will not be a Guild extracting profit.

If the question of profit is satisfactorily eliminated,
it is surely evident that sale is a proper Guild function,
to be conducted either through a distributive or
merchant Guild or Guilds, or through the producing
Guilds themselves.

Investment is the hardest problem. At present, as
we have seen, investment is left to find its own level
by means of the investor's sagacity in picking out the
most profitable enterprises. This process is accompanied by colossal waste and fraud, and has nothing to
recommend it, except to the speculator and the company
promoter. Under National Guilds, investment, or the
determination of the flow of Capital, would obviously
be a matter for communal decision, since every penny
saved is so much future wealth, instead of so much
immediate consumption for the community. It is, in
fact, the employment of labour in making capital
instead of perishable commodities. It reduces the
immediate divisible total of the national income, and
must, therefore, be communally determined. The particular Guild desiring new capital or the placing of a
heavy sum to reserve will, no doubt, have great weight
in placing its recommendations before the community ;
but the ultimate decision cannot rest with the individual

Guild. The State, as the representative of the consumers, must have in it a voice equal to that of all the
producers gathered in the Guilds Congress.

We see, then, that in the sphere of control over the
product, though the National Guildsman cannot so limit
his claims in the period of transition, they must, in the
maturity of the system, be a division of power between
the Guilds and the State. We have now to glance
briefly at the other side of the picture—the control of
production.

Here it must be evident that the normal conduct of,
and responsibility for, industry, will be absolutely in
the hands of the Guilds, and that neither the State, nor
any outside body, should have any say in nominating
Guild officers or managers. State intervention in this
sphere should, I think, be limited to making representations on the joint body representing it, together with
the Guilds Congress, and to playing a part in taking
decisions on that body. The exact power of intervention in the affairs of a particular Guild that ought to
be possessed by the Guilds Congress is more difficult
to determine, and probably should not be determined
in advance. There is an obvious danger in making
our system too rigid ; and I, at least, feel that not the
least important elements in the Guild system will be
a vigorous and largely autonomous local life, and the
preservation by federal systems of the individuality
of the smaller industrial groups, and of groups within
the larger industries.

We are now in a position to sum up our argument.
Our immediate policy must always be determined by
the end which we have in view ; but the immediate
measures which we advocate cannot be, in all cases,
themselves a part of the end. We may have to secure

in the transitional period forms of control which it will be our business to discard at a later stage. Thus, we may have in certain cases to accept now joint action (*not* partnership) with the employers ; but our aim is none the less the total elimination of the employers. Similarly, we may have to advocate in the transitional period, forms of control over the product which the workers will have, at a later stage, to hand over to the State. If, on the one hand, we have to beware of becoming reformists and forgetting our ideal altogether, we have to beware also of becoming doctrinaires to whom nothing short of the whole is worth having, and to whom any course is sufficiently condemned if it is clear that it will have to be repudiated at a later stage.

We must, at all hazards, seek economic power in the present, because only by our economic power can we hope to establish our ideal.

CHAPTER V

STATE OWNERSHIP AND CONTROL

I

" MUNICIPAL debt is only municipal capital." How
easily, in their anxiety to find an answer to Moderates
grousing at the growth of municipal indebtedness,
Socialists swallowed that plausible debating answer of
Mr. Shaw's.[1] A municipality desires to own its tramways : it therefore buys out the existing company.
It then owns its trams ; but in acquiring them it has
run up a debt. But, we are told, just as the indebtedness of any company is its capital, so municipal debt is
municipal capital. True ; and, by a parity of reason-
ing, Municipal Socialism is Municipal Capitalism, and
nothing else. Just as the company pays interest to its
shareholders, the municipality continues to pay interest
to private capitalists. It merely guarantees their dividends, which were before more or less precarious.

The same argument applies to nationalisation by
purchase. It results, not in Socialism, but in a guaranteed State Capitalism, which is its direct opposite.
National debt may be in a sense national capital : it
is in effect the capital of the few to whom interest upon
it is paid.

Of course, the Collectivist will explain that he uses
the argument that ' debt is capital ' only to ' dish the

[1] See p. 263.

125

Moderates.' He knows well, he will tell you, that the debt incurred in taking over industries must be wiped out subsequently, in order that the whole product may go to the community. But, if he is pressed, as Mr. Belloc and others have pressed him, it soon becomes clear that the process of expropriation by sinking fund, annuity, or even such taxation as he can plausibly suggest, is going to be one, not of decades, but of centuries. Willy nilly, the tame Collectivist, Liberal, Labour or Fabian-Socialist, becomes a mere nationaliser and ceases to be a socialiser.

It is, indeed, a 'Fabian'—or should I say a 'damned'?—pity, as well as a clear indication of the tendencies of British Socialist thought, that we have of late years ceased to distinguish between nationalisation and socialisation, and even dropped the latter word altogether. For there are clearly two directions in which the State may extend its power over industry. It may own more; and it may manage more. Nationalisation, in the true sense of the word as it is used in common by capitalist and by Labour advocates, means national management; socialisation, whether in the mouth of a Social-Democrat or of a hireling of the Anti-Socialist Union, means national ownership.

Now, is it not clear that, in its economic aspect, Socialism means the absorption of surplus value by the community as a whole? Therefore Socialism implies national ownership. Surplus value can only be communised if the ownership of the land and the means of production is in the hands of the community.

National management, on the other hand, is quite a different story. Provided the communal absorption of surplus value is secured, as it would be under the

Guild system, we are free to devise what scheme we will for the control of the nation's industry. It has been the aim of National Guildsmen to show that national management is not a satisfactory scheme.

The Collectivist, as we have seen, admits, when he is also in the wide sense a Socialist, that national management is by itself inadequate. He wishes to supplement it by national ownership. The National Guildsman replies that national management is not inadequate but wrong. The control of actual production, he says, is the business of the producer, and not of the consumer. Only by giving the maker control over his own work can we satisfy the true principle of democracy ; for self-government is no less applicable to industrial than to political affairs.

It is not, however, my object to rehearse in this place the arguments in favour of Guild control. I desire to point out that there are these two ways in which the State can extend its power—over ownership and over management. And is it not clear at a glance that society is heading to-day straight for national management, and that it is not advancing at anything like the same speed in the direction of national ownership ? We nationalise, but we do not, save to an insignificant extent, socialise.

Furthermore, even if we go on to socialise, we couple national ownership with a system of controlling industry which National Guildsmen hold to be both morally and economically wrong. Even if, at the end of a thousand years or so, we succeed in freeing ourselves from the burden of interest which nationalisation lays upon us, we shall still be saddled with a bureaucratic control of industry that will leave us as far as ever from the true industrial democracy. If, after a voyage almost as lasting as that of the Flying Dutchman, we round in the end the Cape of State Capitalism, we shall only find ourselves on the other side in a Sargossa Sea of State Socialism, which will continue to repress all initiative, clog all endeavour, and deny all freedom to the workers.

Yet the position is not so easy as it appears to those who bid us, on these grounds, oppose all nationalisation as the highroad to the Servile State. I desire in this chapter to confront the whole problem of nationalisation from the point of view of National Guilds. The advanced section of the Labour movement must decide what its attitude on this question is to be ; for upon this depends many important questions of immediate policy. And we cannot afford, in contemplating the perfection of our final victory, to neglect the task of planning our own campaign, and of trying to foresee the plans of our adversaries.

II

What, then, should be the attitude of Guildsmen towards nationalisation ? Forming a discontented minority in the Socialist movement, they find themselves, if they belong to any of the Socialist societies, associating with others who make nationalisation the head and forefront of their programme. If they oppose the extension of national trading, they are told that they are not Socialists, but Syndicalists, who have no business in a Socialist body. If they support nationalisation, but maintain that along with national ownership must go Guild control, their fellow-members make haste to inform them that there is, after all, no difference of principle, that they can all agree for the moment upon national ownership, and that the precise amount of control to be *given* to the workers can be determined later on. The Collectivist is full of sympathy for the idea behind the Guild system, provided that he need not in any way commit himself to the vital principle of industrial self-government.

Guildsmen, therefore, find themselves in a dilemma. They are in favour of national ownership, but only on conditions. The difficulty is to define their attitude when nationalisation is offered them without conditions. There are several positions which they may take up ; and I propose to examine each of these in turn.

In the first place, they may agree with the authors of *The Miners' Next Step*,[1] at least where the method of transition is concerned. They may simply oppose nationalisation and rely wholly on industrial action They may hold that the best way of securing control is to oust the capitalist by direct action. According to this plan, a series of strikes must be declared, and the victory of the workers in each of these must leave the capitalists poorer than before. The rate of profits must fall, and at the same time the workers must secure a continually greater share in the actual management of the industry, till at last the capitalists, finding business no longer profitable, clear out and leave the workers in undisputed possession. So far, this is pure Syndicalism ; the Guild Socialist who adopts this attitude adds a rider. Then, and not till then, must the State assume the ownership of the means of production, while their control remains in the hands of the Trade Union.

This view would be clearly the right one if the Unions could rely upon the capitalists to sit still and

[1] See p. 264.

do nothing. But what, we must ask ourselves, would be in reality the capitalists' 'next step'? First, it is by no means clear that what is ordinarily called a 'successful' strike causes the rate of profits to fall. Especially in a more or less monopolistic industry, the capitalist, as a rule, recovers from the public in enhanced prices as much as, if not more than, he is forced to concede as wages to the workers. Even if each strike, imbued with a new purpose, gives the Union a greater foothold in control, it will not, by this means alone, succeed in abolishing profits. "But," the advocates of pure industrialism will say, "even if this is so, the series of strikes for partial control will be followed by a successful strike for complete control, and the demand in this case will include the entire transference of profits to the workers. Or, rather, if strikes do not cause profits to fall, the workers will, long before, have coupled their demand for a greater share in control with one for a transference of the profits of the enterprise."

This view ignores the capitalists' second step. Confronted with the risk of having their profits filched from them by the workers, the possessing classes will unload on the State. They will demand to be nationalised in order that their dividends may be guaranteed by the Government. In this case, the workers will suddenly find themselves striking not, as they had planned, against a body of private capitalists, but against the State. Their action will be none the worse for that; and, if their demands are refused, it is to be hoped that, under such conditions, they will strike all the more persistently; but, whatever they do, their plans will have to be remade—that is, if they are out for control in conjunction with a democratic State.

If they are Syndicalists, it will make no difference to them against whom they are striking—except that the State is a more dangerous enemy. Their aim being in that case the complete absorption of the surplus value created in their industry, they will presumably go on until that end is achieved. Guildsmen, on the other hand, believe in a partnership between the State and the Unions, and, being Socialists, stand for the communal absorption of surplus value. They have no wish to set up forms of collective profiteering in the various industries. They will desire to strike, not in order to compel the State to yield up a property which is no longer profitable, but to secure control over production; and for this control they will be prepared to pay, according to their ability, as it is measured by the productivity of their industry.

To this aspect of the question we shall return. What is relevant now is to point out that, if all this is granted, a part at least of the case we are criticising falls to the ground. The pure industrialist of this first type leaves nationalisation out of account in his argument. It is not enough for him to say that he is opposed to nationalisation. It is of no use to be opposed to the enemy's plan of campaign, which, at no distant date, nationalisation may well become. The skilful strategist thinks out what the enemy will do, and considers how he can meet it. Our industrialist, then, must either defeat or accept nationalisation. But can he, holding the view that industrial power precedes political power, or can anyone, doubt that, if the capitalists want nationalisation, they will get it? The doctors might possibly succeed in resisting a proposal to establish a national medical service, because they are capitalists as well as workers; but it is ridiculous to suppose that any class of manual workers could resist nationalisation if the State and the employers alike wanted it. Nationalisation is inevitable, not because it is the policy of the Labour Party, but because it is rapidly becoming sound capitalist economics.

Let us be quite clear. The only industries in which the organisation of the workers is anything like complete enough for such a policy as *The Miners' Next Step* suggests are certain public utility services which are in the nature of natural monopolies. Let us confine our survey to these industries—say, to the mines and the railways. In both cases, is it not obvious that the first sign that such a policy was being consciously and successfully adopted would be the signal for nationalisation ? And is it not equally clear that, for the present, a strike against nationalisation is unthinkable ?

Indeed, such a strike would be in itself an absurd paradox. It is not *against* nationalisation that the workers must strike, but *for* control. It is admitted, however, on all hands, that the workers are not yet ready for complete control. Till they are ready, a strike against nationalisation would inevitably be a strike for the retention of private ownership in the hands of the present holders. It would be a strike to save the capitalists from themselves, or at least from their *alter ego*, the State. Though such a strike might be represented by its advocates as an attempt to save the fatted calf of Capitalism from being carried off by the enemy, the situation is evidently too absurd to contemplate. Even if it were logically justifiable, which it is not, it would be a hopeless position to adopt.

It is therefore futile to oppose or obstruct the nationalisation of such public utility services as the mines and the railways. In other industries, in which there is not yet awhile any likelihood of nationalisation, it matters little whether Socialists propose or oppose nationalisation. There is, as we shall see, at least one case—banking—in which they ought actively to forward it. For the purposes of our present argument, it is enough to say that, where it seems likely, opposition is futile ; where it seems unlikely, advocacy is at present useless.

The argument which we have brought to bear upon thorough-going opponents of nationalisation applies also to those who say that the time for nationalisation will come, but that the workers are not yet ripe for it. Of course, the workers are not ready for it, and that is precisely why it will come. Were the working class as a whole imbued with the idea of control and endowed with the power that idea gives, nationalisation would no longer serve the capitalists' ends. It would be the signal for the complete overthrow of Capitalism—State or private—and for the substitution of the Guild system. Nationalisation is coming now, and coming inevitably, because it is the capitalists' last card. When their dividends are no longer safe from the direct action of the workers, they trust to the State to save them by nationalisation—at any rate, for the time. But until those who say that the workers are not ready for nationalisation explain how the workers, being admittedly unready and badly organised, are to defeat it, the argument I have used in criticism of pure industrialism holds against them also. It is waste of breath, ink, and energy to oppose the inevitable. Let us, then, seek to discover what effect the nationalisation of mines and railways will have on the chances of Guild control.[1]

[1] See p. 264.

III

I ended the last section with a question. What will be the effect of nationalisation—State Capitalism, if you will—upon the prospects of Guild control ? Will it make the path to the Guild easier or more difficult ? In the attempt to answer this question, it is natural to appeal to the actual working of those enterprises which are now run by States or Municipalities. What, in these cases, has been the effect of national ownership ? When the general question of nationalisation is at issue, advocates and opponents alike make this appeal. The State Socialist will tell us that the State is on the whole a better employer than the private capitalist, that in public employment the worker enjoys prefer- ential conditions and greater security of tenure, and that the publicity afforded by Parliamentary control secures the remedy of any crying injustice. On the other hand, the opponent of Collectivism will point to the dangers and annoyances, petty and great, which bureaucracy entails ; he will cite existing State services as showing the inevitable growth of bureaucracy under a system of national management ; he will point out that such ' advantages ' as the Government employee enjoys are more than balanced by losses of civil and industrial rights ; and he will urge that the publicity secured through Parliament has been shown to be use- less unless the weapon of industrial action is behind it. Both sides will cite instances in support of their views with equal facility ; but they will, as a rule, be different instances, drawn not necessarily from different public enterprises, but from different points in the working of the same services.

Thus, the Collectivist assures us that the State is not

a bad sweater, and that, in most cases, it pays Trade Union rates. Where this is not so, he can, as a rule, show that the workers are getting an equivalent in pensions or the like. Supernumerary men are indeed often underpaid; but, judged by the capitalist standard, the State is a fair employer to its established staff of workers. With more exceptions and in a less degree the same may be said of the Municipalities. They do not, from whatever cause, normally pay less than the Trade Union rates. The exceptions, of which every one knows not a few, do not alter the rule. In the scale of capitalist employers, the State stands perhaps a little above the average.

It may be true, further, that it occupies this position partly as a result of Parliamentary publicity and control. Members of Parliament have an interested—in many cases even a disinterested—dislike of the worse forms of sweated labour, or at least of being openly and publicly responsible for them. So far, therefore, as wages are concerned, Parliament may intervene, when a certain amount of publicity has been secured, to bring the condition of public employees up to the standard rates. Further than this they have no desire to go ; they will try to be as ' good ' as the average private employer, but they will do anything short of losing their seats rather than be any better. Where any question of discipline or management, in short, of control, is concerned, they are adamantine in defence of the bureaucratic omnipotence and all-wisdom of the permanent officials.

The plausibility of all the *argumenta ad opificem* in favour of national management rests on the same fallacy as the arguments for compulsory arbitration. Because the effect may be at first to screw up wages all round to the standard rate, it is argued that this proves the system right. It proves nothing of the sort : wages fixed by Parliament or by bodies depending on Parliament attain to the standard rates ; but there they invariably stagnate. Every new demand, that cannot be shown to be the habitual practice of most employers or of all the best employers, is resisted to the death by the public authority, dominated as it is in every case by officialism, conservatism, and bureaucracy. If the Guildsman is asked to accept nationalisation on the ground that Parliament and the officials will be anxious to grant every reasonable demand, his answer is obvious and complete. For the purpose which they have in view, Parliamentary control is not only valueless, but definitely obstructive.

Turn now to the picture of national management as the Syndicalist paints it. Let us take as our example ' democratic ' France, the home of Syndicalism. Take three State enterprises—the schools, the Post Office and the State railway. The teachers have had their Trade Unions suppressed ; a French Premier, nominally a Socialist, has defeated a railway strike by calling the railwaymen to the colours ; the Post Office, as M. Beaubois has shown in his admirable pamphlet, *La Crise Postale et les Monopoles d'Etat*, is a hot-bed of bureaucracy, favouritism and inefficiency. The French worker knows well that the accompaniment of State ownership is administrative tyranny.

Are we then to conclude that nationalisation is always bad from the Guildsman's point of view ? If so, since we have decided that it is futile to oppose it, we are indeed in a bad way. What we have said, however, need not bear that construction. Nationalisation is dangerous only in proportion as Trade Unionism is weak. Were French Trade Unionism strong, instead of weak, the public enterprises could not be conducted with the inefficiency and tyranny that characterise them now. The vice of the administration is limited by the virtue of the employees.

State departments and municipalities, while on the whole they pay at least as good wages as the general run of employers, are, we admit, naturally inimical to any interference in management by the managed. Every extension of Trade Union activity is repressed by them as subversive of discipline, or, if they have been brought up to be philosophers as well as bureaucrats, as cases of rebellion by the worker against himself—for the citizens, they will tell you, are the State. Every obstacle will be put by administrators in the way of the extension of Guild control. Yet none the less the public and semi-public services are the soil in which the Guild idea is growing most fruitfully, and may be expected to grow.

We have too long repeated the Marxian phrase that the emancipation of Labour must be the work of Labour without understanding it. The Syndicalists and the National Guildsmen are fundamentally right in regarding the industrial consciousness of the workers as the pivot on which the whole social system swings. The fundamentally important thing about the various forms which the capitalist organisation of industry assumes is not whether they are harsh or gentle, whether they feed the workers well or ill, but whether they foster or destroy the spirit of liberty in men's hearts. Wherever, under the present system, we find growing up a revolt that is not merely blind anger or blind despair, wherever we find in revolt the constructive idea of industrial democracy, there is the social structure best fitted to further the cause good men have at heart.   Wherever there is no such spirit of construction, there, whatever the material position of the workers, no hope of the ending of Capitalism exists.

This gives us a measure of the new spirit which is not merely quantitative.   Not where men are most angry or most rebellious, but where they realise most clearly what needs ending or mending and how it may be ended or mended, is the cause of Labour most hopeful.   Only an idea can slay an idea : until the workers are animated with the desire to be their own masters they cannot supplant the idea that their class is born for wage-slavery.

But is it not in public and semi-public services that the idea of control seems to be taking root ?   The Postal and Telegraph Clerks' Association had the honour of being the first Union to make a public and open demand for joint control—a proposal characteristically stigmatised by the dotards of the *New Statesman* as fantastic.[1]   In the Post Office, as we shall see, the demand for control is, and has long been, a vital and practical question.   A generation in advance of their time, the Postal workers are fighting, against odds, the battle of National Guilds.   It is significant that the demand for control should have come so far in its most articulate form in such a public service as the Post Office.   Moreover, we have already noticed that the same demand has been made by the Postal workers of France.

The second case in which the question of control has of late years forced its way to the front is the railway service.   The railway workers, regarded until recently as among the most backward of Trade Unionists, have now practically assumed the lead among the ' forward '

[1] See p. 264.

section in the world of Labour. The railways of this country are not indeed nationalised, though they are now State controlled ; but of late years there has been so much State interference with them that from the point of view that concerns us here they might as well have been so.[1] What then has caused the Guild idea to take spontaneous form in these branches of industry rather than in those which are under distinctively private management ?

One main reason is not far to seek. Nothing tends so greatly to promote the idea of control as unified management. Where an industry is split up among a number of wholly or almost wholly separate manage-ments acting on different principles and with very little co-ordination, the twin demands for recognition and control cannot so easily be made as where a whole industry is gathered up under one supreme direction. For, in the first place, with divided management Trade Union activity tends to be concentrated on the attempt to bring the worse employers up to the level of those who are better. Trade Unionism remains wrapped up in the old attempt to maintain and improve the standard rate. Wages questions tend to hold the first place, though they do not, of course, monopolise the energies of the Union. But where questions of discipline or management arise, they are usually in this type of industry questions affecting a single management, and when they are settled, no demand arises for a uniform and recognised right of interference with the acts of all firms in the industry. The case remains isolated and unimportant : no new principle is established.

With a unified management, on the other hand, the accumulating series of individual demands have all to do with the same authority, and are soon inductively

[1] See p. 264.

recognised as instances of a general principle, which at once becomes a general demand. Recognition of the Union is claimed ; and recognition, once won, soon arrogates to itself wider and wider definitions. Sooner or later the Union gets a real foothold in the control of the industry, and a step has been taken in the direction of National Guilds.

Secondly, the very bureaucracy which is characteristic of State departments, accompanying unified management, both irritates the workers and gives them an obvious target for their irritation. They readily come to see not only that something is the matter, but what the matter is and, sick and tired of official bungling, they claim to take the place of the bunglers. The natural impulse we all feel to push aside anyone whom we see doing badly what we can do better comes to their aid; and their anger is transformed into a rational, but none the less righteously angry, demand for joint control of their industry. Is it not nationalised industry that best answers this description, and, if so, is not nationalised industry a good seeding-ground for the Guild idea ?

IV

' Trust-busting ' is the favourite pastime of American ' fake ' reformers. In the United States, Government regulation of big business is the approved ' progressive ' alternative to ending the wage-system —as transparent a device of Capitalism as the most flagrant pieces of Lloyd-Georgism that we in this country have to endure. The futility of such attempts to play the Mrs. Partington has all along been appreciated by the revolutionary wing of American Socialism.

W. D. Haywood and Frank Bohn, in their book, *Industrial Socialism*, declare with emphasis against the anti-trust campaigning of the politicians. They have seen that it is none of their business to decide between rival forms of capitalist organisation. They are out to end Capitalism, and not to adapt it.

If, as the Syndicalists would have us believe, all nationalisation is simply and solely State Capitalism, it does not follow that it should be opposed. If the State is the *alter ego* of the employer, what does it matter which of them rules the roast ? If it is futile to oppose trusts, is it not equally futile to oppose nationalisation, which is only the trust in its most perfect form ? Are not both stages, not indeed necessary, but in many cases convenient, in the passage from individual Capitalism to the system of workers' control over industry ?

For the State and the trust, cartel and combine clearly have this in common. Both involve a high degree of unified management ; both incline to centralisation and bureaucracy ; both, even when they pay fair rates of wages, tend to annoy their workers with galling restrictions and red tape. It is among the employees of the trusts in America that the revolutionary Unionism of the Industrial Workers of the World has taken root ; it is among the wage-slaves of the State and of the combines of Great Britain that National Guildsmen are destined to be made.

What matters, then, is not so much whether an industry is State-run or not—that is for the present mainly a question of capitalist convenience—as whether a whole industry has come under a unified management. For it cannot be too often emphasised that the organisation of industry which the Guild system

connotes is a national organisation, as the Trade
Unionism out of which it must grow is a national
Trade Unionism. Generally speaking, we may say
that the battle for Guild control will be fought in the
great industries, and above all in those in which the
combination and concentration of capital are closest.
If we leave State-run industries out of account, no
one will for a moment dispute this statement ; as soon
as it is realised that State-run industry is only concentrated Capitalism to the *n*th power the case is
equally clear there also. The State will be the leading
antagonist of the Guilds ; but it will also be, in
many cases, their chief begetter—a sort of *médécin
malgré lui* of the malady it has itself created.

It is no lingering illusion about the benefits of State
employment that should cause Guildsmen to refrain
from joining hands with Tories and Whig advocates
of *laisser-faire* in opposing nationalisation. Bill Haywood[1] refuses to help the reformers in America to
destroy trusts, not because he loves trusts, but because
Capitalism is destined to self-destruction, and through
the trust lies the road to its ruin. Combination is the
capitalists' last card but one ; nationalisation will
prove to be their last card of all. It is not for us to
interfere with their method of playing their hands ;
let us rather trump the trick when the capitalists' ace
has been played.

We must not, however, push the analogy between
the State and the trust too far. There are certain
differences between them ; but these, too, are far from
inducing us to oppose the extension of State industry
to-day. Suppose we had to choose whether a given
industry should be run by a trust or by the State.
What, we should ask ourselves, would be the position

[1] See p. 265.

of the workers in the two cases ? Wages would probably be much the same under both systems ; but there might be a tendency, if the management were national, to assure a higher standard to the worst paid employees. Hours, too, would probably be much the same ; but, if there was a difference, they would probably be shorter under the State. In status, especially in the consciousness of status, the government employee would be likely to have a distinct advantage. But the consciousness of status is the beginning of wisdom, and an essential prerequisite of the Guild idea.

What then becomes of the familiar view that nationalisation means the Servile State ? We are all well acquainted with the argument ; and many of us are fully conscious of its force. Yet, if nationalisation has all the effects we have been claiming for it, is not the whole theory of the Servile State utterly untrue ?

Not altogether, though it is at least half untrue. The broadest of all oppositions between rival schools of Socialist strategy is that between the evolutionist who holds that, bad as Capitalism is, if we go on improving it, it will some day turn into Socialism, and the revolutionist who maintains that Socialism will come about when Capitalism has become so bad as to be absolutely intolerable. Good arguments are brought forward in support of both positions. The evolutionist will say that the better off a man is the more likely he is to realise the injustice of his position, and to ask for still better conditions. He will point triumphantly to the fact that it is among the better-paid workers that Socialism and Trade Unionism alike make most headway ; and he will urge that this conclusively proves his case. The revolutionist, on the other hand, will point to the success with which ' benevolent ' employers have managed to lull their workmen into apathy, to the growth of sedative movements like profit-sharing and copartnership, and to the effects of Australasian labour legislation, his knowledge of which, being based on out-of-date text-books, will stop short some years back, before the present period of unrest began. Each will seem to have a strong case, because each is in the main speaking the truth in what he asserts, but suppressing or failing to perceive other truths that are no less important.

On the one hand, it is abundantly clear that high wages make men more, and not less, discontented. This is true generally, but more especially when high wages are the result of industrial action. In such a case the effect is immediate, and new demands almost invariably follow on the first favourable opportunity. When a rise is due to some external cause, such as legislation that is not the response to direct industrial pressure, the immediate effect may be a lull ; but none the less the workers will be, in the long run, more inclined to make demands than before. The evolutionist is right in his view of the psychological effects of high wages.

On the other hand, it is equally demonstrable that copartnership and all forms of ' coddling ' by employers who are astute or benevolent, or more often both, do devitalise the workers who receive them, and make rebellion more difficult. The copartnership employee does not make a good Trade Unionist, nor does the ' almshouse and pension ' type of benevolent employment foster the spirit of independence. Here, then, the revolutionist is right in his psychological inductions.

But is it not evident that these views are perfectly

compatible ? Low wages, supplemented by benevolent and considerate management, may secure a fair standard of material comfort for the employee ; but they are demoralising and degrading ; they produce a spirit of subordination and acquiescence, in which the Guild idea cannot grow. They breed such stuff as Nietzsche's ' Ultimate Men,' servile in word and thought and act. High wages, on the other hand, are themselves an incitement to demand higher ; where they are combined with harsh or bureaucratic management, they are the forerunners and the creators of revolt.

It is hypocritical, and even real but stupid, benevolence and not malignant opposition that Guildsmen have to fear. Some day, the State may learn to play the game of benevolence in a last effort to lull the workers again to sleep. But we may reasonably hope that the State will be so long in learning that lesson that the attempt will be made too late. For the State has one great disadvantage when it sets out to imitate the Levers and Cadburys of private capitalism. The ' benevolent ' employer is working on a comparatively small scale : he makes full play with the idea that the business is a family, a home, an idea to which the employees' trade patriotism can cling. He makes, wherever he can, a sentimental appeal and calls for ' loyalty to the firm.' All this the State cannot easily imitate. For, first of all, State industry tends to fall into the hands of temperamental bureaucrats, and will continue to do so till the workers themselves assume control. But the bureaucrat is always likely to rub the average man up the wrong way. Herein lies the State's first handicap. Secondly, the State-run industry possesses a unified management, and the centralisation which this involves only gives the bureaucrats a bigger chance of making themselves unpleasant. On all accounts, therefore, though the State will probably try some day to play the benevolent employer, it will probably fail in its attempt to send the workers to sleep. If it pays high wages, it will only rouse them to ask for more ; if it tries the more underhand method of supplementing wages by conditional benefits, it will only rouse the workers by the pin-pricks of bureaucratic ' benevolence.'

The nationalisation, therefore, which capitalists will bring about in order to save their dividends, and reformers urge upon us in the interests of social peace, we may accept, at least in certain industries, because we believe that it will bring, not peace, but a sword.

V

Advocates of nationalisation admit that their policy is immediately practicable only in a few cases. There is little chance that the State will as yet take over any save a very special class of industries. Broadly speaking, these will be public services which naturally tend towards monopoly. But the possession of these characteristics will not by itself be enough to cause nationalisation ; the additional impetus will come, at any rate in great industries, from the growth in numbers and in consciousness of the Trade Unions. In these cases, the very strength with which the workers make their demands will hasten their transference to State employment ; where Trade Unionism is strong and intelligent, nationalisation will be inevitable.

We can therefore say with confidence that in some cases national management will precede National Guilds. This, however, need apply only to industries which are in the nature of public services. While we may be confident that nationalisation of mines and railways will come before Guild control can be achieved, it does not follow that the same order will be observed in the textile industries, in engineering, or in the building industry. For the nationalisation of an essentially monopolistic public utility service, such as the railways, the trams, or even the mines, is one thing; but it is quite another to take over an industry which is not a public service, and of which the stoppage does not dislocate the national life to anything like the same extent. A strike of cotton operatives only indirectly affects the industry of the country; the effect of a national stoppage of miners or railwaymen is immediate and devastating. Only in industries of this latter type is the State, for some time to come, likely to step in with any complete system of nationalisation or control, except as a purely temporary war-time expedient.

National management is inevitable, as a transitional stage, in the mines and on the railways, for two reasons which may seem contradictory : first, because there Trade Unionism is strong, or at least will soon be strong enough to frighten the employers into getting their profits guaranteed by the State; and secondly, because even there Trade Unionism is weak—too weak, that is, and too little self-conscious to assume full control. For even the most advanced Trade Unions have a long road to travel before they fit themselves for the control of industry. Militant class-consciousness is still far enough from realisation; and class-consciousness itself is but the foundation on which a constructive idealism remains to be built.

It is probable, therefore, that the most the railwaymen or the miners will at first secure, when their industry comes to be nationalised, will be recognition together with an organised power of making representations to the bureaucrats who will still be in control. In the first instance, they can hardly hope to do more than entrench themselves firmly in the disputed territory. Once fully recognised through their Unions, the workers will go on to make new demands ; but the demand for the actual control of industry will come later than the claim to criticise those who control it. The introduction of State management will be the signal for a long battle between bureaucracy and freedom.

The industries that will then be nationalised are, however, precisely those in which the demand for control is already most articulate. To this demand the bureaucracy incidental to State management will afford a stimulus, and the result will be a great growth of the spirit of unrest. After nationalisation, we may expect the Unions in the nationalised industries to lead the way. With the possible exception of a few small industries, it seems likely that the Guild system of national ownership and producers' management will be established first in those industries which pass first through the stage of national management.

Every approach to the Guild system made by a Trade Union in one of these State-run industries will act as an incentive to every other Union. The principles established by one Union soon become the programmes of all the rest. While, therefore, the workers in some industries are feeling their way towards producers' control in face of the opposition of the State, the rest of the workers will be learning to make the same demand of the private capitalist. And, if we may expect the equilibrium of joint control to be reached first in some one of the nationalised industries, we may expect also that there will have been in many others, both State-run and private, a greater or less encroachment of the workers upon control.

When the workers have this training in constructive class-consciousness behind them, there will be no longer any need for an intermediate stage of national management. The workers, grown wise enough to exercise, and strong enough to win, control, will at once assume management when the State assumes ownership of the means of production. In those industries which will then remain in the hands of the private capitalist, it will then be both possible and right to pass at once to the stage of Guild control. In all these cases, the workers will no doubt have already gained a considerable share in control; the transference to them of the whole management will therefore present no difficulty, while the State will slip naturally into ownership, and will deal as it thinks fit with the owners it supplants. At the same time, the workers in the various nationalised industries, who will also have gained already a large share in control, will make good their claim to management, while the State will restrict itself to ownership and criticism of the workers' managerial methods. The first industry in which the State and the Trade Union arrive at a satisfactory demarcation of the functions of ownership and management will serve as a ' new model ' for all the rest, just as the Amalgamated Society of Engineers served as the model for Trade Unionism in the past.

It is impossible to say how many industries will pass through the intervening stage of national management. That, we have seen, is a matter of capitalist organisation, with which we can hardly interfere one way or the other. At the one end of the industrial chain, it seems clear that the railways and the mines will be national-ised. The same fate very probably awaits the dock-yards, and possibly the shipyards also. On the other hand, it is very unlikely that the pottery trades, the brass trades, ironfounding, tinplate making, and many others of the same kind will ever pass through the stage of national ownership. The battle between the rival systems of Capitalism and National Guilds will be fought out in the great industries; and the system which wins the day will then be more generally applied. Of the cotton industry it is impossible to speak; for on the one hand it seems in itself admirably adapted for producers' control; but the consciousness of the workers seems to be on the whole so little developed in the direction of control that nationalisation, remote as it seems, may have its turn. All we can say with confidence is that there will be some industries in each class, and that it rests with Capitalism and the ruling caste to draw the line.

To Guildsmen, the whole question should appear secondary. Their first business is to forward the idea of working-class control of industry. Whether control has to be wrested from the State or from the private capitalist is irrelevant. Opposition to and advocacy of nationalisation are alike, viewed purely from this standpoint, waste of time; they mean the diversion of the movement on to a side-issue. In season and out of season, Guildsmen should be preaching control; and when nationalisation is suggested, they ought not to oppose it; they ought to redouble their efforts and reiterate their original demand. They have not so much surplus energy that they can afford to waste it upon irrelevancies.

VI

The main object of this chapter has been to prove that it is not the business of the Guildsman either to advocate or to oppose nationalisation ; but it by no means follows that he should have no policy in relation to it. It is indeed of the first importance that he should seize the occasion of nationalisation to push forward his own alternative to national management. Those who, like the Syndicalists, are content to oppose every extension of State action are merely disarming in face of the inevitable : powerless to stop nationalisation, they are leaving the State to stew in its own juice. But, even if we admit that the best bargain the workers can hope to drive with the State must be a bad one, it is none the less our manifest duty to make the best of it. Instead of a mere repudiation of the principle of national management, the National Guildsman must present a definite and concrete demand for a share in control. We cannot hope to bring in National Guilds all round by a *coup de main* ; we must first lay the foundation of our edifice.

I have already referred to the resolutions recently passed by several important Trade Unions on the subject of the control of industry. I must here again refer to two of these. Trade Unionists in the Postal Service unite in demanding, in one form or another, a system of joint control with the State department. This demand comes continually to the surface in the evidence volumes of the Holt Committee,[1] especially in the examination of Mr. C. G. Ammon of the Fawcett Association, who, putting his demand in the form of a suggestion that the Unions should be consulted before the making of any change that would affect the workers,

[1] See p. 265.

clearly has in mind a system of joint control. The claim has been reiterated far more clearly by the Postal and Telegraph Clerks at their annual conferences ; and it is significant that they have made an open demand for joint control. This is evidently largely the result of the dissatisfaction caused by the Holt Report and by the subsequent debates upon it in the House of Commons. Here then we have a clear demand made in a service which is already State-run.

But the Postal workers have not been content with a vague generalisation ; they have also offered definite suggestions as to the methods of extending to them a share in control. They have urged in the first place a great extension of the principle of recognition, and secondly, the standardising of this recognition in the form of Trade Union advisory councils, local and national, sectional and general, which would have to be consulted before any change in organisation could be made. Such a system of advisory councils would no doubt fail to achieve much at first ; but it would afford the workers a valuable experience and would serve both to fit them to exercise a more real control and to stimulate them to lay claim to it. Recognition, backed by a system of advisory councils, is for them the half-way house to control.

The policy of the bureaucrats, when they are driven to make some concession, will be to establish a single national advisory council for all grades and localities, or else a series of national councils for each grade. Either system will be by itself almost worthless. The chief value of these councils will lie in the training they are able to afford ; and from this point of view a national council is of little use. It is local training and local recognition that is the greatest need ; and accordingly local as well as national advisory powers must at all costs be secured. For, if the workers are to assume control, they must create a local as well as a national organisation capable of managing industry.

I have dwelt so long upon the particular demands of the Postal workers because they are, in great measure, typical of the demands which will have to be made wherever an industry comes under national management. In the Post Office, it is the privilege of workers who are already State employees to show the way to those who will ere long become like them. The Postal Unions are working out half unconsciously the methods of transition from the servile to the free organisation of Labour.

The second case to which it is necessary to refer again is that of the Railwaymen. For many years, the N.U.R. has invariably passed at its conferences a resolution in favour of nationalisation. The habit of years is too strong to be suddenly broken ; but at their 1914 conference this resolution changed its form. " Whilst reaffirming " their old resolutions in favour of nationalisation, the railwaymen declared that " no system of national ownership could be satisfactory " to them which did not assure them a say in the management of the industry. Like the Postal workers, the railwaymen have begun to demand joint control. They have not yet formulated any scheme by which this partnership could be assured ; but such a formulation will no doubt follow in good time.[1] The main thing is that they have recognised the principle ; for, apart from the survival of a certain amount of historical phraseology, their demand amounts to a claim for a National Guild.

This has become still clearer in the last three years,

[1] See p. 265.

during which the Guild demand has spread rapidly among the rank and file. An instance of its growth will serve. Early in 1917 a National Conference of the District Councils of the National Union of Railwaymen carried the following resolution :

" That this Conference, seeing that the railways are being controlled by the State for the benefit of the nation during the war, is of opinion that they should not revert to private ownership afterwards. Further, we believe that national welfare demands that they should be acquired by the State to be jointly controlled and managed by the State and representatives of the National Union of Railwaymen." [1]

Instead, then, of urging or opposing nationalisation, Guildsmen have a far more important duty to perform. The idea of control, which is at last taking root in the minds of the workers, must not be allowed to remain a mere idea. The first thing, no doubt, is to secure acceptance and understanding of the idea ; but this must be complemented by the elaboration of a practical programme. Guildsmen must be ready, when the day of nationalisation comes, to urge the railwaymen to make certain specific demands ; nay more, they must try to provide the railwaymen with a policy before nationalisation becomes imminent. In thinking of the Guild State which we would fain see in being, we are too apt to neglect the transitional stages through which we must pass on the way to our ideal ; but our foresight, and the foresight of the workers, in making im-

[1] For further discussion of the application of the Guild idea to the railway service, see *Towards a National Railway Guild* (National Guilds League, 2d.). See also, for railway matters generally, *Trade Unionism on the Railways*, by G. D. H. Cole and R. Page Arnot (Allen & Unwin, 2/6), concluding chapter. For the mines, see *Towards a Miners' Guild* (N.G.L. 1d.).

mediate and intermediate demands will be the measure
of final success.   At every stage, the movement towards the establishment of self-government in industry
runs the risk of being side-tracked or put off by specious
concessions ; it is the task of those who know definitely
what they want so to leaven the great inert mass of the
workers that it will be impossible to delude them with
false offerings.   On those few who are alive to the ideal
aspirations of Labour rests the whole burden of clothing
that ideal with a practical programme.   They are as
yet few, and they have no easy task before them.
Above all, they are bound to fail if they believe that,
once they are clear in their minds about the general
outline of the system they wish to establish, their
thinking is done.   It is only begun ; for the city of
our dreams has to be built with the bricks and mortar
that lie to our hands amid the dilapidation and decay
of the capitalist edifice.   We are the world's builders ;
and, unless we lay our foundations truly, the whole
structure which we rear will come tumbling to the
ground, no matter how fine our architecture may be.
Guildsmen are well pleased with their architects ; they
have now to make equally sure of their builders.

CHAPTER VI

FREEDOM IN THE GUILD

I

THE Collectivist's first line of attack upon the Guild system is usually, in form at least, made in the interests of the consumer. He seeks to show that the Guild would inevitably ' exploit the community.' But, defeated on this point, he goes on to appeal to the producers themselves, and asks whether the Guild system would in fact secure greater freedom for the individual worker. Modern methods of production, he declares, are so intensely complicated and on so large a scale that it is impossible to restore the individual freedom of the craftsman. That being so, it matters not, from the point of view of freedom, how industry is organised : the only wise course is to concentrate on securing the greatest efficiency of production and the best possible distribution of the product. Since neither under Capitalism, nor under Collectivism, nor under a gigantic system of National Guilds, can the individual be free, why bother any longer about freedom, at any rate in the industrial sphere ?

That is, I believe, a fair statement of the Collectivist argument : and it rests on two fallacies. It is contended, first, that Collectivism, which is the trust system *in excelsis*, makes for productive efficiency, and secondly, that the system of National Guilds cannot but be bureaucratic. I shall deal with these two points in turn : but my real concern is with the second, because I believe that it rests on a complete misconception of the system of industrial organisation Guildsmen desire.

The first argument rests on the double fallacy that self-government has nothing to do with efficiency and that freedom has nothing to do with self-government. This is a denial of the whole philosophy of all good men. It is against this very view that the main attack upon Collectivism is directed. The key to real efficiency is self-government ; and any system that is not based upon self-government is not only servile, but also inefficient. Just as even the labour of the wage-slave is better than the labour of the chattel-slave, so, and a thousand times more so, will the labour of the free man be better than either.

" That may be so," the Collectivist will answer, " but under modern conditions freedom is out of the question. With machine production, man must be reduced to the position of a cog in the wheel. Let us work, then, for Collectivism, in order that, by paying good wages, we may secure at least the highest mechanical efficiency."

Such an argument not only ignores the humanity of labour, but also totally misconceives the nature of freedom. Freedom is not simply the absence of restraint ; it assumes a higher form when it becomes self-government. A man is not free in himself while he allows himself to remain at the mercy of every idle whim : he is free when he governs his own life according to a dominant purpose or system of purposes. In just the same way, man in Society is not free where there is no law ; he is most free where he co-operates best with his equals in the making of laws. Over and over again, Socialists have used this argument in answer to the anarchical individualism of Herbert Spencer ;[1] yet they have been the first to direct against National Guilds what is, after all, only a repetition of the most palpable fallacy of Individualism. They contend that it matters whether a man governs himself politically or not ; but they refuse to admit that it matters no less whether he governs himself industrially.

A hundred years ago, it was a theory almost generally accepted that democracy, good as it might be for the small City-State, could not be applied to the great Nation-State. Rousseau himself, the father of modern democratic idealism, expressed this view in the *Social Contract*, and it was held in his time equally by philosophers of the most diverse schools. Yet now political democracy of a sort is applied to the governance even of the largest States, and the surviving exponents of autocracy no longer seek to base their case on the size of the modern State. It is generally admitted that, however great a community may be, the individual is more free under a democratic than under an autocratic system. And his freedom is seen to lie less in the absence of restraint than in the realisation of self-government.

The view of Rousseau and his generation was doubtless largely due to the fact that the possibilities of local and sectional self-government had not in his time been appreciated. To the application of these methods of decentralisation I shall come, in the next section, in dealing with the second fallacy behind the Collectivist's argument. I wish now to speak of the application of the principle of self-government to industry in its most general form.

[1] See p. 265.

That community is most free in which all the individuals have the greatest share in the government of
their common life. In every struggle for liberty, the
enslaved have always demanded, as an essential pre-
liminary to all self-government, the right to choose
their own rulers. This applies in industry no less than
in politics. While the citizen has his King and his
Parliament imposed on him independently of his will,
he cannot be free. Similarly, while the workman has
his foremen and his managers set over him by an external authority, then, however kindly they use him,
he has not freedom. He must claim, as a necessary
step on the road to industrial emancipation, the right
to choose his own leaders. To deny this is to adopt
towards industrial democracy exactly the attitude that
the defenders of autocracy or aristocracy adopt towards
political democracy.

The reception of the Guild idea among Socialists has
shown that many Socialists have forgotten their democracy. In political self-government they see nothing
more than a convenient practice of ' counting heads
to save the trouble of breaking them.' They regard
government as essentially a mechanism, designed with
the object of securing mechanical efficiency ; they do
not see that the problem of self-government is a moral
problem, and that the task of social organisation is
that of expressing human will. Their theory is in-
human, because they neglect will, which is the measure
of human values.

The Guildsman approaches the problem in a more
philosophic spirit. He desires not merely to provide a
mechanism for the more equal distribution of material
commodities ; he wishes also, and more intensely, to
change the moral basis of Society, and to make it

everywhere express the personality of those who compose it.   He seeks, not only in politics, but in every department of life, to give free play to the conscious will of the individual.   Admitting the failure of political democracy to achieve all that its pioneers promised, he refuses to be disillusioned, or to give up his belief in the ideal for which they strove.   Behind the failure of actual political democracies his eyes are keen enough to descry the eternal rightness of democracy itself, and his wits sharp enough to understand why we have failed in applying it.   We have erred because we have had too little faith : driven by the logic of events, we have pressed for democracy in the political domain, but we have still regarded it mainly as a means of securing certain material ends.   We have never really believed in democracy ; for, if we had, we should have tried to apply it, not to politics alone, but to every aspect of human life.   We should not have been democrats in politics and autocrats in industry : we should have stood for self-government all round.

Democracy rests essentially on a trust in human nature.   It asserts, if it asserts anything, that man is fit to govern himself.   Yet every criticism passed upon the Guild system by Collectivists, who are loud in their lip-service to the democratic principle, reveals that they are fundamentally distrustful of human nature and human capacity.   They admit the right of the worker, as a citizen, to a vote in the choice of his political rulers ; but they refuse to the same man the right to elect his industrial rulers.   The contradiction is flagrant : the explanation of it is discreditable.

Political democracy is accepted because it has so largely failed : it is the very fact that it has not made effective the will of the individual citizen that has

caused the opposition to it to die down.   The fear of
many of those who oppose industrial democracy is that
it would be effective, that the individual would at last
come to his own, and that, in learning to control his
own industry, he would learn also to control the political machine.   The day on which he learnt that would
certainly be a black day for the bureaucratic jugglers
in human lives whom we still call statesmen—or sometimes New Statesmen.

Collectivists may take their choice : they are knaves,
who hate freedom, or they are fools, who do not know
what freedom means, or they are a bit of both.   The
knaves are not Socialists at all ; they are divorced by
their whole theory of life from the democratic idea
that is essential to all true Socialism.   The fools may
become Socialists if they get a philosophy : if, ceasing
to think of social organisation as a mere mechanism
and of self-government merely as a means, they try
for themselves to understand the moral basis on which
Socialism rests.   If they do that, they cannot but
realise that political democracy by itself is useless and
that industrial democracy is its essential foundation :
the expression of the same principle in another sphere.
They will see that the Collectivist theory is built upon
distrust, and, if they are good men, they will reject it
on that ground alone.

It is a view deeply rooted in the British mind that
the nastiest medicines are the most wholesome.   In
the same way, we have been too ready to believe that
the most nauseating system of social organisation will
be the most efficient.   How many Socialists of the old
sort really believe in their hearts that Collectivism
would lead to a system of production more efficient, in
the capitalistic sense, than that we have now ?   The

fact that they hasten to advance against National
Guilds the very arguments that Anti-Socialists have
always urged, with at least equal justice, against themselves, proves that they have always doubted.   They
reject as absurd the Guildsman's argument that a good
system of production demands good men, and that a
man cannot be good, as a maker or producer, unless
he is free.   Collectivism is the ' doubting Thomas '
of the Socialist faith ; there is but a veneer of humani-
tarianism over its belief in the mid-Victorian heresy
of original sin.   Upon such a gloomy gospel of despair,
no great Society can be built.   And, after all, if men
are like that, is it worth while to build anything ?

II

I come now to the second fallacy upon which the
Collectivist bases his argument that the Guild system
would not bring freedom to the individual worker.
When the Guildsman urges the dangers of bureaucracy
in the Collectivist State he is met with a *tu quoque* ; the
Guilds, he is told, will be no less bureaucratic.   Nay,
they will be even more so ; for they will substitute for
the single great tyranny of the centralised State a
multitude of petty tyrants, each of whom will be to
the full as oppressive to the individual as the responsible
civil servant is likely to be.   As Sir Leo Chiozza Money
has put it, a tyrant is none the less tyrannical for being
a petty tyrant.

This view, or some view resembling it, is taken by
critics of the most diverse types.   On the one hand, it
is the argument of the bureaucrat who would reduce
all aspirations after freedom to an absurdity ; on the
other, a very similar view is advanced by some lovers

of freedom who, while they wish to realise industrial democracy, fear the centralisation which they believe to be essential to the system of National Guilds. The two types of objection demand very different answers, though it is not possible to keep them wholly distinct. I shall deal in this section with the former line of attack, and shall come in the next to that which is more dangerous, because the motive behind it is more worthy.

It will be well, however, to guillotine the Girondins before turning our attention to the Jacobins. The Collectivist urges that the workman has to choose between two tyrannies, and that the tyranny of State Socialism will be less oppressive, as well as more efficient than that of the Guild. The tyranny of the State Department, or the tyranny of the great corporation, which is it to be ?

It is here once more necessary to remind the Collectivist that he is dealing with men, and not with machines. The answer to the problem is in terms of human character. We have to ask ourselves which of the two alternative systems is the more likely to call into play the qualities of initiative and independence. For the danger of bureaucracy in any system of organisation varies inversely with the spirit of independence displayed by the individuals whom it governs.

Political democracy, we have agreed, is ineffective because, resting upon an autocratic industrial system, it does not call into play the energy needed to control it. Over the vast mechanism of modern politics the individual has no control, not because the State is too big, but because he is given no chance of learning the rudiments of self-government within a smaller unit. In the business of his daily life he is subject to an autocracy which at every turn stifles, instead of developing, his natural capacities for self-government and self-assertion. Autocracy in industry finds its inevitable reflection in political bureaucracy. On this ground it has too often been concluded that all institutions are naturally bureaucratic, and, despairing of freedom, men have concentrated on the task of reducing the number of responsible bureaucrats. But democracy in industry is very different from political democracy. In industry the individual is dealing with something that he himself understands, with something free from the vague glamour with which the politician contrives to surround his own sphere of operations. The Guild officer will not be able to go the way of all politicians, because the Guild member will soon find him out and learn to control him.

No Guildsman denies the need for discipline and order within the Guild. What he does deny is the Prussian theory that discipline can only be secured through tyranny. Given a Guild permeated by the spirit of equality and well provided with democratic institutions, all needful discipline will follow. For man is not naturally a rebel against order, unless the order is itself unjust.

I have many times heard employers of labour advance, almost in the same breath, two contradictory opinions which bear upon this point. Having told you that all workmen are lazy dogs and that the only thing for them is the iron heel, the Capitalist will go on, without a break, to declare that his workers give him no trouble, because he always puts the right men over them. There is, behind this contradiction, an important truth. It does matter very much what kind of foremen the workers have set over them. Where,

as in too many modern factories, the foreman is chosen
for his slave-driving capacities, the worker is naturally
and justifiably a ' lazy dog ' ; what work he does is
done grudgingly, because it is exacted by means of a
suspicious compulsion.   Where, on the other hand, the
employer has sense enough, from his own point of view,
to choose foremen who trust their men and treat them
as human beings, there are many cases in which work
is done well and cheerfully, even despite the permanent
exploitation under which the worker is suffering.   So
ready are most men to obey and to work willingly that
they are prepared, in return for so small a concession,
to forget the great injustice of Capitalism itself.

If this is true under the present system, how much
more will it be so in the Guild, where there will be no
consciousness of exploitation to stay a man's hand
from giving manfully of his best !   To do good work
for a capitalist employer is merely, if we view the
situation rationally, to help a thief to steal more successfully ;   good work done for the Guild will be done in
the interests of a society of equals, and will appeal to
the highest and strongest of human motives—the sense
of fellowship.   Even a purely rational man would work
well for his Guild : how much more willing will be the
service of the average man, a creature of sentiment,
ever more inclined to give than to take, if only he
can feel that in giving he is serving a fellow and an
equal !

All this will seem the veriest nonsense to the hard-
headed business-men who have of late years become
converts to Collectivism, and even to the more sentimental rank and file of the Socialist movement, who
combine with an almost maudlin personal benevolence
a capacity for swallowing the most cynical doctrines

on the subject of human nature. The Fabian heresy of distrust has sunk deep into our souls ; even if we admit the vast difference that a good foreman can make to the spirit of the workshop, the most part of us cannot believe that the workers in the Guild would know how to choose the right foremen. Just as democracy in politics is assailed because it brings the demagogue to power, democracy in industry is feared because the workers might elect to be led by industrial demagogues.

The fact that in politics this fear is not groundless lends the argument plausibility. But the Guildsman's whole answer is based on the difference between politics and industry. The demagogue can succeed in political life because the individual voter has so little check upon him ; there is no political check-weighman to tell the worker when he is being cheated. The politician makes his election speeches and is triumphantly returned—on promises. He remains in power for a number of years, during which things happen. He and another man very much like him, who poses as his opponent, then return to his constituency and make more promises. Even if the worker has suffered inconvenience and oppression he can hardly bring it home to the bland and persuasive gentleman in the frock-coat. He listens again to the specious rhetoric, and the demagogue is again returned to power. Or, if he decides in favour of a change, and elects the other fellow—" plus ça change, plus c'est la même chose." The misdeeds of politicians come not home to roost.

But can any reasonable man suppose that democracy in industry will follow the same course ? Let us face the worst possibilities of the case. In the Guild there will be many kinds of officials to elect, from the foreman of the individual shop to the members of the national executive council. Let us take the two extreme cases separately.

Suppose, when the workers first win the right of choosing their leaders, they show a general tendency to elect incompetent foremen. Very possibly they will do so ; but what will follow ? At every turn, every hour of every day, the workers in the shop will be conscious of the incompetence of the man they have chosen. He will be dealing with matters that they themselves understand, and his interference will soon be resented by men who know his business better than he knows it himself. When the day of re-election comes round they will have had enough of him and his sort to make them choose a more capable man in his place. The workers will have to learn the art of choosing the right foremen ; but, given these conditions, can it be doubted that the lesson will be learnt, and learnt without delay ?

On this point the case is clear ; but what of the other extreme ? Will the workers know how to elect their national officers, above all those in whom the higher kinds of technical, commercial and professional capacity will be essential ? Let us admit that this is not so easy, though here too the method of trial and error will produce its effect. Moreover, in learning to choose the right local officers, the members will have mastered the first great lesson of self-government ; they will be able to go on and master its further lessons.

As we shall see in more detail later on, the national executive of the Guild need not be selected by means of a simple mass ballot of all the members. Many and various forms of local and sectional election could be employed, according to the needs of the various Guilds. Thus, the corporate capacity of each district and of each craft within the industry would be called into play, and the same incentives to a right choice as apply in the election of foremen would operate here also. One of the main problems of Guild government will be the securing of a national executive that represents the General Will of the members.

Of this more hereafter. But what of the more distinctly professional officers of the Guild ; what of those who will correspond to the technical experts, general managers, and heads of departments in the industry of to-day ? For these there is no need to adopt the method of mass election ; in many cases they would no doubt be appointed by the executive committee. The technical expert can hardly be chosen by a mass vote, for his expertness is *ex hypothesi* something which the majority of the members of the Guild cannot hope to understand. The same contention applies with equal force to the commercial experts, who will be in charge of the trading operations of the Guild. They, too, cannot be well chosen by a general vote. It is enough that they should be the servants of an authority directly representing the whole Guild ; for it is the business of the expert to provide the means of securing the ends which the democracy has in view. The executive might well select and control all such experts. Then, if the expert made himself unpleasant, and the executive refused to remove him on direct protest from the branches of the Guild, the affair might be thrashed out in the delegate meeting, which would be, in such a case, supreme.

I have put the position concretely and dogmatically for the sake of clearness ; but, of course, the Guild may always play the game of ' Cheat the Prophet.' It will be for the Guild to decide on its own methods of democratic government ; I am only stating what seems the most obvious solution.

It seems, then, that the Guild can be fitted to choose its leaders at both ends of the series, both in the small shop unit and in the great national unit. Doubtless it will learn the art of self-government gradually, and there will be mistakes at first ; but these mistakes will be largely got over in the intermediate period when the Guild has still only a partial foothold in control. Men may become democrats by conviction, but they become good democrats only by practice. Every new system must fall into errors ; it will survive its errors if the ideal behind it is worthy of humanity.

III

Any old stick was good enough for beating the dull dog of Collectivism ; I have now to deal with an attack that is more deserving of respect. We have seen that the Collectivist argument, reduced to its logical elements, amounts to a denial that freedom is either possible or desirable for the mass of mankind. I come now to those who, while calling themselves ' Guildsmen,' believe that a system of National Guilds would not secure the freedom or the initiative they require. They are frightened by the word ' national,' upon which *The New Age* has always strongly insisted.[1] My answer to them brings me to the heart of the argument I am trying to develop ; for my main object is to prove, first, that a national system of industrial organisation is essential, and secondly, that such a national system need not mean bureaucracy and centralisation.

[1] I am here speaking of the word ' national ' as opposed to ' local.' I am not raising the issue of nationalism *v.* internationalism, for which see my *Labour in War-Time*, Ch. I.

It will be well to begin by defining the case against
National Guilds more exactly. The attack comes
mainly from the mediævalists, and finds its chief expression in the writings of Mr. A. J. Penty.[1] I should
not be taken as attributing to him all the opinions that
follow ; I merely mention his name as that of one of the
foremost defenders of the mediævalist position.[2]

" The defect of the Socialist movement to-day,"
Mr. Penty once wrote in *The New Age*, " is a certain
timidity which comes from it still having some faith
in Industrialism." " Having given up the hope of
saving existing society, it will be able to lay the foundations of a new one by setting in motion forces which
run counter to modern tendencies."

Mr. Penty's immediate object in the article from
which I quote was to convict me of being, at bottom,
an "Industrialist ' or a ' Modernist,' masquerading in
the thinnest and most transparent of mediæval gauzes.
Applied to the system of National Guilds, his argument
would run something like this—or so I have heard it
put by some who profess to agree with him.

" Your National Guilds are an attempt at compromise.   You are trying to save machine-production and
Industrialism, which you hate, simply because you
believe the tide of circumstance to be too strong for
you.   You have fallen into that economic determinism
which has been the curse of modern Socialism ; instead
of striving for what you see to be good, you are merely
drifting with the current.   You differ, in fact, from the
Collectivists much less than you think ; you accept,
like them, large scale production.   That once conceded,

[1] Mr. Penty has, I know, since modified his view of National Guilds ;
but he will forgive me for using his admirable expression of his earlier view
as a text on which to hang my comments.
[2] See p. 266.

all your aspirations after freedom must be futile ; you are trying to patch the rotten structure, when you ought to go out and smash it.   Your National Guilds, based on the Capitalism of to-day, and the inheritors of its tradition of meanness and slavery, will themselves be almost as mean and servile as the system they arise to replace."

That is a view which I understand and respect, though I hold it to be wrong.   It is at least the error of a man, and not of an automaton.

I cannot here repeat the arguments for and against machinery, or do more than state the view, that machines, rightly used, may be beneficial over a great part of industry, harmful as they undoubtedly are to many skilled crafts.   Assuming that the right spirit in which to approach machinery is not that which would destroy it everywhere, but that which would change it from a master to a servant, I want to inquire whether the accusations levelled at National Guilds are really justified.   Does mechanical, large-scale pro-duction inevitably mean bureaucracy and the loss of individual freedom ?

As we saw in the first section of this chapter, there is a sense in which everything that makes life more complicated means a loss of freedom.   But that is to conceive freedom after a fashion that renders every form of human co-operation an instrument of slavery.   Such a view rests on a fundamental disbelief in the power of men to organise their lives on any but the simplest basis.   It is the standpoint of those who repudiate the Nation-State, and demand a return to the City or the local Commune.   Those who believe in National Guilds hold that it is possible for the demands of freedom to be satisfied over a larger area.   But they are fully alive to the dangers of this wider central-isation.

The Nation-State, we saw, cannot but be false to its profession of democracy so long as it remains a great, undigested mass of individuals, whose sole recognised bond one with another is their citizenship in the great Society.   If the community is to be truly self-governing there must be within it many forms of grouping, political, industrial and the like, local as well as central, uniting men by bonds at once more narrow and more intense than those which link them together one and all in the community.   There must be a strong municipal life and a strong Guild life, or there will be bureaucracy at the centre and rottenness and apathy in the members.   But if this is true of the community as a whole, is it not true equally of the smaller communities within it ?   Will not the Guilds too have to be complicated in structure and government, if their democracy is to be more than a sham ?   And, if a free constitution can be secured within the Guild, will not this go far to meet the objections of those who fear that the new system will be bureaucratic like the old ?

There are not a few people who are frightened of the centralisation which seems to them to be implied in such a name as National Guilds !   But surely they are wrong in believing that centralisation is implied.   Local initiative can be given free play within a national system.

The first point on which Guildsmen insist is that the system should be national.   Here they come into con-flict with an opposing school, represented chiefly by the French Syndicalists and their forbears, the Com-munists.   Bakunin and those who derive their doctrines from him have always believed in the autonomous local

Commune as the basis on which a national or inter-national system should be built.[1] Everything larger than the Commune has been, to their mind, *federal* in character : the freedom of the locality has been the cornerstone of the whole system. In extreme opposi-tion to them stand the *centralisers*, who believe in the large unit for its own sake and for the sake of efficiency, and who are quite unmoved by the dangers of bureau-cracy which it involves. Both these schools of thought I believe to be wrong.

The third view I will call that of *decentralisation*. It is important to realise in what respect it differs from the federal view, which, superficially, it seems to resemble. Federalism implies that all power rests originally in the small unit, which may then, of its own free will, surrender a certain amount of it to a larger body. The larger the unit, the less the power ; for each unit can only hand on a part of the power it has received from the unit below it, and there is accord-ingly a continually decreasing scale of power from the local to the national body. Federalism begins at the bottom and builds up. As we shall see shortly, its failure in the sphere of modern Trade Unionism has been flagrant : nor is there greater hope for it, at least in Great Britain, as a basis for the future industrial society.

Decentralisation, on the other hand, begins at the centre—in this sphere, with the democratic, equali-tarian, national, industrial Guild. Those who advocate it realise that with the dead ideal of the self-contained and almost self-sufficing City-State must pass away the corresponding ideal of the isolated local workshop or group of workshops. The national organisation of the community demands a national organisation of

[1] See p. 266.

industry, and, under such conditions, it is only possible to maintain freedom by giving it scope within the larger unit. As surely as no Nation-State can avoid autocracy unless it possesses an effective system of local and sectional institutions, the National Guild can avoid bureaucracy only by setting its house in order from within. If the State is to be healthy, industry must be made self-governing ; but no less certainly, if industry is to be healthy, must the workshop and the locality be given freedom within the Guilds.

Syndicalism and the craftsman's attitude which we have been examining alike arise from a despair of ever getting truly representative government. It is to the honour of the National Guildsman that, even in the midst of the misrepresentative institutions under which we now suffer, he has never despaired. He has sought, instead, to find out why representation has failed in the past, and has seen that the solution lies in applying the democratic principle in every sphere. The small unit, he has realised, is essential ; and, under modern conditions, this can only be secured by sectionalising the larger unit, *i.e.* by decentralisation. But if this principle holds good in the political sphere, it is clearly no less true of industry.

If critics of the Guilds are still unsatisfied, there is a further line of attack they can pursue. It may be urged that the whole tendency of modern Trade Unionism is towards centralisation, which is almost universally admitted to be essential to the success of the Unions as fighting organisations. This being so, is it not reasonable to fear that the Guilds, which Guildsmen hope to see grow out of the existing Unions, will inherit their centralisation, even when the need for it has passed ? To this question I shall turn shortly. What is important for the moment is to bring out the full implications of the argument. The ' Federalists,' those who believe in the independent small unit and not in decentralisation within the large unit, must, if they are to be logical, despair, not only of Industrialism, but also of Trade Unionism, which is the product of the conditions it will in time supplant. But if, having despaired of representative government, we go on to despair of industrial democracy as well, then wherein lies our hope ?

We are, as a rule, bidden to rely upon a return to Mediævalism, to run boldly counter to the stream of modern tendencies, and to aim at restoring the productive methods of a period in which artist and craftsman were not yet divorced. I believe this statement of the mediævalist case, right as it undoubtedly is for certain ' artistic ' crafts, to be based on a confusion of thought. It is true that William Morris went straight to the heart of the problem when he pointed out that the mediæval workmen had joy, because he had freedom, *in his work.* The Middle Ages, at their best, before the decadence, combined the two characteristics of localism and freedom. The industrial world of the period was a world of towns, each more or less completely isolated from its neighbours, within whose boundaries much the same free small-scale production was carried on. Upon these conservative communities burst the bombshell of Capitalism, the invention in the first instance not of the producer, but of the trader exploiting the new-found possibilities of a world-market. Capitalistic trading, national or international even at that date, was inevitably far more than a match for the small local communes and townships, each of which stood by itself. Had the cities controlled such national

governments as there were, there might well have been
a different story to tell ; but the rising national States
were in every case hostile to the pretensions of the
cities, which they saw only as barriers in the way
of centralised government. The capitalist trader
triumphed, and gradually he became the industrial
magnate. Finance, the pioneer as usual of large-scale
organisation, conquered production and annihilated
freedom.

This, however, does not prove that large-scale production is necessarily inimical to freedom. Freedom
fell, not because the City gave place to the Nation,
but because it was the trader, who was also the financier,
by whom the revolution was accomplished. Autocracy organised on a grand scale, while democracy still
clung to the small unit. The result was that autocracy
overcame, as the large unit will always overcome the
small, whenever a conflict arises. It is only possible
to beat the enemy with an army his own size. Split
up the army if you will : have your corps, brigades,
regiments, companies, platoons ; but let it be one army,
or it will go to disaster. In short, federalism and the
policy of comparative isolation must give place to
decentralisation, which differentiates without disinte-
grating. The future for the great industries lies, not
with local Guilds, but with National Guilds allowing
local and sectional freedom.

IV

" You can only beat the enemy with an army his
own size." If the holding of that opinion makes us
' Modernists,' let us be ' Modernists ' by all means.
If Capitalism is to be overthrown, the workers must

not only be animated by a common spirit of class-consciousness ; they must present a solid front. They must organise again *la grande armée* of the Revolution, and, whatever sub-divisions it may contain, it must be one army, marching, under the impulse of a common idea, against the common enemy.

It is unnecessary greatly to labour the point that, if we are to have a great change, it must come by means of big battalions. The whole history of Trade Unionism forces this conclusion upon every competent observer. Everywhere is found, among the small Unions, stagnation or failure, among the larger Unions, growth and comparative prosperity. Among national Unions, craft gradually gives place to industry as the basis of organisation ; while local Unions are swallowed up one by one by those of national extent. It is the latter process which chiefly concerns the present argument.

Take, for instance, the case of the miners. We have here an edifice of three, or, in some cases, of four stories. Everywhere the structure is based, in origin and intention, on the pit lodge, including the men working in a single pit. These lodges are combined in various ways—I omit all points of detail—into County Associations. Sometimes several of these are grouped in a larger, but still an intermediate, body, such as the Midland Miners' Federation or, till recently, the Scottish Miners' Federation. Lastly, the various County Associations, or larger units, where such exist, are united in the Miners' Federation of Great Britain. Thus, there are at the least three degrees of grouping—the pit, the county and the nation. There may even be five—the pit, the district, the county, the federated counties, and the nation. I can omit altogether the district, which is never more than a part of the administrative machinery of the county unit.

The whole intention of this structure is clearly federal, and federal in many respects it actually remains. The current, however, is setting more and more strongly towards centralisation, and the recent history of the miners is a good instance of federalism denying itself in practice.

In some places, the lodge, which means the pit unit, is still more or less autonomous. There is, however, no case that I know of in which the lodge continues to rely simply on its own funds. Even where the lodge preserves, wholly or largely unimpaired, the right to declare a local strike on its own responsibility, it has some claim to call upon the county funds in support of such a dispute. But this means the creation of a central fund in the hands of the County Association, and with centralised funds goes either a considerable amount of central control or else disaster. The reformers in the South Wales Miners' Federation complain that in the past their central funds have been continually depleted by local strikes—usually unsuccessful—and that, as a result, they have never been able to meet the employers on equal terms. When occasion has arisen for a strike extending over the whole county area, they have found their coffers empty ; they have been forced either to remain inactive, or to court defeat or, at best, unsatisfying compromise. Thus, in the national miners' strike of 1912, it was only the poverty of the S.W.M.F. that made South Wales favour a settlement.

Local autonomy, or, at any rate, pit autonomy, will not work in the mining industry. Where the local strike continues, it can only be effective if it has the financial support and the countenance of a larger body. A centralised South Wales Miners' Federation is an organisation on so large a scale as to give rise to very difficult problems of democratic control. This the authors of the *Miners' Next Step* have clearly seen, and we shall have to return to the question of control later on. What concerns us now is that the large-scale organisation is seen to be so necessary for fighting efficiency that the only course is to provide good government, which means freedom, within it.

We see, then, the South Wales Miners' Federation abandoning lodge autonomy and passing from a Federation to what is practically a Union.[1] Still more significant is the case of the Scottish Miners ; for here, until quite recently, there were a number of distinct county associations, each more or less centralised in itself, federated into a larger body covering the whole of Scotland. In 1914, the Scottish Miners' Federation became the Scottish Miners' Union. For sick benefits and the like, local finance and local customs are retained ; but for trade purposes, the Scottish Miners now form a single unit. As the various County Associations in the Midlands drew together in the Midland Federation, the Scotch had their national Federation : they have now outstripped England in forming themselves into an amalgamation. Once more the principle of federalism has been denied ; instead of delegating a part of their powers to a larger and looser body, the various Associations have merged their unity in the interests of fighting strength. Federalism has given place to centralisation : such powers as the localities retain must be accounted as decentralisation, and no longer as federalism.

The same forces are at work in the Miners' Federa-

[1] See p. 266.

tion of Great Britain itself.[1]   More and more, in face of
national combination on the side of the employers, the
workers are being forced to come closer together, and
the Federation to take action as a single unit.   When
such common action becomes normal, the weakness
of the federal organisation at once makes itself felt.
For, while in strikes confined to a single county area,
or to South Wales, or Scotland, or the Midlands, it is
possible, by means of the levy which the M.F.G.B. can
impose at need, to strengthen the district concerned,
the case is quite different as soon as the dispute is of
national extent.   Then, as was seen only too clearly
in 1912, the strength of the whole Federation is the
strength of its weakest link, of that county which has
least money in its war-chest.   The 1912 strike collapsed
because of the bankruptcy of some of the districts.   As
soon as this is realised, there follows the demand for
centralised finance and control of national policy, the
demand for the conversion of the Miners' Federation
of Great Britain, in fact, if not in name, into something
more like a national union.

I have taken but a single example of the tendency
towards centralisation, because it is necessary to go
into some detail if a true idea of the situation is to be
given.   Much the same facts apply wherever a system
of local autonomous organisations more or less loosely
federated is attempting to cope with the massed force
of Capitalism.   Everywhere the federal principle tends
to break down and to give place to a more centralised
system.   Thus, the same forces are beginning to
operate in the cotton industry, long regarded as the
chosen home of federalism, and probably in fact the
sphere in which federalism will linger longest.   I have,
however, no space to deal with any other case in detail.

[1] See p. 266.

The miners must serve as typical of the general tendency.

This movement towards centralisation is, it should be noticed, no mere drifting with the tide. It is the conscious statesmanship of the workers, and in its success lies their one chance of supplanting and over-throwing Capitalism. Labour must centralise, or it will be beaten ; but as soon as it centralises, new problems of self-government arise within the Unions themselves.

It is no part of my aim here to travel again over ground I have already to some extent covered in *The World of Labour* (Chapter VIII). It is enough to repeat that, if the great Union is not to fall into bureaucracy, if it is to represent effectively the will of its members, if it is to do successfully its work of fighting the em-ployers, it must give all possible freedom to craft and local interests within itself. This is true even from the point of view of the old, defensive Trade Unionism : much more is it true as soon as the Union passes from the stage of fighting to that of control. It is clear that the mediævalists are right in believing that a highly centralised system of control would be fatal to that freedom in production which the Guilds are to realise. I shall therefore try next to describe, with a full consciousness of the fallibility of all prophets, the method of internal organisation that a Guild might adopt. The aims of this model Guild constitution will be at once to ensure unity and co-ordinate pro-duction on a national scale, and to safeguard diversity by giving the locality and the craft free play and fair representation within the industrial Guild.

V

In applying ourselves to the task of prophecy, it will be well to begin with general principles. Our model Guild statutes will be to some extent unlike any actual statutes that could ever exist, just because they are formed on general principles without regard for the particular moment or sphere of their application. Let us try to see first of all what these principles are.

In the first place, the Guild statutes must make the individual self-governing not only in name, but in fact. They must embody not a ' paper ' democracy, but a real democracy which will encourage, and not merely allow, the individual to express himself. They must aim at giving to every man the feeling of freedom, which is the basis of true self-government. Furthermore, they must enable the workers not only to choose their leaders, but also to exercise a check upon those whom they choose.

Secondly, the statutes must try to combine freedom with efficiency—not that capitalistic efficiency which turns man into a machine and secures a dead level of mediocrity by the destruction of all native genius ; but an efficiency based throughout on the development of individual initiative, emphasising valuable differences, bringing out all that is most distinctive in individual, locality or nation.

Both these objects, we have seen, can be secured only by means of a decentralised constitution. The gathering-up of all power to a single centre means bureaucracy, and means just that dead-alive mediocrity which goes to-day by the name of ' industrial efficiency.' On this point, we may take a lesson from Capitalism itself. Not so long ago, the world awoke to the gravity of a new industrial phenomenon which it called ' the trust problem.'   The trust, in its earlier and cruder Transatlantic form, was simply the ' big business ' —it concentrated capital and management into one colossal accumulation, and, in the process, it very often swept away the difference between firms : in short, it standardised production.   We all know the line the Socialists took when confronted with this super-Dreadnought type of Capitalism.   They attacked the abuses of the trust system, and pointed out the exploitation of the consumer which resulted from it ; but their remedy was not the destruction of trusts, but their nationalisation.   They never realised the human dangers of ' big business ' ; not they, but the Anti-Socialists showed how the trust resulted in the crushing-out of initiative, in the world-wide triumph of the man-machine.   At the same time, those who realised this danger were equally short-sighted in their attempt at ' trust-busting ' ; they failed to see that there is no way out of the trust system, public or private, except industrial democracy.

But while the trust movement was gaining ground and attracting universal public attention, a second movement towards industrial combination was quietly at work in Europe.   In the public mind, rings, cartels and trusts are too often lumped together without distinction ; but the difference between them is of the greatest importance for Guildsmen.   The ' ring ' may be only a trust in process of formation ; the fully developed ' cartel ' is a distinct type, and is Capitalism's latest and best form—from the capitalist point of view. Briefly, the cartel, instead of destroying difference, aims at retaining it.   It leaves the management of every ' works ' in separate hands, and only co-ordinates their forces in face of the consumer. It regulates sale, supply and demand, and keeps a watchful eye on efficiency, and often on labour conditions—all of course from the capitalistic standpoint ; but the methods of production it leaves, generally speaking, to each separate factory. In this way it does undoubtedly secure a higher degree of efficiency than the complete trust ; it standardises price, but it avoids the standardising of production.

The Collectivist Utopia would be a world of public trusts ; the Guild Utopia will be a world of producers' cartels, worked in the interest of the whole community. If the Guild is not to fall into mediocrity, it must preserve the distinctness of works from works, of locality from locality, and of nation from nation. It is the organisation of human differences on the basis of human identity.

We shall begin, then, in describing the Guild statutes, with the simplest unit, and shall work up gradually to those which are most complex. At every stage we shall be able to indicate roughly the work to be done and a possible machinery for the doing of it. Thus, we shall find as the lowest stage the single ' shop ' within the works. Next will come the whole works or factory, then the whole district in which the factory is situated, and, lastly, the whole Guild, with its various governing and executive bodies. At each stage, again, we shall have to deal with a double problem. We shall have to ask, first, how the governing bodies are to be chosen and controlled, and secondly, how the Guild officers, from the shop foreman to the head national officers, are to be chosen and controlled. Furthermore, we shall have, in each case, to discuss the distribution of power between officers and representative bodies.

Throughout our system, one principle will be operative. Collectivism means for the worker government from above ; and we have given it as the essence of the Guild idea that it means government from below. At every stage, then, wherever a body of men has to work under the supervision of a leader or officer, it must have the choice of that officer. And, in the same way, every committee must be appointed directly by those over whose work it is to preside. Sweepingly stated, this is the general principle on which Guild democracy must rest. I shall come shortly to its more particular applications.

On the other hand, this insistence on the principle of direct democracy—which is indeed the only real democracy—must not lead us, as it has led many of its supporters, to ignore the unity of the Guild. The cartel leaves its constituent firms free to carry on the normal business of production as they choose ; but it acts as a unit, even a coercive unit, in the regulation of price and supply, and in enforcing general rules which are necessary for the good of the trade—again, be it said, from the capitalist point of view. In the same way, the Guild authority acting in co-operation with, and in the interests of, the consumers must regulate supply and enforce general rules over the whole Guild. The regulation of prices under the Guild system I discuss in the next chapter. Besides these functions, it will clearly be the duty of the Guild to secure the adoption of new inventions and processes, first introduced in one workshop or locality, wherever they may be of use, and to keep a general watch on the working of the various branches. To these points we shall have to return in discussing the constitution of the central authority.

The establishment of the Guilds will be the workers' act of faith in themselves, and we may therefore believe that many of the elaborate precautions which Guildsmen advise will be, in the event, unnecessary. The establishment of a free system of production will not, we believe, be followed by a monstrous attempt on the part of the workers as producers to practise fraud on themselves as consumers. But, since we believe that the workers as consumers would exploit themselves as producers, because consumers' associations can never be democratic in character from the producer's point of view, we see the necessity of answering the critics who have the same fear of National Guilds. Guildsmen ourselves, we do not accept the parallel ; we believe that freedom is natural, and slavery unnatural to man ; indirect ' democracy ' we regard as a form of slavery, only more disguised than other forms ; and we hold that a society which organises its industry on the basis of consumption will be inevitably servile. But a free system, we hold no less strongly, will bring to the front man's natural qualities—his sense of fellowship, his desire to express himself in Rousseau's phrase, his *amour de soi* and not his *amour propre*. Unlike Collectivists, we are ready to trust the people.

But living in an untrusting world, and, worse, in a world where men have so lost the power of trust that it will take long to recover it, we must meet the questions of those who do not share our faith. Of such unbelievers I would ask whether the system of organisation that is being outlined in this chapter does not offer a reasonable prospect of combining with the freedom Guildsmen desire the safeguards Capitalism has taught Collectivists to regard as necessary. I had almost said ' necessary evils ' ; but I fear that many a Collectivist no longer regards such a system of safeguards as an evil.

VI

I now come at last to details. For convenience I shall speak throughout of a single industry ; and I have chosen Engineering, because it seems most fully to illustrate all the points that arise. It should, however, be understood that the Engineering Guild is taken only as an illustration, and that I am even neglecting many features in it which make it abnormal. The proposals I am advancing remain general and typical, and would have to be modified to fit any particular case—even my chosen example of Engineering.

I desire to make it quite clear that I do not imagine myself to be forecasting any form of organisation which will ever actually exist. I am only trying, as far as one can in theory, to make plain the principles of industrial democracy by means of a detailed hypothetical example. This clear, I can go on.

I begin, then, with the methods of electing the various Committees, national and local, by which the Guild will be governed. These it will be best to set out point by point.

(a) *Shop Committees will be elected by ballot of all the workers in the shop concerned.*

The National Guild will include many separate works, corresponding roughly to the ' firms ' or businesses of to-day. In each of these works there will be, as there are now, a number of ' shops.' Thus an engineering works may have its drawing office, pattern shop, foundry, toolroom, planing, milling, turning and boring, grinding, and fitting and erecting shops, its stores, and its various offices, receiving, shipping, financial, etc. In each of these shops, or wherever it may be necessary, the workers will elect a Shop Committee, to look after the interests and the efficiency of the shop. The number of shops, and accordingly of such Committees, will, of course, vary as the whole works is more or less large and complex. The Committee will act as a counterpoise, where one is needed, to the authority of the foreman, and will further serve as the intelligence department and executive of the shop. It will be democratic, in the sense that it will be chosen directly by those with whom it will have to deal.

(b) The Works Committee will be elected sectionally by ballot of the members of each shop.

All the shops will have both interests in common and interests distinctively their own. On the Management Committee of the works as a whole it will therefore be necessary to reconcile these different points of view, both for the securing of harmony and for the co-ordination of the various departments. It is likely that these objects will be most easily secured by allowing each shop to appoint, by direct ballot, its own representative to sit on the Works Committee. Such sectional representation has been found to work well where it has been tried by Trade Unions in the past, as, for instance, by the railwaymen, the dockers, and the steel-smelters.

(c) *The District Committee will consist* (1) *of works representatives, elected by the Works Committee in each separate works, and* (2) *of craft representatives, elected by ballot of all members of each craft working within the district.*

As there will, as a rule, be a number of works in the same neighbourhood, it will be necessary to group these in districts, similar to those in which Trade Union branches are often grouped nowadays. The chief functions of these District Committees will probably be the co-ordination of production over the district as a whole, and the conclusion of arrangements with the municipality or with other Guilds within the district. They will also be the main link between the individual works and the Guild as a whole, and will therefore be of very considerable importance.

On such a body it seems that two forms of representation will be necessary. Each works will have to be represented if the co-ordination of production is to be satisfactorily accomplished ; and the works' representatives will clearly have to come from the Works Committee, the body responsible for the management of the works as a whole. But it is equally clear that craft interests must not be forgotten ; the moulder from the foundry, the patternmaker, and the fitter may all have their distinctive problems to bring before the District Committee, which must therefore represent them also. As there is in this case no question of co-ordinating various managements, direct universal election can be employed. Thus all the moulders in the district will combine to elect one member to the District Committee, and so on for the other crafts.

(*d*) *The National Guild Executive will consist* (1) *of district representatives, elected by general ballot of each district, and* (2) *of craft representatives, elected by general national ballot of each craft.*

It is clearly of the greatest importance that the National Executive of the Guild should be at once as democratic as possible, and as closely as possible in touch with the feeling of the members, which comes to the same thing. It is therefore essential that it should be chosen not by the District Committees, but by some system of universal ballot. But, in a great national body, an indiscriminate vote for a whole executive by the whole body of the members is seldom really democratic in its effects. A man cannot vote for twenty or thirty persons to represent him nationally with the same sense of certainty and responsibility as he can summon up in voting for a single member to represent his own district or his own craft. On the system here suggested every member of the Guild would cast two votes, one for his district and one for his craft representative ; and, on the executive itself, the result would be an equipoise between district and craft interests, from which the general good would be most likely to emerge.

(*e*) *The National Delegate Meeting will be elected by general ballot of the members of each craft in each district.*

The National Executive will not be the ultimate governing body ; power will reside, in the last resort, with a larger body, meeting as often as it may be needed, and serving both as a final appeal court and as the initiator of the general lines of Guild policy. This body, like the Executive, will have to aim at representing the general will of the Guild, and will have the same task of combining the interests and outlook of the crafts with those of the various districts. But in a larger body, consisting in the greater Guilds of at least a hundred members and perhaps of considerably more, it will be possible to adopt a new systen of representation. Delegates will come from each district, and one of each group of delegates will be a member of each craft. Thus, there will be groups of representatives from Sheffield, Newcastle, London, etc. And, from each of these districts will come a patternmaker elected by the patternmakers of the district, a fitter elected by the fitters, a clerk elected by the clerks, and so on. Thus each individual will have someone in the Delegate Meeting who directly represents his interest as a craftsman and as a Sheffield or a Newcastle man.

Such is the general scheme of Committees with the varying methods of election which seem, in general, most applicable to them. The distribution of powers between these various Committees is a more difficult question, with which it will be easier to deal when we have laid down general rules for the election of the various officers of the Guild.

Throughout this system the aim is democracy, reposing upon trust of the individual worker. In each case the power of choice is placed directly in the hands of those over whom each committee has to preside, and the principles of local and sectional or craft representation only come in within this wider system. Provided, however, that special representation is not allowed to contravene this first principle of democracy, it is the chief means of safeguarding the Guild against bureaucracy—and the only means of ensuring real control by the rank and file. The giving to each committeeman of a more restricted but at the same time more alert electorate secures that the individual workers shall not only elect, but also control, their leaders. It converts a paper democracy into a system of true self-government.

VII

I turn now to the question of the officials. We know from experience to what an extent the efficiency of a Trade Union depends upon its permanent officials. In even greater degree will the Guild stand or fall as it selects and controls its officers well or ill. In the first place, since it will be no longer a bargaining, but a producing, body, it must choose men who are capable of replacing the capitalists and professionals of to-day, to whom we cannot deny a high degree of business capacity, however we may dislike the use they make of it. In the second place, if freedom is to be a reality in the Guild, the competent officer must be under the control of those whom he directs, and such control is more than ever necessary because of the wide sphere of influence which he will have to occupy. Unless the problem of the officials is far more satisfactorily settled by the Guilds than it has been by the Trade Unions, there will be grave peril for the whole system. It is therefore of the greatest importance that Guildsmen should attempt to face the problem of the election of officials ; ánd, if they feel more than ever the impossibility of giving a dogmatic answer, at all events to rush in where fools will no doubt abuse them for treading.

We will again set out our scheme point by point.

(a) *Foremen will be elected by ballot of all the workers in the shop concerned. The heads of the clerical departments will be elected by ballot of all the members of their departments.*

More and more strikes of late years have centred round the question of tyranny or slave-driving by foremen, and this has been particularly the case in the engineering industry. The workers have clearly an interest in the choice of their foremen, and any democratisation of industry must begin with the reposing in the workers of the elementary trust of electing those supervisors with whom they come continually into direct contact. On this point, at any rate, there should be no need of further argument.

(b) *The Works Manager will be elected by ballot of all the workers on the manipulative side of the works. The Manager of the Clerical Departments will be elected by ballot of all clerical workers.*

The duty of the works manager will be the co-ordination and supervision of the various productive departments. Under the general manager, he will be the head of the manipulative side of the works ; but he will have nothing to do with the clerical or business side. His election should therefore be the business of the workers directly engaged in production, and not of the clerical staff. Similarly, the workers in the various clerical departments will combine to elect the clerical manager, who will be the head of the clerical side of the works, under the general manager.

(c) *The General Manager of the Works will be selected by the Works Committee.*

The business of the general manager will be the co-ordination of the productive and the clerical sides of

the works. In a wider sense than either the works or
the clerical manager, who will be mainly engaged in
carrying out decisions and devising ways and means,
he will be concerned with questions of policy. By
making him the nominee of the Works Committee,
which represents the various shops within the works,
the democratic control of the whole enterprise will be
secured, and at the same time it will be possible to
avoid the danger of erecting two distinct supreme
authorities, each depending on a direct mandate from
the whole body of the electors.

    (d) *The District Secretary will be selected by the Dis-
        trict Committee.*

The district secretary's functions, as far as can be
seen, will be in the main statistical ; he will have to
play an important part in the co-ordination of supply
and demand within the district, especially in those
industries which produce mainly for a local market.
It is therefore probable that his powers will vary widely
from Guild to Guild, and from district to district.   In
the main, he will have throughout to act under the
control of the District Committee, much as the secretary
of a ring or cartel of employers acts under Capitalism.
His selection by this Committee seems to follow as a
matter of course.

    (e) *The General Secretary of the Guild will be nomi-
        nated by the Executive Committee, but this nomi-
        nation will have to be ratified by the Delegate
        Meeting.*

The general secretary will occupy much the same
position in relation to the National Executive as the
district secretary in relation to the District Committee.

But, as his work will be very much wider in scope, he will require the assistance of a large staff, which will fall under the two divisions we have already noticed in the case of the works. He must, in order to avoid a conflict of authorities, be chosen by the Executive Committee ; but, as his post is one of great responsibility, and one which directly affects the freedom of the subordinate units in the Guild, there must be some check upon this election. Such a check seems to be provided by a power of veto in the hands of the democratically chosen delegate meeting.

(f) *The Assistant Secretaries, who will be the heads of the various departments in the Central Guild offices, will be chosen by ballot of the workers employed in those offices, subject to ratification by the Executive Committee.*

One of the most difficult of the minor problems of Guild organisation is the giving of adequate self-government to the clerical workers employed in the administrative offices of the Guild.   Generally speaking, the Guild office should reproduce in its organisation the structure of the clerical side of the single works.   The clerical workers should choose their own departmental officers, and only at the top should they be controlled by an authority elected on a wider franchise.   The sanction of the Executive Committee may or may not be essential in the case of these assistant secretaries ; it is put in here in view of the close co-operation there must be between them and the general secretary.

So far we have been dealing with the distinctively administrative staff of the Guild ; let us now turn to the more special question of the expert staff.   These, again, will be of several distinct types.

(g) Works Experts will be chosen by the Works Committee.

It might seem natural, at first sight, that the election of works experts should be the business of the various crafts. In certain cases, where the function of the expert is definitely concerned with a single craft group, he may no doubt be elected by that craft ; but, as a general rule, the works expert has a more general task to perform. Not only does his work cover in many instances the spheres of several distinct crafts ; he may be concerned with craft questions that belong to another industry. Thus, in a textile factory, there will be needed an expert on textile machinery, but the making of such machinery will be the work of the Engineering Guild. The expert will have to pass qualifying examinations, which will no doubt be in the charge of a professional organisation similar to, and succeeding, the professional institutes of to-day ; but, subject to this qualification, he will be elected by the Works Committee.

(h) District Experts will be elected by the District Committee.

The same arguments apply in this case, except that the experts will be in this case less concerned with the actual business of production, and will have a more purely advisory capacity, as the function of the District Committee will itself be in the main advisory.

(i) The Travelling Inspectors in the service of the National Executive Committee will be chosen by that Committee.

Clearly, the Central Executive, in its work of coordinating the activities of the localities, will have to retain in its service inspectors, who will visit the districts and works on its behalf. They will succeed to the work of the Mines and Factory Inspectors of to-day, and will play an important part in carrying the latest methods of production from district to district. No longer hostile spies in a strange land, or abettors of the evasions and subterfuges of capitalist producers, they will be the missionaries of Guild enterprise up and down the country. In their case, too, qualifying examinations will play an important part, and they will probably be selected in the main from among the works and district experts.

(*j*) *National Experts in the Central Guild Offices will be chosen by the Executive Committee.*

These advisory officers will be, in the main, of two types. They will have to do either with the technical processes of the Guild to which they belong, in which case they will reproduce on a larger scale the qualifications of the local experts from whose ranks they will be recruited ; or they will be concerned with the relations between one Guild and another. In many cases Guild will be producing for Guild ; and in such cases the producing Guild will often need upon its staff experts in the work of the Guild for which it produces. Sometimes, then, the Guild will draw its expert officer from the ranks of another Guild. In all these cases the election should obviously be in the hands of the Executive Committee. There is no need for a more directly democratic method, because the function of this type of expert is in the main advisory, and he does not come into direct relations with or control any body of workers.

It will be noticed that all through this outline there

has been one very important omission. I have said nothing about either the time for which the various officers will remain in their positions, or about their eligibility for re-election. Annual tenure with re-eligibility will probably hold for foremen and works managers of various sorts ; but in the case of the district and general secretaries probably a longer period is desirable, provided there is a method of removal at any time through the Delegate Meeting, Executive and District Conference, or Committee. Experts will probably hold, in most cases, at the pleasure of the Committee which controls them. But the whole question of length of tenure is a matter of detail of which it is not necessary to suggest dogmatic solutions at the present stage.

In most cases the qualifying examinations will probably play an important part. No candidate will be eligible for election to any position of trust unless he has passed certain tests, ranging from the simple tests of the competence needed in a foreman to the severe examinations imposed by a professional institute of the type now represented by the Chartered Accountants or the Institute of Civil Engineers. These professional associations will assuredly survive and co-operate with the Guilds, and beside them will spring up similar bodies representing the unity of technical interest in the various manual-working crafts. In this way an additional safeguard will be placed in the hands of the crafts, and the craft representatives on the Guild Executives will be able to speak with the authority of a craft association, often extending over several Guilds, at their back. In a wise complexity of this type and not in the artificial ' return to nature ' which is advocated by those who despair of the great industry, lies the road to freedom for the individual worker.

VIII

The sketch of a Guild constitution which has been given in the last two sections of this chapter remains incomplete until something has been said of its actual working. Two leading questions at once suggest themselves. In the first place, what will be the relation between the various Committees on the one hand and the various officers on the other ? And secondly, what will be the relation between the single works and the larger units both local and national ?

The distribution of power among officials, executives and the rank and file is a source of continual difficulty in the Trade Union movement to-day. In one Union there may be constant friction between the Executive and the General Secretary ; in another there may well seem to be an unholy alliance of officials and executive against the rank and file. Even the Delegate Meeting, designed as a more democratic body to counteract bureaucracy and officialism, often seems, from its very size and lack of experience, to be all too easily managed by those whom it was intended to control. It is therefore a fair question to ask whether the faults of Trade Union government of to-day will not reproduce themselves in the Guilds of to-morrow.

To some extent, this question has already been answered by implication. Stress has been laid on the importance of craft and district representation in making the various Executives more really a reflection of the will of the members of the Guild, and, in especial, on the method chosen for electing the Delegate Meeting. When, as in too many Unions to-day, the Delegate

Meeting is merely an enlarged replica of the Executive Committee, elected by the various districts in exactly the same way, the larger body affords no real check over the actions of the smaller body. The one will effectively balance the other only if different methods of election are adopted. I have therefore designed an Executive consisting half of representatives of all grades in each district and half of national representatives of the various crafts ; but over against this body I have set a Delegate Meeting elected by each craft in each district severally. Thus, while the Executive will represent the national craft point of view, the local representatives of each craft will have a chance of criticising its actions in the Delegate Meeting and against the local ' all grades ' point of view on the Executive will be set the local ' craft ' point of view in the Delegate Meeting.

Local and sectional representation will not only secure committees more in harmony with the will of the members ; they will also serve to develop and strengthen that common will. Most of the problems of Trade Union government can be traced, in the last resort, to the apathy of the great bulk of the rank and file. But, if only the rank and file secure, as they must under the Guild system, not only a direct interest in the business of production, but also a means of making their interest effective, they will soon learn the double lesson of controlling their Executives and, thereby as well as directly, of controlling their officials. Interest the members, and give their interest a means of expression, and the problem of industrial democracy will be to a great extent solved.

Let us assume, then, that the Guild Executive, checked by the Delegate Meeting, will be not a bureaucracy, but a true reflection of the popular will. What in that case will be the relation between the Executive and the officials? Clearly the official will be the minister of the Executive and will carry out the commands which it imposes. No doubt, much power will remain in his hands; but he will be subject at every step to the will of an alert democratic body, as the Trade Union official would be to-day if only Trade Union Executives were as a rule alert or really democratic— or let us say rather, as the officials are to-day in the best governed Trade Unions. In the Guilds, this principle will hold at every stage; the official will be an administrator, responsible to and directed by his committee, whether it be the National Guild Executive, the District Committee, or the Works Committee. Sovereignty will reside, not in the official, however elected, but in the representative body, or, in the last resort, in the whole mass of the members.

The problem of the relation between officers and committees is comparatively simple. I come now to the far more difficult question of the relation between the various units of production, local and national, within the single industrial Guild. Something has already been said on this point in the third and fifth sections of this chapter; it remains to draw together the threads of the argument which I have all along been developing. We saw that many of the mediævalists criticise the system of National Guilds for its acceptance of industrialism and of large scale production (Section III), and we have laid it down that the organisation of the Guild must be more like that of a cartel than of a trust, in that it must respect the independence of the individual works or factory (Section V). The question we have now to ask is whether the system of organisation we have laid down will in reality secure the independence of the small unit within the great National Guild. If it will not, I admit that, tried by the fundamental test, National Guilds fail.

How, then, is this independence to be secured ? Not so much by a distribution of powers as by a distribution of functions. We have laid stress on the necessity of a national organisation of industry on the, one hand and of a local organisation of production on the other. Are these two views reconcilable or are they not ?

Let us ask first more precisely what it is that must be organised nationally. It is surely in the main relation now known as ' buying and selling,' or the ' co-ordination of supply and demand.' It is, in fact, not *production*, but *trading* that must be under a national control. The Collectivists have been right in their insistence on the need for a ' national organisation of industry ' ; but the thing that they have aimed at organising nationally has been not so much production as exchange. The quantities of various commodities that are to be produced and the prices that are to be charged for them—these are the questions that must be asked and answered in respect of the whole industrial life of the nation. The organisation of supply and demand and the control of prices in consultation with the consumer will therefore be the main business of the National Guild authority, and of the District Committees which will work in conjunction with it over a smaller area. The National Guild will organise exchange in direct connection with the National State ; the District Committee will perform the same function in conjunction with the Municipality or County Council. I do not suggest that this will be the sole work of

the National Executive or of the District Committee ;
but this, I believe, will be its primary function.

Let us turn now to the individual works. If the
evils of modern industrialism and of large-scale production are to be avoided, the group of workers
employed in the single works must form a self-governing
group. But their need is not so much to govern
exchange as to govern *production*. The Works Committee will no doubt have duties which fall under the
head of exchange, as the National Guild will have
duties belonging to production ; but the primary
function of the works will be to produce and not to
exchange its products. Exchange will be carried on
mainly through the District Committee where the
market is local, or through the National Executive
where it is national or international ; but production
will be carried on in the various works up and down
each district, and unless stagnation and a dead level
of mediocrity are to be the rule, the works must be
free to organise its own business of making things.

Here, then, is our reconciliation. Let each works
be in the first instance self-governing where production is concerned ; but let the organisation of exchange
be carried out by a national authority acting in co-
operation with local authorities. Does not this satisfy
both the demand for a national system in the interest
of the consumer, and the demand for freedom in the
workshop on the producer's behalf ?

Of course, the problem is not altogether so simple as
the solution would seem to suggest. There will have to
be some check on the works in the hands of the district
and, through it, of the national authority. But this
check will be provided most easily through the mechanism of exchange. The works will supply its products

to the District Committee for purposes of distribution, and the District Committee will pay it according to the price-lists fixed by the National Guild for what it produces, quality as well as quantity being, of course, taken into account in fixing the price. By this means, a check will be put upon any attempt by a works to do bad work or to 'scamp' its tasks. The preservation of a high standard of craftsmanship will be a function of the National and District authorities ; but the works will be self-governing, and intervention from without will come only by way of occasional criticism, and in answer to an existing grievance.

Thus, the differences between works and works will be secured ; and each body of workers will be free, until the total demand is exhausted, to specialise in the especial products which it most likes to produce. There will be no standardisation or centralisation of production ; indeed, the need for it will be removed by the standardisation and centralisation of exchange. The individual works will be a free and self-governing unit, and in the works the individual craftsman will find his freedom.

I am convinced that, if once we get clear in our minds the difference between production and exchange, we shall have seen the last of much loose thinking. As we saw earlier in this chapter (Section III) Capitalism is the invention, not of the producing, but of the trading, interest. We live to-day under the domination of the trader, who rules production as well as exchange. Once separate the control of these two, and the way is clear to the combination of a national industrial system with freedom for the producer. It remains to discuss the actual effect which the independence of the works will have upon the methods of production—how far, in fact, the Guild system will smash what Mr. Penty calls ' Industrialism.' To this question I shall turn next in the concluding section of this chapter.

IX

How far will the system of National Guilds smash Industrialism ?   Just as far, I believe, as Industrialism ought to be smashed, and no farther.   But if I am asked precisely how far that is, I can give no direct answer.

We are all familiar, in general, with the effect of Capitalism upon the skilled crafts.   We know that the progress of invention, instead of aiding the craftsman, tends, under modern conditions, to make him more and more the slave of the machine which he operates.   In the engineering industry, for instance, there is a continuous growth in the proportion of semi-skilled workers to skilled and unskilled alike.   If, on the one hand, the number of quite unskilled labourers diminishes, as they are taken on to work the simplified new machines, on the other hand the skilled men have continually to resist the encroachment of these newly recruited semi-skilled workers upon the old-established skilled crafts.   The number of real mechanics diminishes ; the number of machinists increases ; and, of the skilled crafts, only the toolmaker thrives because he ministers to these semi-skilled workers.   The employers use every moment of vantage to secure a foothold for the semi-skilled in the skilled occupations.   Thus, the shortage of mechanics due to the pressure of work for the war has led to an enormous increase in the employment of semi-skilled and unskilled workers, male and female, on skilled work.   Hence, too, the constant demarcation disputes which have prevented solidarity in the engineering industry.

It is from such bickerings that it will be the first mission of the Guilds to deliver modern industry. The self-governing fraternity of the Guild will determine for itself all questions of demarcation, and will have in mind not so much the cheapening of production, which is the sole thought of Capitalism, as the preservation of a high standard of workmanship coupled with reasonable efficiency and cheapness. The ' cheap and nasty ' product will be replaced by well-made goods, sold at a ' fair price,' and produced at a fair cost.

The change will mean not the smashing of large-scale production, but the placing of the workers' industrial destinies in their own hands. It will depend upon the feeling that animates the Guildsmen, as well as upon the material needs production has to meet, whether large-scale industry is to be destroyed or retained. If in any case large-scale production is then found to lead inevitably to the turning out of shoddy work, or to the brutalisation of the worker, then the Guild will see to it that such production shall cease, or be transformed. But the scrapping of machines, where it comes at all, will come not of a general movement against machinery, but in response to the definite discovery that this or that machine is degrading the industry to which it belongs. The method of destroying the bad machine will be experimental ; and this method will have the advantage that it will enable us both to preserve the good ones, and, in many cases, to transform those that are bad. Here, too, the process will be gradual and not catastrophic ; but it will be none the less revolutionary.

There are some who urge that modern Industrialism is altogether degrading, and that all attempts to reform it are doomed to failure. The fault of the reformers, on this showing, was that they come to believe in the very thing they set out to reform : their vision of the Socialist State becomes only the vision of a more democratic Industrialism. In short, they offer the workers self-government, perhaps ; but they do not offer them freedom.

I reply in essence that even if those who use this argument are right in their ideal, and right in wishing to inspire men with a faith in that ideal, revolutionaries have to consider not only ends, but also means. It is not enough to have ' news from nowhere,' unless we have also a true conception of ' the wage-system and the way out.' For, after all, we have not only to dream dreams—which we must do to keep our sanity —but also to bring about the revolution. We have to hew our statue out of the block of marble, and the material on which we have to work is the modern wage-slave.

My complaint against the mediævalist is that there are no stages to his revolution. It is a spiritual revolution, which it is hoped may be accompanied by a convulsion in the material world. I too desire a spiritual revolution ; but I do not believe that hearts are changed all of a sudden any more than institutions. Let us work for a change of heart, by all means ; but at the same time let us begin to alter our institutions. Above all, let us set out to develop *dans le sein du système capitaliste*, as a French writer has said, institutions capable of supplanting Capitalism.

I do not know, and I do not believe that any man can know, the part machinery will play in the coming society. We have so regularly used the machine to enslave man that we have no idea how it could be used to free him. A civilisation in which machines do the skilled work and men the dirty work cannot understand the potentialities of the opposite system. There will, we may hope, be always a growing number of machines to do the dirty work of the community. But, if machinery is to be put in its proper place, if it is to do only work that is both necessary and dirty or mechanical, the first need is that the craftsman should recover the control of his craft, that the Trade Union should once more concern itself with standards of production, and that the unskilled man and his machine should cease to ape the mechanic to the detriment of the quality of the product.

This question of machinery, however, is not the only question involved in the more general problem of Industrialism. We must ask ourselves also how far large-scale production will survive. The two questions are, no doubt, closely connected, since it was the coming of the machine that made large-scale production inevitable ; but they are not, for all that, the same. Large-scale industry might survive with much less machinery; or it might, as electric power, easily divisible and cheaply transmitted, continues to develop, disappear even as machinery increased.

Here again I want to lay stress on the difference between production and trading. The Guilds, we have seen, will preserve the large unit for trading purposes ; but, whatever happens to machinery, it is to be hoped that they will keep the small unit of actual production. Recent investigations of industrial phenomena, particularly Professor Chapman's studies of the Lancashire cotton industry, go to show that the size of the ' model ' business does not necessarily increase with the concentration of capital. That is to say, there is no need for the capitalist to increase his scale of production because he increases his scale of trade. Experience goes to show that the tendency in the past has even been to let the scale of production outrun the limits of economic efficiency, and that the capitalist, even from his own point of view, has let his factories get too big.

But, if a national system does not imply large-scale production, it will clearly rest with the Guilds to determine their own scale. Certain demands of efficiency they will have to satisfy ; but they will determine efficiency by quality as well as quantity. The scale on which they choose to produce will doubtless vary very greatly from industry to industry ; but there is reason to suppose that there will be a decrease rather than an increase on the scales now in vogue.

All this is not so far away as it may sound from the general question of freedom in the Guild ; for freedom will be secured only if the control of the individual over his own work can be made a reality. Make a man a voter among voters in a democratic community ; it is at least a half-truth that the measure of control he will have will vary inversely to the total number of votes. So, in the workshop, the control of the individual will be real in most cases only if the workshop is small, unless, as in a coal mine, only the simplest and most uniform questions have, as a rule, to be decided. Wherever at all a complex government is needed, the National Guild will need to be broken up into the smallest possible units, or else the individual will possess self-government without freedom. For self-government is only a means to freedom ; and freedom is self-government made effective.

Before, however, we can arrange what scale of production the Guilds are to adopt, we have to get the Guilds. ' Smashing Industrialism ' has a fine sound ; but from this point of view it does not help us. Only through the strengthening of Trade Unionism can we hope for a new industrial revolution which man shall govern as he was governed by the last ; only through such a revolution can the craftsman hope to get a chance to be a true craftsman once more. If, then, the eyes of Guildsmen seem too often turned on the ' wage-system and the way out,' or on safeguards and checks upon the power of producer or consumer, and too little on the craftsman's eternal problem of reconciling art and industry, none the less the craftsman must be lenient to us. He is now a voice crying in the wilderness ; we claim that if we had our way he would at least be able to cry in a more promising place. When Trade Unionism, alive and class-conscious, has given birth to the Guilds, we may hope that men, being at last their own masters, will have the strength and the leisure to understand William Morris. The Guild System will bring Morris into his own : under Collectivism, he would be remembered only as a quite unpractical Socialist who was so little ' in the swim ' that he refused to join the Fabian Society.[1]

[1] See p. 266.

CHAPTER VII

THERE is a school of Socialists which is forever talking glibly about the ' consumer.' These ' consumptive Collectivists ' urge that the Guild system fails to protect the consumer ; that, while Collectivism orders production in the interests of the whole, there would be nothing to prevent the Guild from raising prices at will and so exploiting Society in the interests of its own members. Against Syndicalism, at any rate in some of its forms, this criticism may be valid : but it has no application whatsoever to the Guild-Socialist idea.

In previous chapters, we have analysed the State and tried to make clear its economic function. We have seen that Collectivism would be, not production in the interests of the whole community, but production organised by and for the consumer. We have concluded, then, that the only way in which industry can be organised in the interests of the whole community is by a system in which the right of the producer to control production and that of the consumer to control consumption are recognised and established. This, we believe, would be accomplished by the balance of powers and functions which is the fundamental idea of National Guilds.

This, however, does not satisfy the critics, and I must therefore reason with them in more detail with a view to answering a few of their more frequent criticisms.

To every exchange there are two parties, and in every indirect exchange under a monetary system, the two stand in the relation of producer and consumer, or buyer and seller. Our problem is that of securing a fair exchange between these two, under whatever system our Society may be organised. Under Capitalism, we hear complaints from the capitalist producer of the tyranny of the middleman and the consumer, of the severity of foreign competition, and generally, of the impossibility of securing a fair price for what he has made ; while from the consumer we hear that rings and combines are forcing up prices, that profiteering is going on, and that the producer and the middleman, who stands in a double relation and is the scapegoat of both parties, are guilty of exploitation.

The same question arises when we begin to discuss our dreams of a future Society. The working-class producer fears that under Collectivism the wage-system will continue, and he will be exploited by the consumer and perhaps the *rentier*, instead of by the capitalist profiteer : the consumer fear that if the producer is given any real control over industry, he will use it to exploit the consumer as rings and combines use their control to-day. To these fears, from whichever side they come, National Guildsmen must have a ready answer.

We may here assume that, if control over production is to be restored to the workers, the Guild will have, by one means or another, to dispose by sale of its products. Short of pure Communism, we shall have

buying and selling : and, whether the Guilds are
retailers or not, they will in any case have to
be wholesalers, dealing with other Guilds, with Co-
operative Societies or Municipalities, and with the
State.

This, say our ' consumptive ' critics, is highly dangerous. It is admitted that the Guilds will possess a
monopoly of Labour, each in its own industry ; and
we all know that the effect of monopoly is to raise
prices or keep them up artificially in nine cases out
of ten. What, then, is to prevent a blackleg-proof,
monopolistic Guild from raising prices at the expense
of the public ?

The answer is to be found in the method of taxation
to be adopted under National Guilds. Because one
industry is more productive than another, because the
exchange-value of its product per head is higher than
that of its neighbour, it will not be allowed to absorb
the surplus, any more than the urban landowner ought
to absorb the surplus value of urban land. But,
our critics inquire, is not this precisely what will
happen under the Guild system, whether we like it
or not ?

The answer is in the negative. They have forgotten
the ' substitute for economic rent ' which the State is
to receive from the Guilds in return for the use of the
industrial plant. Each Guild will pay to the State an
annual quasi-rent corresponding in some measure to the
' rent ' of to-day. Each year, the State will estimate
its total expenditure, as it does now. But, instead of
raising its revenue by means of a number of cumbrous
and costly taxes which are for the most part unjust
in their incidence and often easily evaded or passed
on to others, it will demand a lump sum from the Guild

Congress, upon which, and upon the various Guilds, the business of collection will fall.

The total sum required being known, there will remain the task of dividing it equitably among the tax payers. To each Guild must be assigned its quota, and the heaviest burdens must be laid upon the broadest backs. This assigning of proportionate burdens may be carried out either by the Guild Congress or, more probably, by a body representing equally the Guild Congress and the State. Each Guild, then, will be expected to contribute its share to the national exchequer.

Clearly, in apportioning burdens, the competent authority will take into account the productivity of each industry. Just as, in the Census of Production nowadays, the net product per worker employed is calculated for each industry, productivity will be capable of estimation under the Guild system. But as productivities can only be compared in terms of a common standard of value, the product, being expressed in pounds, shillings and pence, obviously depends upon the price. If more is charged for the finished commodity, then, *ceteris paribus*, the net product, in terms of exchange value, will appear as higher.

It is clear, therefore, that, since ' economic quasi-rent ' will be calculated on a basis of productivity, and since the product depends upon the price, price and ' economic quasi-rent ' must stand in a fixed relation.

Even then, if each individual Guild were left to fix prices at its good pleasure, the consumer would run no risk of exploitation by a ' profiteering ' Guild. Any Guild which increased prices would thereby increase the measure of its own productivity, and, consequently, would have to pay a higher rent to the

State.   The State would thus receive in revenue what
the consumer paid as enhanced price.

But, though it must be evident that, under such a
system, no Guild would seek to force up prices, that is
not to say that prices would be best fixed in all cases
by the individual Guilds.   If they were so fixed, there
would certainly be an approximation of prices to what
we may call ' natural values.'   The price of each
commodity would tend, far more than nowadays, to
be determined by the cost of raw material plus the
income of the Guildsman reckoned on a basis approxi-
mating more or less nearly to a common time-standard
of value.   So far from being exploited, the community
would most often find itself paying, for every article
or service, very roughly what it was, economically
speaking, really worth.   Under a system in which remuneration tended to equality this would involve no
great hardship.   If, therefore, the control of prices is
not to be left solely to each individual Guild, this is
not because such a method involves any risk of exploitation to the consumer.   The State and the Guild
Congress could always counter any tendency to
advance prices unduly by an adjustment of the Guild
rent.

What is by no means clear is that the ' natural
economic ' price of which I have spoken is in all cases
the best price.   Indeed, we continually recognise, alike
in theory and in practice, that it is undesirable that
prices should in all cases be thus mechanically settled.
Socialists have always maintained that it is desirable
that many services should be rendered free, and Mr.
Shaw has even made the ' communisation ' or free
distribution of bread a plank in his platform.   And if
it is expedient to give some services and commodities

free, may it not also be good to cheapen others ? We may well have, under Guild-Socialism, free transit, free bread, free milk, etc., as well as free education and perhaps a free Public Health Service. We may also have cheap theatres, libraries, and so on. We need not commit ourselves to the particular instances : it is enough to say that Society will probably give free all things which most men need in fairly equal measure, and cheap those things which it wishes, for one reason or another, to see more widely used.

Is it not evident, therefore, that ' rent ' or prices will be fixed by the same authority ? A joint Congress, equally representative of the State, or the consumers, and the Guild Congress, or the producers, is the body suggested for this office. The matter is clearly one which affects producers and consumers alike ; equally clearly, in assuming a share of control in this sphere, the State will not be interfering with the autonomy of the industrial republic. The producer will remain in command of the productive process : the consumer will share with him the control of the price charged for the product. It is in this sphere, and not in a divided control in the workshop itself, that the interests of producers and consumers can be reconciled. The control of industry does not involve unchecked control of prices ; even apart from any question of exploitation, which, as we have seen, does not arise in any case under the Guild system, the determination of prices is a ' social function.' It is no less foolish to allow prices to be fixed by a competitive standard than to allow remuneration to be so fixed. Both alike should be decided by the organised will of the community, irrespective of the economic standards of ' competition ' or ' supply and demand.'

If, then, Collectivists will consider a little more carefully and with rather more honesty of purpose than in the past, they will cease from trying to scotch the Guild idea with the weapons of the economist. For National Guilds is, in one of its aspects, an assertion of the right of the community to defy old-fashioned economic conventions.

There are two points arising out of this argument on which it is necessary to dwell further. In the first place, let me say that I do not for a moment suppose that precisely the system I have outlined above will ever come into force. Nor, for that matter, do I imagine that we shall ever have National Guilds exactly as we forecast them. I am not so foolish as to be ignorant that history does not work in that way. We formulate and define our ideas not in the hope of realising them completely in the domain of practice, but because only ideas that are clearly formulated and defined really help in the building of a better world. I go into more detail than otherwise I should, because only by going into detail can I answer the points of detail which critics bring up against me. Even if the system of taxation I have outlined never comes into existence, my argument none the less holds ; for I have explained a method (not necessarily the only method) which secures the consumer absolutely against exploitation by a ' profiteering ' Guild. I have, then, proved that there is nothing to justify the criticism that the Guild system would lead to profiteering. In fact, I think I have shown more than that : the system of National Guilds provides the best possible safeguard against exploitation, either of consumer by producer, or of producer by consumer.

The second point is also important. There are some

persons who, some pages back, will have held up their hands in holy horror and cried " What ! buying and selling under National Guilds ! " To them I reply, " Yes, my friends ; buying and selling under National Guilds. Why not ? "

To some people, the mere buying and selling of things at once suggests Capitalism, or, as they would say, " production for profit and not for use." In fact, the two have no necessary connection. Buying and selling existed long before Capitalism, and before them existed barter, which differs only in complexity and convenience. Buying and selling will go on long after Capitalism has passed away ; but they will be buying and selling not for profit but for use.

The amount of goods and services in the community is, and will continue under National Guilds to be, limited. Nor is this limitation only of the total supply of such goods and services : it is also of the particular supplies of particular goods and services. Of some goods and services we can produce as much as we want, but we can do this only if we produce less of others. Of other goods and services the supply is limited by nature. Salmon is scarcer than cod, and gold than coal. Even, therefore, if there were enough commodities and services in the aggregate to give every member of the community as much as he wanted, there would not be enough of each particular commodity or service. For most men prefer salmon to cod.

This is why, under a democratic system, buying and selling are still necessary and desirable. It is good that every man should have the fullest possible control of the expenditure of his own income, after necessary communal services have been provided for. This he can only have if he can choose to what use he will put that income—*i.e.* what he will buy with it. Sure of getting his commodities and services at a just price, he is in the best possible position to expend his income according to his taste and individuality. One man will choose to spend his surplus on theatres, another on books : some no doubt, under any system, on things less desirable in themselves. But if men are to have freedom at all, they must have freedom to spend, and this involves buying and selling. Indeed, the only practical alternative would be a compulsory rationing system, and for this surely no social idealist will pine.

I come now to a quite different argument with which opponents of National Guilds make great play. This point is that any system under which industry is controlled by the producers will tend to industrial stagnation. This argument used to be an especial favourite with that unregenerate Collectivist, Sir Leo Chiozza Money ;[1] and I shall be able to answer it most easily if I take certain articles of his as my text. His longest and most detailed statement of his view appeared in the *New Statesman* of March 14th, 1914. His article, which was entitled " Delimitation and Transmutation of Industries," attacked the Guild system on the ground that it would not leave the labour power of the community sufficiently mobile, and that it would tend to stereotype the forms and methods of production in an age which demands rapid and continual change. This article in the *New Statesman* would seem to be an amplification of some remarks he made on my book, *The World of Labour*, in the *British Weekly* of February 19th, 1914. As he there stated his position more briefly, I will begin by quoting a sentence from his earlier article.

[1] See p. 268.

" It seems to me that the Syndicalist conception takes too little account of the swift development and change of trades and industries which is likely to be one of the distinguishing features of this our new century. It hardly seems to provide for the ever accelerating transmutation of occupations, and it presents the very real danger of stereotyping industrial development and of setting up as States within the State gigantic vested interests in a form very difficult to remould."

There are clearly in this indictment several distinct points, which I will discuss in turn. If in my answer I seem at some points to go beyond the terms of Sir Leo Money's criticism, it will be in the endeavour to answer in advance certain supplementary points which readily arise out of it.

It is easiest to begin with a comparatively small point, which may, or may not, have been in the critic's mind when he wrote. What, I am often asked, will be the effect of the Guild system on initiative and invention within any given trade ? How, that is to say, will it influence change in the workshop itself ? Will it make the workers better or worse at inventing new processes, and more or less ready to accept such as may have been invented ? Trade Unions, we are told, have opposed at every stage the introduction of new machinery, no matter how ' good for trade ' its advent might be. Will not the Trade Unions or Guilds of the future show a like disregard for economic advance ?

This whole argument, I believe, rests on a misconception. Trade Unions have resisted new machinery —the linotype, for instance—not because it is new, or because of any rooted objection to newness as such, but merely because a new process nearly always tends, for the moment, to throw men out of employment or to reduce rates of wages, or both. To men without economic resource, the moment is everything ; they cannot afford to take long views. Where the workers oppose new machinery, they do so simply and solely because they are faced with the prospect of starvation if the new labour-saving device is adopted. Anyone who has studied the history of the Industrial Revolution in Great Britain, and the effects on the hand-loom weavers of the introduction of textile machinery, will have realised that the workers became Luddites not by choice, but from hard necessity.[1]

Most dislocations of employment caused by new machines being temporary and the reduction of standard rates being an effect of the wage-system which would vanish with it, there would be no such opposition on the part of the Guild. For the Guildsman, the new machine would be, not an inanimate competitor for the rights of wage-slavery, but an aid to the lightening of the daily task. Machinery would no longer be dreaded as the enemy of man ; it would be welcomed as his servant and his helper. Each Guild would have its inventive departments, as increasingly great factories are now coming to have them ; and these departments would aim at making production as efficient and the lot of the worker as easy as might be.

However, this question of change within a trade was, at any rare, not uppermost in our critic's mind. The ' transmutation ' of which he was thinking is the transmutation of the industries themselves, the growth of one and the decline of another, the extinction of one and the uprising of a new one in its place. It is in this connection that he complains that the Guild system would

[1]See p. 269.

' stereotype ' production. He assumes throughout an absolute rigidity in the Guild groupings : he speaks of " a State consisting of a number of large and small delimited groups or guilds of labour, each concerned with a separate department of work." This may be Sir Leo Money's conception of National Guilds ; it is certainly not my conception, though he seems to assume that all who advocate the control of industry by the producers must accept it. He offers no reason for this attitude ; he merely assumes that the Guild will be a close corporation of workers, apparently absolutely incapable of being shifted to another occupation. This is surely to isolate Guild from Guild in a wholly unwarrantable manner. If the Guild system grows out of the present structure of Trade Unionism, it will come, not by a sharp separation of Union from Union, but by their close co-operation and coherence. There will be easy transference from Guild to Guild, and even considerable fluidity in the structure of the Guilds themselves, as there was in Florence in the Middle Ages. While, then, each Guild will be charged with the maintenance of such reserve of labour as it may require, there will certainly be in all cases a considerable passage of men from trade to trade, as the demand of the moment dictates. I fail to see what difficulty there is in combining this system of easy transfer with effective control of industry by the producers. Sir Leo Money seems to confuse the Guild system with the ideal of the Universal self-governing workshop of Co-operative Production, which is, indeed, open to the objection he suggests.

Let us take his chosen example, which gives his case at its strongest :—

" If we erect and exaggerate and magnify the Trade

Union into a definite branch of nationhood, what is to become of the Trade Union when Science sweeps away the very foundations of its work ?   If, for example, we erect and exalt and magnify Coal into a self-governing body, a very State within the State, what will become of Coal when Science makes it obsolete, as it may easily do within fifty years from this time ? "

I wholly fail to see in what way the problem is more difficult for the Guildsman than for anybody else.   It seems to me, at any rate, much easier than it is for the pure Syndicalist.   If Coal goes, it goes ; and the Miners have to be transferred to other occupations. Even a State-Socialist like Mr. Money would find this no easy matter ; but I do not see that it is any harder for the Guildsman than for him.   The problem is, in any case, not quite so bad as he makes it sound.   If Coal ceases to be used, the change will not happen all of a sudden, without warning or breathing space.   Its extinction will be foreseen some time at least in advance, and the demand will decline gradually, and not cease all of a sudden.   In face of a falling demand, what does Sir Leo Money suppose the Miners' Guild will do ? Does he think that it will go on producing as much coal as ever, and accumulate at the pit-head stores which no one is ever likely to use ?   Or does he think the Miners will all work short time, as is done in some trades now, sharing out what work there is and what income results from it ?   Or does he believe that those who remain usefully at work will go on paying their fellows to stay idle for an indefinite period ?   These are the three foolish courses that are open to them. But under any Guild system the result of all these courses would be that there would be less to divide among an equal number of persons.   This being so, the Guild might be trusted to see to the clearance of its surplus members, as soon as a new occupation could be found for them. Those of least standing in the Guild would probably, in such a case, have to retire, and these men could be supported by the Guild, or by the whole body of the Guilds in case of need, till a new occupation was found for them. It would only be possible for the Guild to maintain an industry which had ceased to be economically necessary *if the Guild controlled demand* ; and Mr. Money advances not a shadow of reason for supposing that any producers' organisation can control demand, or force its wares upon the reluctant consumer. In short, transference from one industry to another would happen under National Guilds much as it would happen under Sir Leo Money's own State-Socialism, and with far greater ease and convenience to the worker than in the Society of to-day.

" This," says Mr. Money, " is a large-scale example, but many more only too probable cases, of many degrees of magnitude, could be produced." I wonder what his other cases would be : I can think of few that are in any sense parallel. There is a sense in which new industries are always coming into existence—motor cars are one instance, and aeroplanes another ; but neither of these, nor most new ' industries,' would demand the creation of a new Guild. The making of motor-cars would be the work of one section of the Engineering Guild, and the invention of aeroplanes would merely make a new section necessary. It would involve no dislocation, no starting of a new and separate enterprise. The invention and manufacture of the new product would in most cases only call for the creation of a new section within one of the existing Guilds.

So far from being static and stereotyped, the great organisations would be the most flexible instruments of production. Neither the analogy of the mediæval Guild nor that of the modern Trade Union holds in this respect. The mediæval Guilds were in many respects conservative, not because they were Guilds, but because they were mediæval : the whole Society in which they existed was static, traditional, if you like, ' unprogressive ' ; it attained to a marvellous skill in craftsmanship, and it possessed a great tradition of ' good work ' which we may hope that the Guild of the future will emulate ; but its conservatism was due not to its organisation, but to its environment. The modern Trade Union has often been against new methods, not because it is a Trade Union, but because it consists of wage-slaves. Its tradition of solidarity will be carried on into the new Guilds ; but ca' canny, sabotage and conservatism are the products of the wage-system, and with it they will die.

Sir Leo Money sums up his assault on the Guilds in the following passage :—

" The various groups or guilds would inevitably consider themselves possessed of monopoly privileges. They would seek to perpetuate their functions, whether they were useful or not. They would seek to induct their children into their kind of employment, whether it was obsolete or not. The very nature of their organisation would cause them to view with suspicion any proper attempt to alter their very definite character and dimensions to the better advantage of the nation as a whole."

It may be doubted whether our critic understands at all clearly ' the very nature of their organisation.' The great Guilds could not do these things if they wished to do them ; and there is no reason that he can show why they should wish to do them. If the mediæval Guilds were conservative in a conservative age, may we not expect the new Guilds to be progressive in a ' scientific ' age ? They will be monopolists, no doubt, whether *de facto* or *de jure* ; but he has not made clear his objection to monopoly. Is not State-Socialism itself a system of monopolies, and have not Guild Socialists clearly laid down the methods by which the State will be enabled to prevent the Guilds from abusing their monopoly privileges ? Is there not in the vocabulary of National Guilds such a term as ' economic rent,' in the sense of rent paid to the State by the Guild for the use of the means of production ? And is it not a good thing that, where temperament is the same and situations are open, son should follow father in the same vocation ?

" But," says Sir Leo Money, having disposed finally of the Guild bogey, " perhaps we are getting a little too fearful of State control. . . . If we are afraid of ' officials,' then let us remember that a Guild or a Trade Union must have officials. If we fear tyrants, then let us remember that the only difference between a little tyrant and a big one is that the former is usually the worse example of tyranny. The essential thing is that men should be so trained from their youth as to resist injustice, to obey reasonable direction, and to submit to common rules of conduct. *That secure, we need not worry about the good government of a State Department, for a worthy people will secure the government they deserve."* (Italics mine.)

These words were written by Lieut. Commander (am I right ?) Sir Leo Money before the war : perhaps it is no longer necessary to answer them. I will only say that they miss the point with a vengeance. National Guildsmen aim at something better than good, in the sense of efficient, government : they stand for self-government. The difference between a Guild and a State Department, however efficient, is just this : the second is government from above and from without ; the first is government from below and from within, self-government. National Guildsmen happen, in fact, to be democrats, and to carry their democracy into the sphere of industry. In this they differ from Liberal (am I still right ?) Collectivists of the type of Sir Leo Money. The system of National Guilds stands for an efficient and self-governing industry ; but the emphasis is, and ought to be, on the second adjective. Our critic is an apostle of efficiency ; but all who seek efficiency alone are doomed to lose it, for the simple reason that workmen, like other people, happen to be men. It is better to choose one's own tyrant than to live under the rule of a benevolent bureaucrat—if indeed bureaucrats are ever even benevolent.

This, however, takes us rather far from our immediate purpose. No one will disagree with the view that, under modern industrial conditions, Labour must be mobile. It is only a little difficult to understand why Collectivists so often regard this assertion as a crushing refutation of National Guilds, which are expressly designed to meet this, among other, objects. Free man is man adventurous, mobile and progressive : it is the man in chains who is conservative, timid and stationary.

The Collectivist is not the only advocate of the control of industry by the consumers with whom National Guildsmen have to reckon. The Co-operator has also a very real claim to be heard as a spokesman on the consumer's behalf. When I speak in this connection of the Co-operator, I am of course speaking not of the Co-operative Societies of Producers, or self-governing Workshops, and still less of Capitalist Co-partnership, sometimes called Labour Co-partnership, but of the great Co-operative movement—of the Stores and the Wholesale Societies. These great trading concerns, with their enormous turn-over and their dividends as a substitute for profits, are the most monumental examples of control by the consumers.

Clearly, if our general position holds, the arguments we have employed against State conduct of industry apply also against its conduct by Co-operative Societies of consumers. The idea of National Guilds and the idea of Consumer's Co-operation are in the last resort incompatible if they are put forward as complete theories of social organisation. While Trade Unionism adhered to its old reformist attitude, while it stood for no more than the maintenance and improvement of its members' position within the wage-system, there was no clash of ideals and no possibility of conflict. But as soon as Trade Unionism embraces a wider ideal, and sets out to secure the control of industry, the conflict of ideals becomes apparent.

In either case, there is of course scope for both disputes and mutual assistance. On the one hand, disputes must arise concerning the conditions of Co-operative employees, especially as many of the democratic Co-operative Societies bear out what we have said of the consumer by paying low wages, giving bad conditions, and even discouraging Trade Unionism. On the other hand, Co-operation can give, and has given on such occasions as the coal strike of 1912 and the Dublin strike of 1913, valuable help to Trade Unions in their disputes with other employers—help which the Unions can repay, and do in some cases repay, by the investment of their funds and by acting as centres of Co-operative propaganda.

When the conflict of ideals arises, two main points for discussion emerge. The Co-operative Stores are in the main distributive agencies, buyers and sellers, and not to any great extent producers. The Wholesale Societies, on the other hand, have their big productive departments, though they still serve as distributing centres for far greater quantities of capitalist products than of their own. The investment of Capital in the Wholesale Societies mainly serves to stimulate Co-operative Production—that is, a form of the control of industry by the consumers.

We must keep distinct the two separate problems— distribution controlled by the consumers, and production controlled by the consumers.

Clearly, if the Guilds supplant Capitalism, they will supplant Co-operative Production as well. The attitude, then, of productive workers employed by Co-operative bodies will not differ materially from the attitude of those employed by the State or by private employers. In any case, the goal is the same, and the way to it is by the strengthening of Trade Unionism and the securing for it of an ever-increasing share in the control of industry. The struggle for industrial freedom will, we may hope, be less bitter in this sphere than elsewhere ; but the normal attitude of the Co-operative movement to-day in dealing with its employees gives no great ground for the belief that it will be altogether peaceful.

The conflict of principle between National Guilds and consumers' Co-operation does not appear in so acute a form in the sphere of Co-operative Distribution.

It is, however, present. Distribution is clearly a Guild function, and the distributive worker has a claim to industrial freedom no less valid than that of the productive worker. But it is none the less evident that of all the Guilds the Distributive Guild would have the closest and most constant relation to the consumer, and it seems probable that in it the consumer would continue to occupy a certain place in the direct management at any rate of the local Store. If this is so, may not the Co-operative movement on its distributive side, including the Wholesale Societies, actually form the nucleus of the Distributive Guild, however different their conception of industrial control may be to-day?

A last point, and I have done. There was a time when the aristocratic sceptic would sit over his wine and say, " The vulgar herd must have a religion." Is there not a danger that in our day the plutocratic sceptic will sit over his money bags and say, " The people must have a philosophy "? For in these days popular philosophy is taking the place of popular religion as the best friend of the governing class. Political evolutionism, the degradation of the General Will into the theory of the common servitude of men to an omnipotent and impersonal State, the facile identification of the State with the nation, of the consumer with the community—these are the legacies of nineteenth-century philosophy, and from them Collectivism derives much of its strength. Machine-made education, the inculcation of a passive patriotism into the child, the brain softening apostrophes of a subsidised Press—all these minister to our rulers' ideal of active citizenship for themselves and passive citizenship for the people.

The idea of National Guilds is the quickening spirit of the century, not because it puts forward new suggestions with regard to the organisation of industry, nor even because it insists on the right of the producer to control his own life, but above all because it is a new philosophy—a philosophy of active citizenship for every man and woman in the community.

The opposite ideal of servility finds expression, not only in the theoretical doctrines of those who hold it, but also in their immediate economic policy. After the war, they tell us, must come an economic war no less bitter, in which the industrial strength of the Allies will be pitted against that of the Central Powers.[1] In the name of this economic war men are preaching the re-organisation of our industrial system upon the lines of German efficiency. It is said, and truly said, that our pre-war system involved prodigious waste and disorganisation. All this is to be changed if only we will imitate the thoroughness of Prussia : all will be well if only we will become that which we set out to crush.

This book is a protest against that ideal. It is a personal appeal to all who still hold dear the ideal of personal freedom, and watch with mistrust the growing domination of Prussian ideas in this country. It is addressed to all who believe that ' efficiency ' is not really the outcome of the suppression of freedom, but finds its fullest realisation in a community based on personal initiative, on the free will and design of its members. The efficiency of the British Prussians is machine-made and unreal ; true efficiency must spring from the native genius of the people themselves.

We must have, then, in our minds an ideal of social and personal freedom which is both consistent with

[1] See p. 269.

our national traditions and in itself a guarantee of national well-being. We must believe that the first need in a community is not that the community should be ' great,' as greatness is now conceived, but that the citizens should be free to order and control their own life and work. No system of government which ignores or falls short of this ideal can we accept as good ; for freedom is the Alpha and the Omega of our social gospel. Freedom for the producer as well as the consumer, for the consumer as well as the producer : above all, freedom for the creative impulse in all of us, for the impulse of free and unfettered service.

> Ours is the host that bears the word,
> NO MASTER HIGH OR LOW—
> A lightning flame, a shearing sword,
> A storm to overthrow.

I end this book with a verse from Morris, because to me Morris seems the greatest of the democratic writers. He believes in the people ; and the abounding joy he found in the good things of life he desired passionately that all the world should share.

APPENDIX A

The Genesis of Syndicalism in France

I

In the campaign of wanton misrepresentation and wilful misunderstanding of which the mass of doctrines connected with the name of Syndicalism has, during the last few years, been the centre, one of the chief methods of discrediting the new idea has been that of rewriting, out of some convenient text-book, the history of the French Labour movement, asserting repeatedly the failure of that movement, and calling the result an adequate criticism of Syndicalism. Other critics, innocent of even a text-book acquaintance with French Trade Unionism, are quite prepared, on the authority of a few penny pamphlets and the leading articles of the capitalist and the official Labour press, to pass final judgment on the whole theory of Syndicalism as a prospect upon the future society. Both these methods are obviously inadequate : Syndicalism must be viewed both in the light of its historical development, and as a more or less finished vision of an ideal community. It is equally absurd to treat doctrines as if they had no history, and to confuse origin with validity. Yet I think every one of the English critics of Syndicalism, from Mr. Ramsay MacDonald to Mr. Graham Wallas,[1] has fallen into one or other of these errors. I expect *The New Age*,[2] which long ago, in a brilliant but all too brief article, set in the clearest light the real meaning and value of the Syndicalist idea. *The New Age*, however, has not developed its view on the historical side, and in this appendix I propose to attempt that long-neglected task.

[1] See p. 270.   [2] See p. 271.

233

Up to a point, there was right on the side of those critics who attempted to pass judgment on Syndicalism in the light of the history of Labour in France. For this country, I believe that any view which bases its treatment solely on French Syndicalism, to the omission of its American form, is bound to be one-sided and inadequate. But since Syndicalism is essentially a product of the French genius, since it began merely as the name of the policy adopted by Trade Unionism in France, an understanding of French history is essential to a true appreciation of it. This, however, implies a very different treatment from that which the critics have adopted. Proceeding, for the most part, from a mere ' text-book ' acquaintance with the subject, their treatment of the French movement fatally isolates the development of the Trade Unions from the general history of the country. They seem to imagine that it is possible to understand and to explain the economic movements of the working-class wholly without reference to the course of the national life or to the changes of the political environment. Or rather, they imagine nothing : they know that ' Le Syndicalisme ' is the French for Trade Unionism, and, without further thought, they take the easy path that leads to destruction. It is so much simpler to translate a few easily accessible facts from the French than to attempt the understanding and interpretation of a great national movement.

But, if once we bring ourselves to see the French Labour movement in its true perspective, as an integral part in the evolution of the national life, acting upon the national temperament, but also in turn acted upon by the chances and changes of the forces encircling it, the whole development of Syndicalism appears in a new light. Then—and then alone—are we able to sift the wheat from the chaff, to realise what is truly central and vital in its theory and practice, and to explain the origin of those unessential elements which most critics have taken for fundamental doctrines.

The name ' Le Syndicalisme,' or ' Le Syndicalisme Révolutionnaire,' acquired its present connotation between

1902 and 1906,during the first period of the C.G.T.'s activity. ' Le Syndicalisme,' which meant originally merely ' Union- ism,' whether of masters or men, came to be applied to the new revolutionary force which then for the first time struck the public imagination. ' Syndicalism,' then, as a definite and identifiable theory, is about fifteen years old. When we remember how vague the meaning of Socialism for a long time remained, we need not be surprised if so young a theory is not furnished with a complete answer to every question that may be asked by wise man, fool, or knave. But like Socialism, and far more definitely, Syndicalism is older than its name. It was rooted firmly in the Labour movement, and had developed most of its distinctive doctrines, long before the Press and the public began to be agitated about its ' menace.' It is to the active and troubled life of the Federation of Bourses du Travail and to the work of their secretary and inspirer, Fernand Pelloutier, that we should look in great part for the explanation of Syndicalist origins. This much is realised even by English critics ; but they have one and all failed lamentably to make plain what were the forces at work behind the Bourses du Travail, and why the French movement took a direction so contrary to that of our own Trade Unions or to that of the German Gewerkschaften.

The history of France in the nineteenth century is, of course, punctuated by a series of political revolutions. To whatever deeper causes these may be traced, they have, in their own causal action, profoundly modified the history of the Labour movement. With every political revolution, in 1830, in 1848, and again with the Commune of 1871, comes a sharp break in the history of Labour organisation. Industrial causes alone would have made Trade Unionism in France a later and a weaker growth than in England, which, during the industrial revolution and again in the Napoleonic wars, obtained the lead over the rest of Europe in commerce and industry ; but since to these causes France added the solvent force of political revolution, industrial organisation could not be expected to develop either rapidly or securely. The Reform Bill agitation, Chartism and Owenism barely ruffled the surface of Great Britain ; France, at least in the industrial districts, was profoundly stirred by an undying revolutionary enthusiasm, and this enthusiasm flowed naturally into the channels of political activity, and neglected industrial organisation. Scattered industry remained a prevailing type in France, and no effort was made to organise the workers in such industries : where the town workers combined, they remained isolated in small local societies, proscribed by law and liable to instant suppression. The presence of political revolution as an everyday possibility, therefore, in itself prevented the growth of strong Trade Unions. Moreover, reaction invariably followed revolution; and every revolution was made the pretext for a ruthless destruction of working-class organisations. Trade Unionism smouldered in darkness, and was snuffed out as soon as the political unrest fanned it into flame. After every revolution, the workers lost many of their leaders, and the hopeless process of industrial organisation had to begin anew, only to perish again in the next conflagration.

It was undoubtedly due to the weakness of the Trade Union impulse in such an environment that the ban upon all forms of association within the State, imposed by the triumphant bourgeoisie in 1791, was not removed from the Unions until 1884. They were indeed tolerated by Napoleon III, as a matter of policy, from about 1864 ; and, after the period of repression which, throughout France, succeeded the collapse of the Paris Commune, there followed a second period of toleration. But it was only in 1884 that the right of combination was formally granted to the workers, and a good deal of the restrictive legislation abolished. Even so, the Act which Waldeck-Rousseau succeeded in getting carried was in many respects unsatisfactory : it failed notably to establish the right of picketing in any effective form, and it is certain that much of the ill-directed violence that has characterised French trade disputes has been due to the impossibility of maintaining efficient picketing by peaceful means. From this cause spring many forms of sabotage, the *chasse aux renards*, etc.

All the same, the legislation of 1884 did mark a great advance, and Waldeck-Rousseau's theories, though they were vitiated by a false idea of social peace and readjustment, were in some respects far in advance of his time. He does seem to have looked forward to a partnership of some sort between the State and the Unions, and to a development of Trade Union control of industry—ideas which, in a reformist spirit, have been considerably developed by some of his followers, notably by M. Paul-Boncour in his two brilliant books, *Le Fédéralisme Economique* and *Les Syndicats de Fonctionnaires*. The first Ministry of Waldeck-Rousseau achieved for Trade Unionism at least the right of free development. His constructive ideas were not equally fruitful. A clause was inserted in the Act compelling all Unions to register under the State, and to give the names of their responsible officials. The workers, with the memory of their long oppression still fresh, naturally regarded such a clause not as a first step towards fuller recognition by the State, but as an attempt to continue a repressive policy. Waldeck-Rousseau's very idealism did much to ruin his plans : he estranged the Unions by trying to bring them too closely into touch with the State before the State was fit to consort with them. His premature suggestions of social peace with partnership merely estranged the Trade Unions and paved the way for an anti-political propaganda.

The first result, however, was to fling the Unions into the arms of the political Socialists. A national Federation of Trade Unions arose out of a conference of protest against the Act of 1884, and this fell almost at once into the hands of M. Jules Guesde and the Marxians. The one idea of Guesde and his friends was the ' conquest of political power ' by the creation of a strong Socialist Party in Parliament. Trade Unionism they regarded as either a useless side-tracking of the workers' efforts, or as a useful method of electioneering. They did their best to turn the Unions into purely political bodies, aiming at the political revolution by peaceful means, which, they held, alone could emancipate the workers. Naturally, a Trade Union organisation, conducted on such lines as a mere adjunct to the *Parti Ouvrier Français*, made little progress. If political action was the only method, clearly Trade Unionism ought not to exist : to create an organisation nominally for one purpose and then use it solely for another is not the right way to build up a strong and self-reliant movement.

There was, however, another reason why at that stage of French political and industrial development it was impossible to create a strong ' National Federation of Trade Unions.' In nearly every case, the Trade Union was a purely local body, including only the workers in a particular trade within a particular district. This localisation was due partly to the local character of French industry, but far more to the circumstances in which the Unions had arisen. Liable to instant suppression, unable to organise save in secret, continually coming into and going out of existence, the Unions had been quite impotent to pass the boundaries of their own localities, or to link up into any national bodies. The local ' Syndicats ' remained helpless and isolated in the midst of a hostile civilisation.

In 1887 a project long mooted by reformers of all schools at last bore fruit in the foundation of the Paris Bourse du Travail, or Chamber of Labour, designed to serve for Labour the purposes a Chamber of Commerce serves for Capital. It was to be a Labour Exchange, a centre for the Trade Union bodies of the district, and a sort of workmen's club. At Paris, the Bourse soon became a centre of revolutionary activity, and there was trouble with the municipal authorities, who had subsidised, and been responsible for starting, it. But the example of Paris was soon imitated, and Bourses began to spring up in many of the large towns. To the surprise and chagrin of the municipalities, the Bourses instead of peaceably serving the interests of Capital, invariably developed revolutionary characteristics, and in most cases became the centres of the first effective Trade Union movement France had ever seen. In 1893 the Federation of Bourses du Travail was formed, and in 1894 this absorbed the National Federation of Trade Unions.

These facts are gravely retailed to the public by most writers on Syndicalism, but the attempt is hardly ever made to explain why the Bourses succeeded where the National Federation had failed, or to show how the Bourses have left their mark indelibly on the whole history of the Labour movement in France. Yet this is the whole point. It was out of the Bourses du Travail that Syndicalism, as a distinctive mass of doctrines, arose and developed. The National Federation attempted the impossible task of linking up a number of isolated local Unions into a general organisation, without any intermediate step. Such an attempt could not succeed : a national organisation must be based either on a number of strong national Trade Unions, or on a number of strong local Trade Councils, or on both. There is no fourth course.

The French conditions at the time made local very much easier than national organisation, and the foundation of a number of Bourses du Travail came precisely at the opportune moment. At this stage, there entered actively into the Labour movement a man who saw how something could be made out of the existing chaos rapidly and effectively, if only the occasion were seized. Fernand Pelloutier, the Anarchist and idealist, who became secretary and inspiring genius of the Federation of Bourses du Travail, saw at once how history could be made—and proceeded to make it. In his hands the number of Bourses grew from 34 in 1894 to 96 in 1902, and, of these, 83 were in the Federation. During this period of growth and prosperity, the doctrines of Syndicalism were developed, in the Congresses of the Federation and in the local Bourses, under the guidance and inspiration of Pelloutier. It is therefore essential to know something of his views.

Those critics who say that Syndicalism is merely a new name for Anarchism have seized an essential element in the truth and exaggerated it till it has become folly. Anarchism is the father of Syndicalism ; but Trade Unionism is its mother, and it was in the fertile womb of Trade Unionism that, in the 'nineties, the Anarchist seed grew unseen. Pelloutier was inspired throughout by the Anarchist-Communist idea of free association, in which the control of industry by free groups of workers played an integral part. This idea, which may be found writ large all through his *Histoire des Bourses du Travail*, Pelloutier applied to the problem as he found it in the Trade Unionism of his day, and there resulted a theory which was as new as any reasonable theory can be. This theory Pelloutier could put before the workers with the more confidence because the Trade Unionists were still few in number, and, therefore, included only a select and conscious body of workers, and because the political upheavals had familiarised men with Anarchistic ideas. The memory of the Commune was still fresh, and Anarchism has always taken root easily in a Latin soil.

It is, then, from the ideas which germinated in the Bourses du Travail during the 'nineties, and under Pelloutier's guidance grew into a definite theory of the new Society, that we must begin if we would understand the genesis of Syndicalism in France. Recently the leaders of the Confédération Générale du Travail have often declared themselves averse from theorising about the future, and Syndicalism has become far more a theory of Direct Action in the present than a vision of the Producers' Commonwealth of to-morrow. But, in this early stage, there was speculation enough and to spare : the Bourses drew up plans for the organisation of the Co-operative Commonwealth, and Pelloutier theorised to his heart's content.

II

The vision of the coming Society which inspired the ' militants ' of the Bourses du Travail was the natural outcome of their environment. They had to base their hopes on the revolutionary enthusiasm of a few ; the possibility of the ' Great Change ' depended on the power of these few to draw after them ' the recalcitrant mass.' The theory of the ' conscious minority ' naturally appealed with peculiar force to men so circumstanced : it appeared as the right, even as the duty, of the few that they should assert themselves on behalf of the unconscious many. In their embryonic organisations, weak and unstable as these were, they saw the germ of the new Society. Face to face with a social structure which denied them their most elementary rights, they were prepared to sweep everything away, and to put in its place the institutions they had themselves created.

The theory of *National* Guilds could only arise in a society where Labour was organised in strong *National* Trade Unions. Syndicalism, at least in its early forms of which the later are, as we shall see, only readjustments, was based throughout upon the small, independent *local* Trade Union. The foundation of the Bourses du Travail with municipal subsidies afforded an opportunity for the linking up of these Unions, but still on a *local* basis. Trade Unionism, instead of developing a system of national craft Unions, as in Great Britain, developed a complicated network of Trades Councils, covering all the big industrial centres.

Anarchist Communism, we have seen, had always been strong in France. It had looked to a great political revolution in which the State and all its dependencies would be overthrown, and to the substitution of a new Society of free groups or Communes, which were to be the units of production and social organisation in the future. Under the guidance of Pelloutier and others like him, the Bourses whole-heartedly accepted this type of Communism, only modifying it by making the local Trade Unions the future units of production and the Bourses the co-ordinating forces and the units of social organisation. The Society to which they looked forward was essentially still Bakunin's federation of free Communes, and the workers were to be linked up nationally and internationally, not on the basis of their particular industry, but solely by a system of local federation, having the free and independent Commune as its foundation and its dynamic conception.

Such a theory, as it is set forth in the reports of the

congresses of the Bourses du Travail and in Pelloutier's history of them, was obviously not open to many popular objections to modern Syndicalism. There was no question of a great National Union of Miners or Railwaymen holding up or exploiting the community as a whole. Indeed, the whole question of the rights of the consumer, on which the Collectivist criticism of Syndicalism is mainly based, has no application to this earlier form. The Bourse du Travail, which is to determine the amount and character of production, is the free local community, reconciling the interests of the various sections ; the national Federation of Bourses is the national community, co-ordinating the various local interests. In Pelloutier's book, and in the reports prepared by the various Bourses, ultimate control over production is claimed, not for the individual Trade Union, but for the Bourse itself, which is in effect the municipality of the future. The essential features of Syndicalism are present : the control of industrial pro-cesses is demanded for the sections of producers, and Communism has been transformed by taking Trade Union-ism as its basis ; but the theory is still purely *local* in character. It looks, for the overthrow of Capitalism, not to the economic power of great national Industrial Unions enjoying a monopoly of labour, but to the local organisa-tion of a conscious and militant minority : and, while it sees in the Bourses the germ of the future Society, it still contemplates a catastrophic social revolution, less a general strike than a general insurrection similar in type to the revolutions of 1789, 1848 and 1871.

There is doubtless in this statement some artificial simplification ; but I believe it fairly represents the point of view of the leaders of the Bourses du Travail in the earlier period of their existence. Out of this germ grew by gradual stages the developed theory of the leaders of the C.G.T.—an evolution which proceeded simultaneously with the changes in industrial conditions and in Trade Unionism itself.

The first, and the most important, of these changes was the gradual growth of national Trade Unions and

Federations in the various industries. The old General Federation of Labour failed, as we saw, because it attempted a general national grouping of the workers without the intermediate link of national Trade Unions. The new Confédération Générale du Travail was enabled to keep alive because, under the influence of the Fédération des Bourses, Trade Unionism had begun to develop on national lines. Founded in 1895, the C.G.T. remained very weak until its fusion with the Bourses in 1902 ; its own reports freely confess its weakness and acknowledge the superior efficiency of the Bourses. But the change was coming surely, if slowly ; and the fusion of 1902 ushered in the final period in the growth of French Syndicalism.

From 1895 to 1902 the Federation of Bourses and the C.G.T. were continually at variance, and it can hardly be doubted that, in the minds of some of the leaders at least, the conflict was between two rival methods of organisation. Two theories, alike of the proper conduct of the class struggle in the present and of the constitution of the future Society, were really contending for the mastery. Syndicalism was passing from Anarchist-Communism, with its essentially local basis, to a theory founded on Trade Unionism in its national form.

Into the amalgamation of 1902 the Federation of Bourses entered as still overwhelmingly the predominant partner. Both in membership and in prestige it was far ahead of the C.G.T., which consisted at this time of national Trade Unions, local Trade Unions, national Federations, and Bourses du Travail. The fusion at once made a more systematic arrangement possible : the new C.G.T. was divided into two sections, the one a Federation of Bourses with its national Executive, the other a Federation of national Federations (craft or industrial), and national Unions, with its separate Executive. The Executive Committee of the whole C.G.T. was formed by joint session of the two sectional Executives. According to the rules of the new organisation, every local Trade Union must join both its Bourse du Travail and its national Craft or Industrial Federation.

The adoption of this double basis of affiliation shows that the leaders of the working-class movement had already realised the inadequacy of the purely local bond, and had seen the importance of linking up nationally the local Unions in each distinct industry. But they did not at all anticipate the disappearance, or even the weakening, of the local bond, which they still regarded as the more fundamental of the two. Yet, in fact, the whole history of the C.G.T. since 1902 is the history of the decline of the Bourses and the rise of the national Federations. This has been the outcome partly of essential and partly of purely accidental causes : its general result has been a far-reaching modification of Syndicalist practice and theory alike. From the ideal of local solidarity such as Mr. Larkin seems to have had in mind in forming the Irish Transport Workers' Union,[1] the C.G.T. passed to the ideal of national solidarity of Labour such as the more advanced Trade Unionists of Great Britain have set before themselves the task of achieving.

One cause of this transformation was external and accidental. The Bourses had grown to greatness by means of municipal subsidies granted them in their capacity as Labour Exchanges. As they became centres of revolutionary activity, these subsidies were gradually withdrawn, and the widening breach between the C.G.T. and the Socialist Party caused them to be discontinued even where the Socialists had conquered the municipal councils. Thus compelled to rely upon their own resources, the Bourses failed to rise to the occasion. One great weakness of Trade Unionism in France, even more than in Great Britain, has always been the workers' unwillingness to pay for reasonably efficient organisation. Compelled either to demand higher dues from their members, or else to give up their most valuable activities, the Bourses were compelled in many cases to take the latter course. Many were ejected from the buildings which the municipalities had placed at their disposal, and, as few were in a position to erect buildings of their own, most of them lost their character of general workmen's clubs, and became mere Trades

[1] See p. 272.

Councils of delegates, with all the weaknesses we have learnt to associate with Trades Councils in England.[1] In their migration, the Bourses lost their function of Labour Exchanges and lost also their name : they became local Unions de Syndicats, alongside of which the old Bourse often persisted merely as a municipal Labour Exchange.

The Bourses would have been better able to survive the withdrawal of municipal assistance had not the natural development of the C.G.T. itself also tended to undermine their position. The national Federations were all the time steadily gaining in power and influence ; they were developing national policies of their own, and coming to be the centres of Trade Union action and organisation. National movements of a single industry were seen to be as a rule more effective than local movements of all industries, and the old ideal of the local general strike began to give way before the ideal of a national strike organised by the various Federations—the general strike on a national, instead of a local, basis. Probably the full importance of this change was not realised by the leaders of the C.G.T. itself—in fact, it may be doubted if they quite understood what was happening ; but undoubtedly the general effect has necessitated a very considerable revision of Syndicalist theory and practice. The breakdown of the local bond has been a grave cause of weakness which the growth of the national Federations has failed to counteract : the period of the greatest strength of the C.G.T. included the few years after 1902 when both systems were in full action ; then, as the Bourses began to decline, the C.G.T. became less efficient, and the rapid progress of the earlier years sustained a check. This has been clearly seen by the leaders themselves, and they are now attempting to meet the want by means of *Unions Départmentales* or County Trades Councils, linking up the Unions on a local basis, but covering a wider area. It is too early to judge the new scheme ; but clearly some such method must be adopted. The local bond is still of the greatest importance, and, as long as it is neglected, the movement will make no progress. The weakness of our own Trade Councils

[1] See p. 272.

is largely responsible for the failure of Trade Unionism in Great Britain (where the national Unions are really strong) to penetrate sooner into the unorganised trades.

With the growth of the national industrial Federation and the decline of the Bourse du Travail, the simplicity of the older Syndicalist theory was bound to give place to a more complex doctrine. Syndicalism could no longer leave the national organisation out of account and build solely on a local basis ; for the inadequacy of the local bond of union, taken by itself, had been clearly manifested. If Syndicalism was to maintain itself as a theory tenable under modern conditions of production and working-class organisations, it had to find a place in its scheme for the great national Unions. But as soon as it came to be proposed to vest control in the national Union or Federation, the Bourse ceased to be an adequate owning and co-ordinating force. The old facile reconciliation of producer and consumer in the Bourses no longer met the need : the new reconciliation must be national instead of local. Syndicalists therefore came to anticipate the vesting of ownership, partly at least, in some such body as the C.G.T. itself, the Trade Union Congress of the future, the legitimate successor of the Capitalist State, but organised still on the basis of production.

In French theory this transformation is by no means complete, because the national organisations in the various industries are nearly all Federations, and not Unions. The local Union has still, in most cases, most of the funds and most of the power, and the whole bias of the French mind is still in the direction of preserving, as much as possible, local independence, and local initiative. But, willing or unwilling, the Unions are clearly tending to greater centralisation ; and, as they grow in numbers and in power, the central control, which was originally forced on them largely by the breakdown of the Bourses, will inevitably become stronger.

Syndicalists and their critics very often talk at cross-purposes because the Syndicalist is dreaming of a mainly local form of organisation, while his critic is assuming a

developed system of national Trade Unions. I know of
no ostensibly Syndicalist work which faces, or seems fully
to realise, the importance of this point. A few British
Syndicalists, with more consistency than common sense,
have advocated the absolute ownership and control, by
the national Union, of the means and methods of production
in its particular occupation : French Syndicalists have, as
a rule, omitted to face the difficulty. Yet Syndicalism
can only stand by its power to adjust itself to this new
situation, and to develop, out of a theory based on Anarchist
Communism and the local Trade Union, a new theory
grounded on the acceptance of the national Union as the
necessary unit of industrial action and organisation. But
this new theory could only arise in some country which
is industrially more developed than France. It will be
evolved wherever strong national Unions, confronted with
important problems of industrial action, can be brought
to re-examine their fundamental dogmas, and to confront
in earnest the question of the control of industry in the
society of the future.

III

Wherever it manifests itself, Syndicalism has two distinct aspects. It is at once a policy of Direct Action in
the present and a vision of the coming Society. Of late
years, Syndicalism in France has curiously confused these
two points of view : professing to repudiate all theory
about the future and to be merely a plan of campaign for
immediate use, it has continually affirmed, almost in the
same breath, its faith in a new Industrial Commonwealth,
based solely on organisations of producers. The confusion
is plainest in the work of M. Sorel, whose philosophy of
Violence, for all its denial of prophetic intention, is but
the continuation of his first work, *L'Avenir Socialiste des
Syndicats*, a distinct and definite attempt to found a new
Society on a Trade Union basis.[1] M. Pouget, again, repudiates the idea of forecasting the future, and gives an
exposition of Syndicalism as a method of Trade Union

[1] See p. 272.

action,[1] but also writes, along with M. Pataud, the elaborate prophetic romance, *Comment nous ferons la Révolution*. But on the whole, it cannot be disputed that there has been in France a considerable reaction against long views and Utopian speculations.[2]

This change can hardly be dissociated from the actual change in industrial organisation. It will be found that, where French Syndicalism remains prophetic, it still cleaves in the main to the old concepts of local autonomy and Anarchist-Communism. *Comment nous ferons la Révolution* is, in most of its essentials, a Communist romance ; it might almost have been written, long before Syndicalism was heard of, by a disciple of Kropotkin or even of Bakunin.[3] French Syndicalists, in fact, have tended to give up theorising largely because a great deal of their theory has already become obsolete. They have not thought out a new system of organisation capable of supplanting Capitalism in such a way as to accept as its basis a national Trade Unionism. They have not carried their speculations beyond the embryonic stage of local organisation : they have produced no theorist great enough to work out the conception of Pelloutier in the light of more recent developments. We shall not be wronging them if we maintain that they have kept silence because they have nothing new to say—because, realising the inadequacy of their first sketch of the future, they have failed to put in its place a profounder analysis and a more complete reconstruction.

Syndicalists in the country would do well to realise the full meaning of this change in the attitude of their friends in France. Syndicalism in England has been too apt to exalt the unessential : a good many English Syndicalists, mainly recruits from the Anarchist ranks, have gone on preaching the principle of federation and local autonomy as the basis upon which the whole movement rests. But Trade Unionism in England is so predominantly national in character, the ' craft ' or ' industrial ' bond is so strong and the local bond so weak, that no theory which aims at a federal system based on general

<hr>

[1] See p. 272.   [2] See p. 273.   [3] See p. 273.

local associations of producers can possibly make headway. The really vital doctrine of Syndicalism is the doctrine of producers' control : it asserts fundamentally that the producers must secure the control of their work, if the work is to be honourable and the community real. Anything that undermines this doctrine is contrary to the whole aim of Syndicalism ; but, if this be accepted, the question of machinery remains secondary, to be settled according to the actual conditions under which modern industry is, or can be, carried on. The federal basis of Anarchism is no essential part of Syndicalism : it came to be regarded as vital because Syndicalism arose in France at a time when local organisation was easiest, and because there was already there a strong Anarchist movement to serve as a basis.

The Syndicalism, therefore, which is most commonly preached by those who call themselves Syndicalists, is, if they would but realise the fact, essentially a national product of French conditions. Moreover, it is at the present time, even for France, something of a back number. It can only emerge revitalised and fruitful if its advocates consent to re-examine their first principles and to rebuild in view of national differences and modern conditions.

As we have seen, there is at least one school of Syndicalists in Great Britain which has attempted this reconstruction ; but most schools still persist in denying its necessity. The French type of Syndicalist often becomes impatient when he is told that his aim is to secure " the mines for the miners, the railways for the railwaymen, and the patients for the doctors." He maintains quite truly that he has never upheld the right of any section of the community to *own* the means of production, or to use them for the exploitation of the consumer. In his system, the conflicting interests of different sections of producers were to be reconciled locally in the Bourse du Travail : the local Unions of miners, etc., had an important function in the control of production, but the national Unions or Federations were, comparatively speaking, unimportant. This type of Syndicalist is therefore contemptuous of the criticism that he is merely substituting a multitude of profiteers for the profiteering of a few. The weakness of his critics is that they have failed to realise the difference between his point of view and that which they are denouncing; if once they see this, they can easily point out to him that, where strong national Unions already exist, the interests of the various sections cannot be reconciled locally : interests nationally organised must be nationally reconciled.

This reconciliation has, indeed, been attempted by another school of 'industrialists' who have drawn their main inspiration, not from France, but from America. The Industrial Unionists agree with the Syndicalists in desiring complete control of industry by the producers, but base their case upon national Trade Unionism federated in a strong central organisation, or even combined in 'One Big Union.'

This, however, does not meet the case. It was possible to suppose that, if sectional organisation remained chiefly local, the Bourses would be able to hold the balance among the different bodies of producers ; but clearly national Trade Unions demand a far stronger co-ordinating force. The power of the national Unions would be so great, and there would be such possibilities of exploitation that it is no longer possible, if the controlling force of producers is national, to dispense altogether with an authority standing for the consumer. The attempt is sometimes made to supply this force in the body of the Trade Union Congress, or, in France, the *Confédération Générale du Travail* itself; but clearly such a body would either be too weak for the purpose, or would reproduce the defects of the State which the Syndicalist sets out to abolish. A Trade Union Congress invested with supreme power would be no less liable to develop tyrannical tendencies than a State invested with supreme power. It would be in fact a quasi-State elected on an industrial, instead of a territorial, basis ; whereas the real need is for a division of Sovereign power, and a distinct representation of the functions of production or ' making ' and consumption or ' use.'

It is not desirable that the ultimate Sovereign body

should be either political or industrial. In that case, it would only reflect, instead of reconciling, the divergence. What is needed is a division of functions between producers and consumers. Syndicalists make the mistake of imagining that the State of the future must necessarily resemble, in all its essential features, the State of to-day, that it must remain capitalistic, bureaucratic and oppressive. But the democratic State is the expression of the structure of Society as an association of consumers ; as the class-structure finds its natural expression in the class-State, so democracy, based on Trade Unionism, will find political expression in the consumers' State, which will be the expression of the consumers' point of view. Confronted with Trade Unions which are their own masters in the industrial sphere, the State will cease to be the natural enemy of the worker, and will become the natural partner of the producers' organisations in the ordering of the national life.

If, then, it be regarded as fundamentally anti-political, not merely in the sense that it holds the State of to-day to be only an instrument in the hands of the oppressor, but also in the sense that it aims at the entire destruction of every vestige of communal expression outside the producers' organisations themselves, Syndicalism is a theory of which no serious account need be taken. If, on the other hand, it is realised that Syndicalism only implies the satisfaction of the workers' demand to control their life and work, it remains still a vitalising force, capable of transforming Socialism into something better than a bureaucratic Collectivism. Out of it must grow a doctrine which will reconcile the conception of social solidarity which was fundamental to Communism with the development of Trade Unionism on a national basis, and at the same time preserve its insistence on the need of control, by the actual workers in each industry, of the processes of production and distribution. In short, the idea of National Guilds is, for this country, the essential parallel to Syndicalism in France. The theory of National Guilds is the restatement of local Syndicalism in terms of national Trade Unionism.

EDITOR'S APPENDIX

THIS 1972 edition consists of the original chapter layout and material of the 1917 edition, leaving out two leading chapters which were concerned specifically with labour conditions during the First World War. The argument therefore starts from Cole's examination of the nature of the State (transferred by Cole in the fourth edition to the centre of the book); and the editor has followed Cole's original plan to present the case for self-government as a series of related steps.

The book was first planned (in 1913) as a sequel to *The World of Labour*, but was put aside on the outbreak of war. The manuscript was extensively revised during 1916 and was completed in June 1917. The bibliophile may trace antecedents and various fragments in various journals issued between 1914 and 1917: notably in *The New Age*; *Nation*; *Church Socialist*; *Herald*; *Highway* and *Labour Leader*. The first edition appeared before the Russian revolution—an event which could hardly be ignored by any social theoretician.[1] In the introduction to the fourth edition (1919), Cole claims that 'the Soviet idea is the Guild idea, or at least has very much in common with it', while drawing the all-important distinction that 'it cannot be too

---

[1] This edition appeared, after the March revolution, at a time when the Soviets were not yet subsumed under Bolshevik control.

clearly understood that there is no essential connection between the Soviet form of organisation and Bolshevism'.[1]

Modern readers, who may find the background to *Self-Government in Industry* hard to recapture, are urged to discover for themselves the ferment of ideas from the literature of the time.[2] There are no really thorough studies of Guild Socialism as a theory, although historical studies of the Guild movement and the shop stewards movement have been (and will probably remain) a rich mine for generations of research workers.[3] Even so, most historical studies lack a definitive touch and Cole in his own historical works was naturally inclined to underplay the significance of the Guild ideas. Readers who wish to re-create the flavour of the trade union situation of the pre-1914 era will find some useful sources to hand.[4] But the theory of

[1] The 'official' theorists of Marxism–Leninism were later to ignore this analytical distinction when concocting a travesty of Cole's thought on the 'common ground' between Communist and socialist aspirations. See *Fundamentals of Marxism–Leninism. A Manual* (Foreign Languages Publishing House, Moscow, 1961), pp. 446–7.

[2] The following are suggested here for guidance. Files of *Guild Socialist*; *Building Guildsman*; *Guildsman*; and *The New Age*; S. G. Hobson and A. R. Orage, *National Guilds*; G. D. H. Cole, *Guild Socialism Re-stated*; N. Carpenter, *Guild Socialism*; G. D. H. Cole, *Labour in the Commonwealth*; G. D. H. Cole and W. Mellor, *The Meaning of Industrial Freedom*; N. Carpenter, *Guild Socialism*; C. L. Goodrich, *The Frontier of Control*; A. J. Penty, *Old Worlds for New*; and M. B. Reckitt and C. E. Bechofer, *The Meaning of National Guilds*.

[3] For primary fieldwork, students should consult the publications of the Society for the Study of Labour History. Contemporary commentators on modern trends should also consult the publications of the Institute for Workers' Control for viewpoints not entirely unrelated to Guild Socialism.

[4] See G. D. H. Cole, *A Short History of the British Working-Class Movement*; G. D. H. Cole and Raymond Postgate, *The Common People*; H. A. Clegg, Alan Fox and A. F. Thompson, *A History of British Trade Unions Since 1889*; E. H. Phelps Brown, *The Growth of British Industrial Relations*.

collective bargaining—so essential for any appraisal of Guild Socialism—has only recently been subjected to sophisticated analysis,[1] and readers unfamiliar with the study of industrial relations may find the concepts difficult to place in perspective without some knowledge of the history of bargaining.

Readers reared solely in the problems delineated by 'Anglo-Saxon' economics will find very little *concrete* guidance from the extensive literature on economic theory.[2] The theoretical debate on the economics of socialism, although it has developed enormously since the 1930's, has been centred around the economics of Collectivism. The techniques, however, are to a considerable extent independent of institutional assumptions and are adaptable to a Guild system. To draw upon the rich fund of economic technique becomes a hard task for the selective skill and versatility of the general reader. But the rewards are great. He will discover that many pointers on Guild allocation criteria may be detected: for example, by careful reading of theories on general equilibrium systems.[3] The astute reader will also discover that the works of Ragnar Frisch and Jan Tinbergen hold greater relevance for the economic theory of a hypothetical Guild economy than for any economic system that we see in the world around us.

Readers of *Self-Government in Industry* who lack the

[1] See Allan Flanders, 'Collective Bargaining: A Theoretical Analysis', *British Journal of Industrial Relations*, March 1968.

[2] For the more specialised student, careful reading in the British stream of labour economics, e.g. the studies of E. H. Phelps Brown, is highly recommended.

[3] Readers, for example, would find much in the standard generalisations of the von Neumann model; and would gain a fresh slant by reading Walras's theoretical writings *in conjunction* with his socio-economic contributions.

time to fan out background knowledge should at least remember a few dates when trying to focus on its context. Industrial action and agitation were part of the social atmosphere of the pre-1914 years: an exciting time of strikes and class conflict in which the ideas of French syndicalism and American industrial unionism jostled in various combinations and permutations to win over the trade unions.[1] The common denominator of all doctrines was the reconstruction of the trade union movement.

When we read *Self-Government in Industry* today, we must recollect that it was written before the formation of the 'modern' Labour Party (1918) and the TUC General Council (1920), before the formation of the British Communist Party (1920), and before the establishment of the industry-wide bargaining system. It would be idle to speculate what would have happened if militant impulses had not spilled into these directions—but it is important to remember that Cole postulated a different working hypothesis for social progress, and readers may reflect on whether this hypothesis holds more relevance for today than it did for the past.

---

[1] General readers with access to a good library can quickly recapture the doctrinal and personal ethos of the British Labour Movement—from the vivid and fascinating books (not always accurate) of the leading American commentator of the time. See Arthur Gleason, *What The Workers Want. A Study of British Labor* (Harcourt, Brace & Howe, New York, 1920). Also Paul U. Kellogg and Arthur Gleason, *British Labor and the War* (New York, 1919).

NOTES ON THE TEXT

THE notes on the text are not intended to be comprehensive, but are merely sidelights on the main themes. Although the text must *not* be narrowly viewed as 'just another source for the labour historian', some historical explanations are necessary to give it full life and drama. Since the new edition is intended to serve students over a wide range of disciplines, which tend to become specialist and disassociated, the purpose is to throw some light on text references which may appear obscure to the general reader.

As a setting for the text, one can hardly better Arthur Gleason's description of the Guildsmen:

> This earnest, tiny group (a few hundred in all the Kingdom) appear in various service uniforms and play many parts. As university graduates, they are at the heart of the University Socialist Federation. As Christians they are Church Socialists, sapping the Established Church. As Guildsmen, they conduct a league, honeycombing the unions. As investigators, they are the Labour Research Department, affiliated to important members of the trade union movement. As Fabians, they buffet Sidney Webb. As journalists, they have entry to powerful newspapers and weeklies. As writers, their books—*Self-Government in Industry* and *The Payment of Wages*—are . . . irreplaceable because of the careful

collection of facts and the understanding of currents of tendency. But their great service has been that of agitators with a smashing generalisation.[1]

Chapter I. The Nature of the State

By 1919 Cole wanted to make a number of detailed modifications to this chapter. The changes mainly centred around two points. First, while Cole was content to regard the State, in so far as it was democratised, as an association of neighbours or 'dwellers together', that is to say as a *territorial* association, he was no longer satisfied with conceiving it as an association of consumers. He came to hold that the representation of men as 'consumers, users and enjoyers' requires a multiplicity of associations dealing with the representation of different groups of purposes and interests. Often, therefore, in this chapter, when he speaks of the 'State', he assigns to it functions which he later came to assign to one or other of the *functional* Congresses.

Secondly, Cole came to regard the problem of territorial representation as far more a question of local or regional, representation than of national representation. Where this chapter tends to lay stress on national organisation, Cole later came to shift the emphasis to the *local* or *regional* bodies, leaving the national functions mainly to federal bodies drawn from them. See G. D. H. Cole, *Social Theory* (rev. edn., 1921) and *Guild Socialism Re-Stated* (1920).

The reference, on page 3, to the Trade Disputes Act refers to the Trade Disputes Act (1906) which cancelled the Taff Vale decision. The reference to the Poor Law Commission highlights the controversy between the Majority and the Minority Reports (1909). Both agreed

[1] Arthur Gleason, *op. cit.*, p. 263.

that the Poor Law was obsolete, but the Minority Report (chiefly the work of the Webbs) proposed a complete break-up of the Poor Law in favour of a social security system: a proposal side-stepped by Lloyd George in the 1911 National Insurance Act. The Charity Organisation Society was, of course, a voluntary association.

The Osborne judgement (1909), referred to on page 10, virtually decided that the unions had no right to spend money on the Labour Party or political activities. A compromise was eventually granted in the Trade Union (Amendment) Act of 1913, which legalised political action by the unions.

The School Boards, referred to on page 14, were set up under the 1870 Education Act to fill the gaps left by the voluntary school system. They provided opportunities for political sponsorship, and the Labour Representation League formed a special committee to fight School Board elections. Elected Boards of Guardians, set up to administer the Poor Law in 1834, were still part of the 1917 political scene.

Chapter II. The Case for National Guilds

Note 1, page 32.

The Independent Labour Party, formed in 1893, avowed its primary objective as 'the collective ownership and control of the means of production, distribution and exchange'

Note 1, page 45.

Throughout the text, where Cole refers to the Collectivists, this is frequently a synonym for the Webbs. The theoretical model of a Trade Union which the Webbs erected in *Industrial Democracy* (1897) was, as Allan Flanders points out, that of a Labour cartel. It had been implicitly assumed that there was no inconsistency in Trade Unions undertaking both a bargaining and a regulative process.

Note 1, page 46.

Here Cole refers to the 1913 Connolly–Larkin strike which gripped the attention of the British Trade Union movement. The Dublin struggle—a sympathetic strike centred around the Irish Transport Union—became a symbolic contest for the New Unionism.

Chapter III. The Re-organisation of Trade Unionism

Note 1, page 54.

The war brought State intervention into industrial life on an unprecedented scale. For the impact on wage negotiations, see Henry Clay, *The Problem of Industrial Relations* (Macmillan, 1929); and Lord Askwith, *Industrial Problems and Disputes* (Murray, 1920). For a racy account of the impact of war on the Labour movement, see Paul U. Kellogg and Arthur Gleason, *British Labor and the War* (New York, 1919). For a brief outline of the events of the war, see N. B. Dearle, *An Economic Chronicle of the Great War for Great Britain and Ireland, 1914–1919* (Oxford, 1929).

Note 1, page 55.

In May 1915 the Labour Party participated in a Coalition Government, under Asquith, with Arthur Henderson as its chief representative. He remained when Lloyd George overthrew Asquith in December 1916 and formed a new coalition.

Note 2, page 55.

As a 'movement', the shop steward system formally

arose from the Committee set up to organise the
unofficial Clyde strike of February 1915. Eventually,
the National Workers' Committee Movement ran into
serious conflict with both Government and Trade
Union executives.

Note 1, page 61.

Both these volumes momentarily gripped the public
imagination, and are interesting examples of the
'social science fiction' of the period. Wells was later to
alter his emphasis in *The New Machiavellians*.

Note 1, page 65.

The A.S.E. is now the Amalgamated Union of
Engineering and Foundry Workers. For a modern view
of the historical development of union morphology, see
H. A. Turner, *Trade Union Growth, Structure and
Policy* (Allen & Unwin, 1962).

Note 1, page 67.

For an historical account of the N.U.R., see Philip S.
Bagwell, *The Railwaymen* (Allen & Unwin, 1963).

Note 1, page 69.

At this time the organisations promoted by the
Committee were strong. Within a few months of the
Armistice the shop stewards movement faded away as
an 'all trades movement', but it left a permanent if
weak impression on Trade Union structure.

Note 1, page 77.

The War Emergency Workers National Committee
did not deal with matters of political policy, or with
strictly Trade Union affairs. Its function was to safeguard working-class interests in matters such as
unemployment relief and the cost of living.

Chapter IV. The Abolition of the Wage-system

It may be argued that there are some affinities, in this chapter, between Cole's treatment of the 'alienation' problem and that of the young Marx in the 'Excerpt—Notes of 1844' and the 'Economic and Philosophic Manuscripts'. See *Writings of the Young Marx on Philosophy and Society*, edited and translated by Lloyd D. Easton and Kurt H. Guddat (New York, 1967).

Note 1, page 89.

Cole refers to Hilaire Belloc and the 'Distributivist' doctrines. These permeated into Catholic Socialism but died away by the late 1920's.

Note 1, page 94.

The Munitions of War Act, 1915, set up a category of 'controlled establishments'. Strikes were forbidden by law and compulsory arbitration was established in all industries concerned with war work. The acceptance of dilution was made legally binding. The Act gave legal force to the system of War Munition Volunteers who could be compulsorily moved from factory to factory, and instituted a system of 'Leaving Certificates' so that munitions workers could not move to other jobs without a certificate of release. To administer the system, a net of Local Munitions Tribunals was set up. In return, the chief concession to the Unions was the legal limitation of excess profits.

Note 1, page 95.

The text refers to the Insurance Act of 1911, and readers should bear in mind that Trade Unions were allowed to administer partly unemployment insurance. Cole, of course, is not referring to the Unemployment

Insurance Act (1920) but still remembers the dishing of the Lib-Labs by Lloyd George on the unemployment issue.

Note 1, page 97.

The 'Ghent system', operating in one of the then largest industrial cities in Europe, supported unemployed workers through the Unions on a principle of Commune responsibility. For an account of a now-forgotten 'Ghent system', see I. G. Gibbon, *Unemployment Insurance* (P. S. King & Son, 1911), pp. 82–107.

Chapter V. State Ownership and Control

The relatively short treatment, in this chapter, should not deceive the reader upon the supreme significance of the current cross-debates on this question. Perspective should be achieved by referring to more general accounts of these debates. See Ken Coates and Anthony Topham, *Industrial Democracy in Britain: a book of readings and witnesses for workers' control* (1968). For a general account of Guild Socialist ideas on State ownership, see S. T. Glass, *The Responsible Society* (Longmans, 1966). For a critical view, see H. A. Clegg, *A New Approach to Industrial Democracy* (1960).

Note 1, page 125.

This reference is to George Bernard Shaw: see Bernard Shaw, *Common Sense of Municipal Trading* (1908). Although a playwright, Shaw served as self-appointed 'economist' to the Fabian Society for many years, acting as a star platform speaker on economic problems.

Note 1, page 129.

The Miners' Next Step was a pamphlet (anonymous) published in 1912 by the 'Unofficial Reform Committee' of the South Wales Miners' Federation. It represented the high-water mark of Syndicalism.

Note 1, page 133.

After this theoretical exposition, Cole seized his opportunity to act as Guild witness on the public ownership of the mines (1919) before the Sankey Commission. His précis of written evidence is singularly biting and still worth reading. From the records, however, Sankey's verbal tactics reveal that the odds were stacked against the Guild Socialists from the start, and it was entirely predictable that Sankey would alight on Haldane's 'public administration' solution rather than on any formulation of workers' control.

Note 1, page 138.

This acid comment refers to the general views of the *New Statesman*, which was founded by the Webbs in 1913, and functioned politically as a voice-piece for 'Collectivist' views.

Note 1, page 139.

This generalisation is not strictly applicable to the era up to 1919, i.e. before the notion of 'joint control' under the Railway Advisory Committee. During the war the railways were under Government control (via the Railway Executive Committee), but, in fact, they were partly self-controlled, because the machinery through which the Government exercised its powers was placed in the hands of the General Managers of the Companies. Only in 1920 were control and financial supervision placed more directly under the Ministry of Transport.

Note 1, page 142.

W. Haywood was a colourful American Syndicalist of the period, and Chairman of the First Convention of the I.W.W. For an account of his role, see Marc Karson, *American Labor Unions and Politics 1900–18* (Southern Illinois Press, 1958).

Note 1, page 151.

The Holt Committee refers to the *Report of the Select Committee on Postal Servants* (1913), whose findings were unanimously rejected by the postal unions. The bitter tone of the time should be recaptured by reading the debates on the *Findings of the Select Committee's Report* in the *T.U.C. Report, 1913*.

Note 1, page 153.

This formulation had not clearly appeared after two years (by 1919). The N.U.R. in *The Railway Review* (15 August 1919) declared that, 'There can be no fixed definition in the meaning of control. Evolution impelled by the aggregate desires of those who share in the labour of production must work its course, and in due order of patience and time our object in spirit will be achieved in fact. The consciousness of our aim must be the guiding line.

Chapter VI. Freedom in the Guild

Note 1, page 158.

The viewpoints of Herbert Spencer (1820–1903), most criticised by Socialists, may be found in *The Principles of Sociology*, *Social Statics*, and (a volume in Cole's personal library at the time) *First Principles* (1910).

Note 2, page 170.

A. J. Penty, architect and somewhat single-minded interpreter of William Morris, idealised the medieval Guilds in a protest against industrialism and the specialisation of labour in *The Restoration of the Guild System* (1906). He later migrated towards the National Guilds League, but in no fundamental theoretical sense can Penty be categorised as an originator of Guild Socialism.

Note 1, page 173.

Here, Cole also has in mind apparently the more medieval-romantic and federal gropings of Kropotkin's *Mutual Aid*—in other ways a quite admirable case for the historical continuity of mutual-aid in society.

Note 1, page 179.

For the fortunes of this group, see E. W. Evans, *The Miners of South Wales* (Cardiff University Press, 1961).

Note 1, page 180.

For the fortunes of the M.F.G.B. and the miners, see R. Page Arnot, *The Miners: Years of Struggle* (Allen & Unwin, 1953); *The Miners in Crisis and War* (Allen & Unwin, 1961).

Note 1, page 210.

Cole's attitudes towards and relationships with the Fabian Society reflected his controversy with the Webbs's views, but were more complicated than this comment implies, and changed over time. George Bernard Shaw gives a somewhat unhistorical but pithy sketch: 'In 1911 the survivors of the Fabian Essayists... resigned their official leadership. . . . The Society immediately replaced them by middle-aged and elderly·

old friends who sat comfortably doing comparatively
nothing until the return to the Society of G. D. H. Cole,
who had begun as a Guild Socialist with an apology for
calling the Essayists fools on the ground that he should
have called them bloody fools, but ended in his suc-
cession to Fabian leadership. . . .' G. D. H. Cole eventually became President of the Fabian Society *and*
Chairman of the *New Statesman and Nation*. Yet in
Fabian pamphlets and in articles Cole never relin-
quished his basic faith in workers' control and the
Guild method. At Oxford, during the 1950's, Cole's
seminars showed no disillusionment with the principle
of self-government in industry, and won over adherents
to the very end.

Chapter VII. National Guilds and the Consumer

In this chapter, where Cole discusses the socialisation
of consumption and the economic activity of Guilds, he
is partly conducting a rear action against both the ideas
of the Co-operative Co-Partnership Federation and the
counter-claims of the Consumer Co-operative Movement.

Orthodox friends of the Co-operative Movement, such
as the renowned father of Cambridge economics, Alfred
Marshall, would admit that 'the State can now look to
the main body of workers as the source of much of that
higher administrative work, which used to belong almost exclusively to the well-to-do'. Neither Marshall
nor Cole had seriously alighted on the idea that the
market mechanism was 'neutral' and could be consciously used as a manipulative device embodying
values other than those of traditional Capitalism. The
modern body of thought on economic planning was only
to be created in the 1960's. But Marshall himself, in

Industry and Trade, pleads for Guild Socialism to take up the technical tools of economic analysis and applied economics, because: 'Unless Guild organisation develops some notion, of which it at present seems to have made no forecast, it may probably drift into chaos . . . the golden age is to bring out latent powers of goodness in human nature; the task of regulation is to be as simple as it would be if all men were as unselfish and earnest as the writer (Mr. Cole) himself: the vast difficulties of modern business organization are so completely left out of account as to imply that they have never been seriously studied.' Careful readers of *Self-Government*, however, will have noted that Cole does make passing reference in the text to S. J. Chapman's study of cotton industry organisation (1904).

Note 1, page 219.

Sir Leo Chiozza Money occupied a leading position as a Liberal-Socialist-Fabian on issues in fiscal policy and income distribution. Cole treats his views critically with a prominence which can only be appreciated by viewing Chiozza Money's political standing. Chiozza Money was a Coalition Liberal M.P. who transferred to the Labour Party. After writing *Riches and Poverty*, republished in 1913, and *The Future of Work* (1914), Chiozza Money sat on the Blockade Committee, the War Trade Advisory Committee, was associated with the Ministry of Munitions, and held a junior post in the Ministry of Shipping. Sidney Webb regarded him as an able 'statistician', and he was elevated to the Coal Commission (Sankey Commission), where he influenced Sankey to embarrass G. D. H. Cole over the details of the Derbyshire pit committees. His writings culminate in *The Triumph of Nationalisation* (1921).

Note 1, page 221.

It is only recently that a thorough investigation of the handloom weavers has been attempted. But it is true that this worker group has received more attention in every book on the Industrial Revolution (up to 1917) than any other. See Duncan Blythell, *The Handloom Weavers* (Cambridge, 1969), for a fascinating study which largely confirms Cole's contentions.

Note 1, page 231.

This allusion to an 'economic war' may puzzle modern readers, who may tend to think of the reparations problem and Keynes's *The Economic Consequences of the Peace*. But this particular notion of an 'economic war' refers specifically to particular proposals and feelings in 1916–17. Readers are urged to look at Paul U. Kellogg and Arthur Gleason, *op. cit.*, pp. 223–8.

After the rejection of the German peace overtures in December 1916 there was a growing suspicion of the influence of economic imperialism behind British and Allied war aims, fed by a wave of war-weariness. The Labour Movement searched, in various ways, for social reconstruction aims: in June 1917 the Leeds Conference (I.L.P.) called for Workers' and Soldiers' Councils in Britain; and in August 1917 the Labour Party Conference adopted the abortive proposal to hold a full conference of the International in Stockholm. In December 1917 the Labour Party and the T.U.C. produced a memorandum on peace conditions which called, among others, for 'the discontinuance of economic war after the declaration of peace'. Lord Robert Cecil, as Government spokesman, then publicly pledged that the Government was not advocating an 'economic war' after an end to the military war.

Appendix A. The Genesis of Syndicalism in France

This appendix to the original edition is kept because it holds the substance of Cole's argument that Syndicalism, as a coherent theory, was of more recent origin than was commonly supposed. The history of French Syndicalism and the fortunes of the C.G.T., now have an extensive literature in French (to a lesser extent in English). However, it is pointless to criticise, on details, 'The Genesis of Syndicalism in France' with a hindsight that was not on hand in 1917. The affinities of Cole's ideas with classical French social theory and its socialistic offspins, with which he was acquainted, are much more rewarding threads to trace. Even today, most works of St. Simon and Fourier remain untranslated from French into English: unknown to the student of social theory or industrial relations except as a vague impression (quite wrong and usually second-hand) that they were Gallic-Utopian schemes. The 'social blueprint' approach, based on a general social theory, is a methodology which Cole adopted and developed: a trait which was largely alien to the Webbs's school of Fabian activity.

However, it may be argued that Cole may have underplayed the residual influence of Proudhonian ideas upon French Syndicalist thought; to throw light on this and on Cole's own intellectual 'lineage' (an un-rewarding task upon an original theorist), see Pierre Ansart, *Sociologie de Proudhon* (Presses Universitaires de France, 1967).

Note 1, page 233.

James Ramsay MacDonald, later to be historically famed, and defamed, as Prime Minister of the National Government, had expressed his attitudes in *Syndicalism* (1912). Graham Wallas, one of the original Fabian

Essayists, was a Professor of Political Science at the LSE and had been a member of the MacDonnell Commission on the Civil Service (1912–15). Later, he was an orthodox witness for nationalisation before the Coal Commission. Walls initiated a 'psychological' approach to social organisation by querying 'rational' motives in *Human Nature in Politics* (1908) and *The Great Society* (1914), an approach which was misrepresented by the anti-Guildsmen. Tawney's attitude to Wallas was that, 'political terms are likely to be strained when transferred to . . . self-government in industry. But is it necessary to prove the psychological malaise which arises when men are unable to exercise any effective control over their social environment? Is it not legitimate to assume it, and to argue on that hypothesis? A more personal view by a Guildsman (in *Graham Wallas on Democracy—the Fabianism of 1895*) was that, 'Wallas has a sort of low-voiced Nonconformist sincerity . . . slightly spoiled by a tendency to occasional bawling . . . in spite of a knowledge of social psychology and an array of modern instances, Graham Wallas is still the enlightened Dreyfusard'.

Note 2, page 233.

This refers to *The New Age* (weekly), edited by A. R. Orage, issued in the new series from May 1907. A. R. Orage and Holbrook Jackson used *The New Age* as an independent platform for launching Guild Socialism (financially helped at one point by Bernard Shaw). Some of Hilaire Belloc's pieces were published in the once-famous *The Servile State* (1912).

In March 1912 *The New Age* swung against Syndicalism, and in April a series of articles (anonymously by S. G. Hobson) produced the first exposition of Guild Socialism. Cole is probably referring to Orage's March article. The Guild platform was transferred to *Guildsman* (National Guilds League) in 1916, which was reformed as *Guild Socialist* (1921–3) and replaced by *New Standards* which ended in 1924.

Note 1, page 244.

James Larkin, in 1908, broke away from the British Dock Labourers' Union and founded the Irish Transport Workers' Union. He was joined by James Connolly, and the militant Union aimed to embrace all un-organised workers under 'one big union' as dreamed of by Connolly and preached by the Industrial Workers of the World. Local solidarity took the form of strike action at single establishments, backed by the threat of sympathetic or guerrilla strikes. At the time, this was new against the usual Union background policies of great stoppages and long negotiations.

Note 1, page 245.

For the weaknesses of Trades Councils, see B. C. Roberts, *Trade Union Government and Administration in Great Britain* (1956).

Note 1, page 247.

Of course, the informed public were more acquainted with G. Sorel's *Réflexions sur la violence* (Paris, 1908; trans., London, 1916). But Cole's diagnosis, in 1917, of Sorel's drift is not far short of the mark: see G. Sorel, *Matériaux d'une théorie du Prolétariat* (Paris, 1921).

Note 1, page 248.

Pouget was an influential Anarcho-Syndicalist French activist, now long-forgotten in England. His leading ideas were in *Le Sabotage* (1910), *Le C.G.T.* (1918), and *Les Bases du Syndicalisme* (1922).

Note 2, page 248.

See Jean Servier, *Histoire de l'Utopie* (Gallimard, 1967).

Note 3, page 248.

Cole is not quite fair to Pouget and Pataud, but he is justified in castigating the vapours of this now-vanished book. To illustrate the facility of the authors in utilising their capacities and that of the French language for airy generalisation, it is worth quoting one futuristic passage to see what the reader can make of it today:

En même temps que disparaissait le prolétariat, devait disparaître tout vestige de subordination. Nul ne devait, à aucun titre, être le salarié, non plus que le subordonné de quiconque: il y aurait, entre les êtres humains, contacts, contrats, associations, enchevêtrements de groupes — mais chacun rendrait service à son semble sur le pied d'égalité et à charge de réciprocité. Et c'est parce qu'il allait en être ainsi, que toute assemblée légiferante était surannée — qu'elle fût nationale, départmentale, cantonale ou communale!